An Annotated Bibliography
of U.S. Scholarship on the
History of the Family

AMS STUDIES IN SOCIAL HISTORY, NO. 6

ISSN 0270-6253

Other Titles in This Series:

1. Esmond Wright, ed. *Red, White & True Blue: The Loyalists in the Revolution.* 1976.
2. Richard V. Francaviglia. *The Mormon Landscape.* 1978.
3. Taylor Stoehr. *Free Love in America.* 1979.
4. Cynthia Huff. *British Women's Diaries: A Descriptive Bibliography of Selected Nineteenth-Century Women's Manuscript Diaries.* 1985.
5. Nan Hackett. *XIX Century British Working-Class Autobiographies: An Annotated Bibliography.* 1985.

An Annotated Bibliography of U.S. Scholarship on the History of the Family

Elizabeth Benson-von der Ohe

Valmari M. Mason

AMS PRESS
New York

Library of Congress Cataloging-in-Publication Data

Benson-von der Ohe, Elizabeth.
  An annotated bibliography of U.S. scholarship on
the history of the family.

  (AMS studies in social history; no. 6)
    Includes index.
    1. Family—United States—History—Biography
Bibliography. 2. Marriage—United States—History
—Bibliography. I. Mason, Valmari M. II. Title. III.
Title: Annotated bibliography of US scholarship on
the history of the family.
Z7164.M2B46 1986 [HQ536] 016.3068'5'0973
85–48008 ISBN 0–404–61606–2

AMS PRESS, INC.
56 East 13th Street, New York, N.Y. 10003, U.S.A.

Manufactured in the United States of America

PREFACE

Family history is an important part of the social history of everyday life. As an academic field in the United States, it was "born" shortly after 1970. There followed an exponential rise in the number of publications, as young and older scholars became intrigued with questions about what marriage, child rearing, and family life had been like in past times. By the mid-seventies the history of the family had already taken shape and was well on its way toward becoming a "mature," established field of study.

There now exists a considerable literature about families in the past. Our bibliography is an attempt to make this knowledge more accessible to those not yet well acquainted with the field. This volume represents one part of a larger study of family history and family historians in the U.S., the initial phases of which were funded by the West German National Science Foundation (Deutsche Forschungsgemeinschaft / DFG)*. Originally intended to make the research of U.S. scholars more easily available to their West German counterparts, this bibliography should be equally useful to American teachers, researchers, and students as well.

We wish to acknowledge the guidance of Professor Werner Conze of the University of Heidelberg, the initiator of the DFG special-emphasis program on family history and also of the idea of studying how and why the field developed so rapidly in the United States. To Professor Harm-Hinrich Brandt, whose support made the study and bibliography possible, goes a very special vote of thanks. Additional appreciation is due to Mary McCormack

---

* DFG grant numbers: Br 239/6 and Br 239/8-2. Principal investigator: Professor Harm-Hinrich Brandt, Department of History, University of Würzburg, Würzburg, Federal Republic of Germany. This project was part of a DFG special-emphasis program entitled "Changes in Family Structures, Gender Roles, and the Life Cycle since the 18th Century."

v

of the Sociology Department at Michigan State University for her considerable assistance in collecting copies of appropriate journal articles, to Daniel Wolter of Munich, West Germany, for the typing of this bibliography, and to those U.S. scholars who took the trouble to provide us with copies of their recent papers and publications. Last but not least, the support and patience of our families -- David, George & April, and Werner & Werner -- is most gratefully acknowledged.

TABLE OF CONTENTS

Volume 3

                                                                    page

Introduction xi

Aids for Using This Volume.. xiii

Detailed Table of Contents.. xv

ANNOTATED BIBLIOGRAPHY
        by Subject-matter Topic

I.   INTRODUCTORY ORIENTATIONS 1

            Broad Surveys of the Literature

      A.   By Historians 1
      B.   By Sociologists·······································3
      C.   By Anthropolgists ····································4
      D.   On the History of the German Family ··················5

            *Introductions to Related
             Bodies of Literature*

      E.   Economics...7
      F.   Women's History & Feminist Theory.....................9
      G.   Psychohistory 12

            History of the Discipline

      H.   The History of Family History 14

            Other General References & Resources

      I.   Bibliographies.......................................16
      J.   Anthologies/Readers 17
      K.   Brief Survey Articles for Students 18

            Other References

      L.   Dissertations..20
      M.   Publications...21

II.   FAMILY/HOUSEHOLD STRUCTURE & COMPOSITION 22

      A.   Conceptual & Theoretical Approaches 22
      B.   Review of Major Books...............................24

            *Studies of Specific Regions
             & Ethnic Groups*

      C.   European Populations 27
      D.   U.S. Populations, General 31
      E.   U.S. Populations, Blacks 33
      F.   Other Regions or Cross-Cultural Comparisons 35

Other References

	G.	Dissertations...37
	H.	Publications..38

III. MARRIAGE: BEGINNINGS & ENDINGS..................................39

    A.   Conceptual & Theoretical Approaches: Gary Becker and
       the "New Home Economics"...................................39
    B.   Marriage..42
    C.   Divorce...44
    D.   Widowhood...45

Other References

    E.   Dissertations..46
    F.   Publications...47

IV. THE LIFE CYCLE..49

    A.   Conceptual & Theoretical Approaches 49
    B.   Reviews of Major Books 53
    C.   The Life Cycle: Empirical Works...........................56
    D.   Life Stages: Childhood & Adolescence.....................59
    E.   Life Stages: Old Age 64
    F.   Methodological Approaches to the Life Cycle..............66

Other References

    G.   Dissertations..67
    H.   Publications...68

V.   WOMEN'S LIVES: STATUS & WORK 70

    A.   Conceptual & Theoretical Approaches 70
    B.   Reviews of Major Books 71
    C.   Status/Power 78
    D.   Employment 81
    E.   Housework & Household Production.........................86

Other References

    F.   Dissertations..89
    G.   Publications...90

VI. FAMILY LIFE: COMPREHENSIVE TREATMENTS..............................91

    A.   Reviews of Major Books 91
    B.   Focus on Mentalité, Values, Emotions····················98
    C.   Other Empirical Works...................................101

Other References

    D.   Dissertations...104
    E.   Publications..106

VII. SEXUALITY, BIRTH, DEATH, & MIGRATION: DEMOGRAPHIC & OTHER
APPROACHES 108

  A. The Field of Historical Demography in Various Countries:
      Overviews...108
  B. Reviews of Major Books 109
  C. Sexuality & Illegitimacy..............................111

Birth & Fertility

  D. Non-demographic Approaches............................115
  E. Demographic Approaches 116

Both Fertility & Mortality

  F. Non-demographic Approaches............................122
  G. Demographic Approaches 123

Death & Mortality

  H. Demographic Approaches 125

Migration

  I. Demographic Approaches 127

Other References

  J. Dissertations...129
  K. Publications..130

VIII. KINSHIP, LINEAGE, & INHERITANCE..................................133

  A. Kinship & Lineage 133
  B. Inheritance 136

Other References

  C. Dissertations...139
  D. Publications..140

IX. OTHER INSTITUTIONS & THE FAMILY 141

The Economy & Education

  A. The Family Economy & Family Strategies................141
  B. The Larger Economy....................................143
  C. Education 146

Welfare & Public Policy

  D. Reviews of Major Books 147
  E. Other Works 151

The Military

  F. War & the Family 153

Other References

  G. Dissertations...154
  H. Publications..155

X.   METHODOLOGY: RESEARCH & TEACHING...................................156

                    Research: Computer Micro-Simulation

    A.   Reviews of Major Books 156
    B.   Other Works 157

              Research: Computer-Assisted Data Analysis

    C.   Quantitative Handling of Anthropological & Cross-
        Cultural Data 160
    D.   Record Linkage & Family Reconstitution.............161
    E.   Inventory Analysis 162
    F.   Multivariate Statistical Analysis: Probit, Logit,
        Tobit, etc. 163

                         Research: Data Sources

    G.   Data Banks & Data Sets 164
    H.   Archival & Other Sources...........................167

                       Research: Other Topics

    I.   Problems in Demographic Analysis...................168
    J.   Oral History 170
    K.   Handling Historical Time-Change....................171
    L.   Other Articles on Research Methodology.............172

                 Teaching: Resources & Methods

    M.   Course Syllabi for College Classes 173
    N.   Textbooks for College Classes 175
    O.   Ideas & Techniques for Teaching Family History 176

                         Other References

    P.   Dissertations......................................178
    Q.   Publications.......................................179

XI.   SPACE & ARCHITECTURE 185

    A.   Domestic Space.....................................185
    B.   Urban Spatial Patterns 186

                         Other References

    C.   Dissertations......................................187
    D.   Publications.......................................188

Name Index...189

INTRODUCTION

This is a bibliography of articles relevant to the historical study of the family. The cited articles come primarily from U.S. journals since 1970, with a focus upon those published after 1975. Via citations of published book reviews, information about a number of key books is also given. Finally, some unpublished papers by American scholars are included.

About the Bibliography

This bibliography is notable for the **extensiveness of its annotations**. The articles cited are summarized and described, not with one or two sentences as is often done, but in considerable detail. Another major feature is the section on **Introductory Orientations** (Section I.). Here the reader will find brief descriptions of works which survey the field-as-a-whole or some major portion thereof; the sources in this section provide both an integrated overview of general trends and extensive listings of additional literature. Overviews of more specialized subareas are located under the appropriate subject headings in the later sections of this volume.

We chose to provide extensive descriptions of a limited number of articles, rather than brief comments on a larger number of citations. It became clear quite early in our literature search that a number of good reviews of the literature already existed (see Section I.) and hence that extensive literature listings were readily available from other sources. Our focus then shifted toward a different kind of bibliography, one which would communicate something of the flavor and specific findings of selected works and provide starting points for locating further literature.

---

* Unpublished papers may be obtained by writing directly to the author in question. If no address is mentioned, refer to our **Directory of U.S. Scholars Engaged in Historical Family-related Work** (Munich: U.S. Family History Project, 1984), available in some university libraries or by writing: Dr. Elizabeth Benson-von der Ohe, U.S. Family History Project, St. Cajetan-Str. 9, 8000 Munich, Fed. Rep. of Germany.

Most of the material cited on the following pages was gathered by searching appropriate American journals in U.S. and German libraries. We did not have the resources to collect all available literature, hence the articles we cite cannot be considered as a random or selected sample thereof. In addition, U.S. scholars who were interviewed or who responded to a questionnaire provided us with some of their papers and publications. Finally, a computerized search of **Dissertation Abstracts*** and of the **Social Science Citation Index** was done; the resulting citations, insofar as they are not annotated elsewhere in the bibliography, are listed at the end of each major section.

On the Uses of this Volume

Such an annotated bibliography can be useful to several different types of readers. The foreign scholar can use it to learn about what his or her U.S. counterparts are doing, to identify key articles which provide an entree into a particular body of specialized literature, or simply to identify which U.S. journals carry which types of articles. The professional who is not a specialist in family history will find guidance for entering a new body of literature and will be able to locate specific publications of interest with minimal library searching. Professionals within family history may find it a convenient way to alert themselves to ideas and works outside of their own particular topics of concentration. Students will find it a useful source for locating term paper and thesis literature. In each case, we trust that the extensive literature descriptions will help readers to identify which publications do and do not fit their specific needs.

Finally, for the reader who is not already familiar with the historical literature on the family or is not well acquainted with the U.S. work on this subject, some sense of the field may be obtained by simply browsing these pages.

---

* For xerox or microfilm copies of U.S. doctoral dissertations, contact: University Microfilms Inc., 300 N. Zeeb Road, Ann Arbor, Michigan 48106.

AIDS TO USING THIS VOLUME

The bibliography is organized according to subject-matter topic. The eleven major topic-sections are identified with a roman numeral. Each is divided into subtopics, identified by a letter (A, B, C, etc.). Within each subtopic, literature citations are listed by number (1, 2, 3, etc.). Hence, to locate citation I.A.1., for example, one turns to Section I (Introductory Orientations), then to subsection A. (Broad Overviews), and locates the first citation in that subsection (Stone 1981).

The table of contents provides an overview of the major topics and subtopics, with page numbers. There is also a detailed table of contents containing additional minor subtopics and a listing of the author and year of all annotated articles and books (for book reviews, also the author and year of the book being reviewed)--also with page numbers.

There are extensive cross-references, both in the text and in the detailed table of contents. However, "Other References"-- i.e., citations listed but not annotated, located at the end of each major section--are not cross-referenced. Hence the reader interested in a particular subtopic should not only check the cross-referenced citations but also peruse those at the end of the appropriate major section.

There is also a name index at the end, including authors of all articles, book reviews, and books being reviewed, as well as most names appearing within the text.

DETAILED
TABLE OF CONTENTS

page

I. INTRODUCTORY ORIENTATIONS...1

Broad Surveys of the Literature

A. By Historians..1

    1. Stone 1979, 1981...1
    2. L. Tilly & Cohen 1981......................................1
    3. D.B. Smith 1982 (see also I.H.1.)..........................1
    4. Himmelfarb 1980: review of Kammen 1980.....................1
    5. Harris 1976..1
    6. Berkner 1973...1
    7. Wrigley 1977...1

    See also: Degler 1980 (V.B.8., V.B.9., IX.D.2.)

B. By Sociologists...3

    1. B. Laslett 1981..3
    2. Elder 1978 (see also IV.A.4.)..............................3
    3. Elder 1980 (see also IV.A.3.)..............................3
    4. B. Laslett 1973..3

    See also: IX.B.1.

C. By Anthropologists..4

    1. Yanigasako 1979..4

D. On the History of the German Family..........................5

    1. Lee 1981...5
    2. Evans & Lee 1981...5
    3. Soliday 1982: review of Evans & Lee 1981, Imhof 1981,
       Mitterauer & Sieder 1982, Weber-Kellermann 1978...........5
    4. Rippley 1976 (see also VI.I.4.)............................5

Introductions to Related Bodies of Literature

E. Economics...7

    1. Sawhill 1977...7
    2. Ferber & Birnbaum 1981.....................................7
    3. Liston 1980..7

    See also: I.A.2., Section III.A.

(I. INTRODUCTORY ORIENTATIONS, continued)

F. Women's History & Feminist Theory 9

(Women's History)

1. Bell 1979: review of Bridenthal & Koonz 1977 9
2. Cott & Pleck 1979 9
3. Lerner 1979 9
4. Lerner 1969 9
5. Sicherman 1975 9
6. Norton 1979 9
7. Lougee 1977 9
8. Shanley 1979 9

See also: I.A.4., V.B.8., V.B.9., IX.D.2.

(Feminist Theory)

9. Rapp, Ross, & Bridenthal 1979 9
10. Bridenthal 1982 9
11. Thorne 1982 9
12. Eisenstein 1979 10
13. Rubin 1975 10
14. Kelly 1979 10
15. MacKinnon 1982 10
16. Benjamin 1978 10

See also: Section V.C.

(Sources & Teaching)

17. Roth 1983: review of Hinding, Bower & Chambers 1979,
     Harrison 1979, Haber 1978, Terris 1980, Tingley & Tingley
     1981, Lerner 1981, Summer Institute on Women in American
     History 1981 11

See also: X.M.6.

G. Psychohistory...12

1. Skolnick 1975 12
2. Sinofsky, Fitzpatrick, Potts, & deMause 1975
    (see also IV.D.1.)......................................12
3. Schoenwald 1973: review of Weinstein & Platt 1973
    (see also VI.A.10.).....................................12
4. Quitt 1976 12
5. Cavallo 1981: review of Stannard 1980 12

See also: Section IV.D., VI.A.9., VI.B.4., VI.A.2.

History of the Discipline

H. The History of Family History 14

1. Ryan 1982 14
2. Hareven 1972 14
3. Hareven 1975 14

(I. INTRODUCTORY ORIENTATIONS, continued)

    4.   Farber 1979 14
    5.   May 1979..14
    6.   J.E. Smith & B. Laslett 1979 14
    7.   Hill 1979...14

    See also: I.A.1., I.A.3., I.J.1.

Other General References & Resources

I.   Bibliographies...16

    1.   Soliday, Hareven, Vann, & Wheaton 1980...............16
    2.   Milden 1977...16
    3.   Skinner & Wolf 1980.................................16

J.   Anthologies/Readers..17

    1.   M. Gordon 1973, 1978, 1983..........................17
    2.   Rosenberg 1975......................................17
    3.   Rabb & Rotberg 1973.................................17
    4.   Demos & Boocock 1978 (see also IV.B.1., IV.B.2.).........17

    See also: Section X.N.

K.   Brief Survey Articles for Students 18

    1.   Hareven 1983..18
    2.   B. Laslett 1983.....................................18
    3.   Kelly 1981..18

    See also: Sections X.M. to X.O. on teaching

Introductory Orientations: Other References

L.   Dissertations..20

M.   Publications...21

II. FAMILY/HOUSEHOLD STRUCTURE & COMPOSITION............................22

  A.   Conceptual & Theoretical Approaches 22

    1.   Verdon 1979 22
    2.   Verdon 1980 22

    See also: I.C.1., II.F.3., IV.A.7.

    Note: for methodology, see especially sections X.A. to X.D.

  B.   Reviews of Major Books 24

    1.   Burr 1979: review of Winch et al. 1977..............24
    2.   Farber 1979: review of Winch et al. 1977, Goody 1976.....24
    3.   Hareven 1975: review of Laslett & Wall 1972.........24
    4.   Vann 1974: review of Laslett & Wall 1972............25

(II. STRUCTURE & COMPOSITION, continued)

    5.   Litchfield 1979: review of P. Laslett 1977, Levine 1977....25
    6.   B. Laslett 1973: review of Anderson 1970 26
    7.   Engerman 1978: review of Gutman 1976 (see also VI.A.12.)...26

Studies of Specific Regions & Ethnic Groups

C.   European Populations...27

    1.   Parming 1979 27
    2.   Schmidtbauer 1980 27
    3.   M. Anderson 1978 27
    4.   Czap 1982...28
    5.   Fügedi 1982 28
    6.   Gunda 1982 28
    7.   Kahk, Palli, & Uibu 1982 28
    8.   Gavazzi 1982 28
    9.   Mitterauer & Kagan 1982 28
   10.   Mitterauer 1981..30

   See also: V.D.1., VIII.A.3., X.C.1-3.

D.   U.S. Populations, General.......................................31

    1.   Kobrin 1976 31
    2.   Modell & Hareven 1978..................................31
    3.   Michael, Fuchs,& Scott 1980............................32
    4.   Zuckerman ca. 1981 32

   See also: VII.I.1.

E.   U.S. Populations, Blacks 33

    1.   Shifflett 1975...33
    2.   Gutman 1975..33
    3.   Furstenberg, Hershberg, & Modell 1975 33
    4.   Harris 1976..34

   See also: VI.A.11., VII.G.2., VII.I.1.

F.   Other Regions or Cross-Cultural Comparisons 35

    1.   Wells 1974...35
    2.   Wheaton 1975...35
    3.   Sanjek 1982..36

Structure & Composition: Other References

G.   Dissertations 37

H.   Publications 38

III. MARRIAGE: BEGINNINGS & ENDINGS 39

    A.   Conceptual & Theoretical Approaches: Gary Becker and the
        "New Home Economics" 39

        1.   Becker 1973 39
        2.   Becker 1974 39
        3.   Freiden 1974 39
        4.   Ben-Porath 1982: review of Becker 1981 40
        5.   Hannan 1982: review of Becker 1981 40
        6.   Huber & Spitze 1980 41

        See also: I.E.1., I.E.2.

    B.   Marriage 42

        1.   Steckel 1980 42
        2.   Safley 1982 42
        3.   Taylor 1982 42

        See also: VI.C.1., X.I.4.

    C.   Divorce 44

        1.   Cott 1976 44
        2.   Schultz 1976 44
        3.   Preston & McDonald 1979 44

    D.   Widowhood 45

        1.   Diefendorf 1982 45
        2.   Wyntjes 1982 45
        3.   I. Brown 1982 45

Marriage: Other References

    E.   Dissertations 46

    F.   Publications 47

IV. THE LIFE CYCLE 49

    A.   Conceptual & Theoretical Approaches 49

        1.   Hareven 1978 49
        2.   Vinovskis 1977 49
        3.   Elder 1980 50
        4.   Elder 1978 50
        5.   Hareven 1977 51
        6.   Elder 1975 51
        7.   Hareven 1974 52
        8.   Keniston 1971 52

        See also: IX.B.2.

(IV. LIFE CYCLE, continued)

B. Reviews of Major Books 53

    1.   Cherlin 1979: review of Demos & Boocock 1978, Hareven
        1978, Hareven & Vinovskis 1978 53
    2.   Watkins 1980: review of Demos & Boocock 1978, Hareven 1978 .54
    3.   Modell 1975: review of Elder 1974 54
    4.   Demos 1973: review of Hunt 1970, McFarlane 1970 54

C. The Life Cycle: Empirical Works 56

    1.   Chudacoff 1980 56
    2.   Elder & Liker 1981 56
    3.   Elder 1981 57
    4.   Runck 1980 57
    5.   Wells 1971 58

    See also: II.D.2., X.I.4.

D. Life Stages: Childhood & Adolescence 59

(Bibliography)

    1.   Lopez 1974 59

    See also: I.G.2.

(Methods: Coding Categories)

    2.   Lyman 1980 59
    3.   Stewart, Winter, & Jones 1975 59

(The History of Childhood)

    4.   Demos 1971 60
    5.   deMause 1974 60
    6.   Ebel 1977 60
    7.   Kozak 1978 61
    8.   Lindemann 1981 61
    9.   Friedberger 1981 62
   10.   Minge-Kalman 1978 62

    See also: IX.E.1.

(The History of Adolescence)

   11.   Hiner 1975 63
   12.   Elder 1980 63

    See also: VII.I.2.

(IV. LIFE CYCLE, continued)

 E. Life Stages: Old Age..64

   1. Uhlenberg 1980.......................................64
   2. Spicker, Woodward, & Van Tassel 1978.....................64
   3. Van Tassel 1979......................................64
   4. Clark 1982...64

  See also: III.D.1., III.D.2., X.I.2.

 F. Methodological Approaches to the Life Cycle........................66

   1. Boocock 1978...66

  See also: IV.B.3.

Life Cycle: Other References

 G. Dissertations..67

 H. Publications...68

V. WOMEN'S LIVES: STATUS & WORK...70

 A. Conceptual & Theoretical Approaches................................70

   1. Hareven 1976 (see also I.A.7.)........................70

  See also: Section I.F., Section V.C.

 B. Reviews of Major Books...71

   1. Lerner 1978: review of Rich 1976, L. Gordon 1976...........71
   2. Interrante & Lasser 1979: review of Cott 1977, Douglas
     1977, Ewen 1976, Ehrenreich & English 1979.................71
   3. Stage 1980: review of Smith-Rosenberg 1975, Cott 1977,
     Ehrenreich & English 1979, Douglas 1977, Gordon 1976.......72
   4. Remy 1980: review of Sacks 1979, Turshen 1980..............73
   5. Cobb 1981: review of B. Smith 1981.........................74
   6. B. Anderson 1982: review of L. Tilly & Scott 1978..........75
   7. Lindemann 1982: review of Norton 1980.....................75
   8. Kerber 1982: review of Degler 1980 (see also IX.D.2.)......75
   9. Riegelhaupt 1982: review of Degler 1980 (see also
     IX.D.2.), Levy, White, & Johnson 1979, Dublin 1979,
     Kennedy 1979, Berkin & Lovett 1980........................76

  See also: XI.B.2.

 C. Status/Power...78

   1. Easton 1978..78
   2. Cooper 1979..78
   3. Folbre 1980..78
   4. Sokoloff 1981..79
   5. Fox-Genovese 1982....................................79

  See also: Section I.F., VI.B.3.

(V. WOMEN'S LIVES, continued)

    D.   Employment 81

        1.   McLaughlin 1971 81
        2.   Walkowitz 1972 81
        3.   Scott & L. Tilly 1976 82
        4.   L. Tilly, Scott, & Cohen 1976 82
        5.   B. Brown 1978 83
        6.   Bolin 1978 83
        7.   Brownlee 1979 84
        8.   Franzoi 1981 84
        9.   Milkman 1981 85

        See also: I.F.10., Section III.A., IX.B.3., X.G.6.

    E.   Housework & Household Production 86

        1.   Cowan 1976 86
        2.   Hartmann 1981 86
        3.   Swerdlow 1978 87
        4.   Jensen 1980 87
        5.   C. Brown 1982 87

        See also: I.F.12., IX.B.5.

Women's Lives: Other References

    F.   Dissertations 89

    G.   Publications 90

VI. FAMILY LIFE: COMPREHENSIVE TREATMENTS 91

    A.   Reviews of Major Books 91

        1.   Breines 1981: review of Flandrin 1979 91
        2.   Ross 1979: review of Poster 1978 91
        3.   Plumb 1977: review of Stone 1977 (see also I.F.8.) 92
        4.   Hill 1978: review of Stone 1977, P. Laslett 1977 92
        5.   L. Tilly 1978: review of Shorter 1975, Zaretsky 1976 93
        6.   Scott 1977: review of Shorter 1975 94
        7.   Kaplow 1977: review of Shorter 1975 94
        8.   Wells 1977: review of Shorter 1975 95
        9.   Dunn 1976: review of Shorter 1975 95
       10.   Lasch 1975: review of Weinstein & Platt 1969
           (see also I.G.3.) 95
       11.   Burton 1981: review of Pleck 1979 96
       12.   Rury 1978: review of Gutman 1976 (see also II.B.7.) 96

        See also: V.B.8., V.B.9., IX.D.2.

(VI. FAMILY LIFE, COMPREHENSIVE, continued)

B.   Focus on Mentalité, Values, Emotions..................................98

    1.   Brobeck 1977.....................................98
    2.   N. Davis 1977....................................98
    3.   Lantz, Schultz, & O'Hara 1977 99
    4.   Demos 1972 99

    See also: I.B.4., II.D.4., VII.C.4.

C.   Other Empirical Studies 101

    1.   Pedlow 1982 101
    2.   Chrisman ca. 1982 101
    3.   Douglass 1980...................................102
    4.   Douglass 1975: review of Brøgger 1971, J. Davis 1973.....102
    5.   K. Brown 1978..................................102

    See also: X.K.2.

Family Life, Comprehensive: Other References

D.   Dissertations..104

E.   Publications...106

VII.   SEXUALITY, BIRTH, DEATH, & MIGRATION: DEMOGRAPHIC &
    OTHER APPROACHES...108

A.   The Field of Historical Demography in Various Countries:
    Overviews..108

    1.   Maynes 1981 108
    2.   Roman 1981 108

B.   Reviews of Major Books 109

    1.   B. Anderson 1981: review of Vinovskis 1979 ....**109**
    2.   Ewbank 1980: review of C. Tilly 1978, Lesthaeghe 1977....109
    3.   Hogan 1982: review of Coale, Anderson, & Härm 1979.......110

    See also: IV.B.1., V.C.5., VIII.B.1., IX.D.2.

C.   Sexuality & Illegitimacy 111

    1.   Freedman 1982...................................111
    2.   Padgug 1979 111
    3.   Ross & Rapp 1981 112
    4.   Gadlin 1976 112
    5.   Shorter 1971 113
    6.   Berlanstein 1980...............................113
    7.   Barrett 1980 114

    See also: V.C.5., V.D.4., VII.C.3., VII.C.5., IX.D.2., X.B.8.

(VII. SEXUALITY, BIRTH, DEATH, & MIGRATION, continued)

Birth & Fertility

D. Non-demographic Approaches....................................115
   1.   Suitor 1981 115
   2.   LaSorte 1976..115

   See also: V.B.1., V.B.3., VIII.A.5.

E. Demographic Approaches 116

                        (Germany)

   1.   Knodel & DeVos 1980 and other Knodel publications........116

                     (U.S.-in-general)

   2.   Tolnay & Guest 1982...................................117
   3.   McFalls & Masnick 1981 118
   4.   Vinovskis 1981..118

   See also: IX.C.1.

                 (U.S. Cities & Regions)

   5.   Haines 1980 118
   6.   Laidig, Schutjer, & Stokes 1981.......................119
   7.   Leet 1976...119
   8.   Steckel 1979 120

                      (Methodology)

   9.   Sanderson 1979..120
   10. Krishnamoorthy 1979...................................121

   See also: Section X.I.

Both Fertility & Mortality

F. Non-demographic Approaches 122
   1.   Davies 1982...122

G. Demographic Approaches.......................................123
   1.   Lithell 1981..123
   2.   Fogel & Engerman 1979.................................123
   3.   D.S. Smith 1972.......................................123

   See also: IV.C.5.

(VII. SEXUALITY, BIRTH, DEATH, & MIGRATION, continued)

Death & Mortality

H.   Demographic Approaches 125

    1. Fogel, Engerman, Trussell, Floud, Pope, & Wimmer 1978 125
    2. Sly & Chi 1972...125
    3. Vinovskis 1972..126

Migration

I.   Demographic Approaches 127

    1. Bodnar, Weber, & Simon 1979...........................127
    2. Moch 1981...127
    3. Swierenga 1980..128
    4. Kamphoefner 1982 (see also I.D.4.)....................128

Sexuality, Birth, Death, Migration: Other References

J.   Dissertations 129

K.   Publications 130

VIII. KINSHIP, LINEAGE, & INHERITANCE 133

A.   Kinship & Lineage 133

    1. Mogey 1976: review of Cuisenier 1975.................133
    2. Dupâquier 1981..133
    3. Plakans 1982..134
    4. Fischer 1982..134
    5. Harrell ca. 1978 135

See also: I.C.1., II.B.1., II.B.2., II.F.2., Section X.C.

B.   Inheritance 136

    1. Vinovskis 1971: review of Greven 1970.................136
    2. Salamon 1980..136
    3. Hoffman 1981..137
    4. Douglass 1981...137
    5. Ditz 1982 138

See also: VI.C.1., X.E.1.

Kinship & Inheritance: Other References

C.   Dissertations 139

D.   Publications 140

IX. OTHER INSTITUTIONS & THE FAMILY.....................................141

The Economy & Education

A. The Family Economy & Family Strategies..........................141

    1. Goldin 1979 and other Goldin Papers 141
    2. Harding 1979 141
    3. Early 1982 142

    See also: VI.B.2., VI.C.1.

B. The Larger Economy...143

    1. Kanter 1978 143
    2. Smelser & Halpern 1978.................................143
    3. Kolko 1978..144
    4. Fruin 1980..144
    5. Vanek 1980..145

    See also: I.B.1., IV.D.7., V.E.2., VI.A.5., X.G.6.

C. Education..146
    1. Graff 1979..146

    See also: IX.B.2.

Welfare & Public Policy

D. Reviews of Major Books...147

    1. Sennett 1980: review of Donzelot 1979 147
    2. Lasch 1980: review of Donzelot 1979, Degler 1980
        (see also V.B.8-9.), Foucault 1978 (see also V.C.5.).....147
    3. Lasch 1977: review of Keniston 1977...................148
    4. Berman 1978: review of Lasch 1977 (see also V.C.2.)......149
    5. Joffe 1978: review of Lasch 1977......................149
    6. Davis 1978: review of Lasch 1977......................149
    7. Rosenberg 1979: review of Lasch 1977..................149

    See also: VI.A.1.

E. Other Works..151

    1. Cavallo 1976..151
    2. Featherstone 1979.....................................151
    3. P. Laslett 1979.......................................152
    4. Zaretsky 1982...152

(IX. OTHER INSTITUTIONS, continued)

The Military

F.   War & the Family 153

    1.   Taylor & Rebel 1981....................................153

Institutions: Other References

G.   Dissertations..154

H.   Publications..155

X. METHODOLOGY: RESEARCH & TEACHING....................................156

Research: Computer Micro-Simulation

A.   Reviews of Major Books....................................156

    1.   Haines 1980: review of Wachter, Hammel, & P. Laslett
       1977/78 (see also X.B.5.) 156

B.   Other Works 157

    1.   Hammel 1979....................................157
    2.   Hammel & Wachter 1977....................................157
    3.   Hammel, Hutchinson, Wachter, Lundy, & Deuel 1976 157
    4.   Hammel & Deuel 1977....................................157
    5.   Fitch 1980: review of Wachter, Hammel, & P. Laslett
       1977/78 (see also X.A.1.) 157
    6.   Hammel 1980a....................................157
    7.   Hammel 1980b....................................157
    8.   Hammel, McDaniel, & Wachter 1980 157
    9.   Hammel 1976....................................158

Research: Computer-Assisted Data Analysis

C.   Quantitative Handling of Anthropological & Cross-cultural Data 160

    1.   Hammel & Soć 1973....................................160
    2.   Hammel 1972 160
    3.   Hammel 1975 160
    4.   Hammel & Yarbrough 1973 160
    5.   Hammel & P. Laslett 1974 160

D.   Record Linkage & Family Reconstitution 161

    1.   Hastings & Harrison 1979....................................161
    2.   Bouchard & Pouyez 1980 161

E.   Inventory Analysis....................................162

    1.   Carr & Walsh 1980 162

(X. METHODOLOGY, continued)

F. Multivariate Statistical Analysis: Probit, Logit, Tobit, etc..........163

    1. Shammas 1981 163
    2. Kousser, Cox, & Galenson 1982 163

Research: Data Sources

G. Data Banks & Data Sets 164

    1. Bean, May, & Skolnick 1978...............................164
    2. Skolnick, Bean, Dintelman, & Mineau 1979 164
    3. Austin 1979 164
    4. Soliday 1971 (see also Imhof under VII.E.1.)............165
    5. National Immigration Archives, forthcoming 165
    6. Kleinberg 1975..166

H. Archival & Other Sources 167

    1. Hughes 1974 167

See also: I.E.3., I.F.17., VII.C.2., X.G.6.

Research: Other Topics

I. Problems in Demographic Analysis..............................168

    1. Spagnoli 1977 168
    2. D.S. Smith 1978...168
    3. D.S. Smith 1979...169
    4. Espenshade & Braun 1982 169

See also: VII.E.9., VII.E.10.

J. Oral History 170

    1. Shopes 1981...170
    2. Blatt 1981..170

K. Handling Historical Time-Change 171

    1. Fogel, Floud, Pope, & Wimmer 1982 (see also VII.H.1.)....171
    2. Patterson 1982 171

See also: IV.B.3.

L. Other Articles on Research Methodology........................172

    1. Kousser 1982 172

See also: IV.D.2., IV.D.3., IV.F.1., VII.E.9., VII.E.10.

(X. METHODOLOGY, continued)

Teaching: Resources & Methods

M. Course Syllabi for College Classes 173

    1. Lyman & Lyman 1981.............................173
    2. Johnson, Slater, White, & Yngvesson 1982 173
    3. Cerullo, Johnson, & White 1981......................173
    4. Lee 1982.......................................173
    5. Goldfrank 1980 (Knodel)..........................173
    6. Thorne 1982 173

N. Textbooks for College Classes...............................175

    1. Watts & Davis 1982..............................175

See also: I.D.3., Section I.J., I.F.1., I.F.2., I.F.14.,
VII.B.1., VII.C.2.

Brief articles: Section I.K., VII.C.4., VII.E.4.

O. Ideas & Techniques for Teaching Family History 176

    1. Beall, Leon, O'Connell, & Rothman 1981.................176
    2. Rothman 1981....................................176
    3. O'Connell 1981..................................176

See also: I.F.17.

Methodology: Other References

P. Dissertations 178

Q. Publications 179

XI. SPACE & ARCHITECTURE 185

A. Domestic Space 185

    1. Clark 1976 185
    2. Lawrence 1982...................................185

See also: X.O.3.

B. Urban Spatial Patterns.......................................186

    1. Modell 1979.....................................186
    2. Wekerle 1980 (see also X.G.6.).......................186

Space: Other References

C. Dissertations 187

D. Publications 188

NAME INDEX...189

I. INTRODUCTORY ORIENTATIONS

BROAD SURVEYS OF THE LITERATURE

I.A. BROAD SURVEYS: BY HISTORIANS

(I.A.1.) Stone, Lawrence
ca. 1979 "Family History." Unpublished manuscript. A revised version has since been published under the following title:

1981 "Family History in the 1980s: Past Achievements and Future Trends." Journal of Interdisciplinary History 12: 51-88.

(I.A.2.) Tilly, Louise A., and Miriam Cohen
1981 "Does the Family have a History? A Review of Theory and Practice in Family History." Unpublished manuscript, to be published in revised form in Social Science History and, in Italian translation, in Passato e Presente.

(I.A.3.) Smith, Daniel Blake
1982 "The Study of the Family in Early America: Trends, Problems, and Prospects." William and Mary Quarterly, 3rd series, 39 (January): 3-28.

(I.A.4.) Himmelfarb, Gertrude
1980 "The New History." New York Times Book Review (August): 3.

Review of: Michael Kammen, editor, 1980, The Past Before Us: Contemporary Historical Writing in the United States. Ithaca, New York: Cornell University Press.

(I.A.5.) Harris, Barbara J.
1976 "Recent Work On the History of the Family: A Review Article." Feminist Studies 3: 159-172.

(I.A.6.) Berkner, Lutz K.
1973 "Recent Research on the History of the Family in Western Europe." Journal of Marriage and the Family 35 (August): 395-405.

(I.A.7.) Wrigley, E. Anthony
1977 "Reflections on the History of the Family." Deadalus 106 (Spring): 71-85.

Several sources are recommended for the professional reader wanting a broad but not-too-lengthy overview of the basic outlines and major findings

of the field of family history. The best starting point for professionals
having little or no background in the field is STONE'S article on the
family in the U.S., France, and England. Subheadings include: demography;
household structure; economics; lineage, kin and family; stages of life;
religion; values and emotions; and sexuality. Reasons for the spectacular
growth in family history and new directions for the future are also illuminated.

TILLY and COHEN'S paper takes a more critical stance and assumes a more-
knowledgeable reader. They identify four major approaches--demographic
(exemplified by Laslett and Wall), sentiments (Shorter, Stone, Degler),
household economics (Tilly and Scott), and hegemonic-institutional
(Lasch, Donzelet)--for which critiques and suggested modifications/
alternatives are given. Using this framework, many recent publications
(most post-1975) on the family in Western Europe and America are discussed.
Finally, feminist critiques of family history are highlighted and future
directions for the field are sketched.

For a comprehensive overview of the literature on the U.S. family up
until about 1800, the article by SMITH is recommended. See Ryan (I.H.1.)
for a briefer treatment, extending into the early 1900s.

For professionals seeking an overview of what U.S. social historians are
doing--not only in family history--the Kammen book is highly recommended
(see the review by HIMMELFARB). It is a collection of review articles
by 20 eminent historians. The essay by Carl Degler on women and the family
deserves special mention. (Those seeking a more comprehensive review
of the history of women and the family in the U.S. are referred to his
book At Odds, discussed in V.B.8., V.B.9., and IX.D.2.) The chapter
on quantitative history will also be of special interest. Other chapters
cover such topics as political, urban, local, intellectual, cultural,
medieval, Latin American, psychoanalytic, oral, and black and ethnic
history.

A less recent but extensive review of the literature on the family,
including also European history, is HARRIS (1976). For Western Europe
see also BERKNER (1973) and WRIGLEY (1977).

(I.B.1.) Laslett, Barbara
            1981 "Production, Reproduction, and Social Change: The
                  Family in Historical Perspective." In James F. Short,
                  Jr., The State of Sociology: Problems and Prospects,
                  239-258. Beverly Hills, California: Sage.

(I.B.2.) Elder, Glen H., Jr.
            1978 "Approaches to Social Change and the Family."
                  American Journal of Sociology 84 (Supplement):
                  S1-S37. (See I.J.4. for book version of this
                  journal supplement.)

(I.B.3.) Elder, Glen H., Jr.
            1980 "History and the Family." Ernest Burgess Award
                  Lecture, held on October 25, 1980, in Portland,
                  Oregon. Later published as:

            1981 "History and the Family: The Discovery of Complexity."
                  Journal of Marriage and the Family 43 (August):
                  489-519.

(I.B.4.) Laslett, Barbara
            1973 "The Family as a Public and Private Institution:
                  A Historical Perspective." Journal of Marriage
                  and the Family 35 (August): 480-492.

Any broad survey of the field of family history is interdisciplinary to
some degree, but those written by sociologists include more of the
sociological literature and hence cover more of the 20th century (where
historians have yet to make much of an inroad). The sociologically
trained reader will find links to familiar theories and studies which
may ease the transition into a new body of literature.

For a concise, but comprehensive, interdisciplinary survey of the field,
LASLETT (1981) is recommended. Her brief, selective introduction (pages
241-244) to 37 major works integrates findings from many disciplines
about interrelated domestic, developmental, and demographic changes. It
provides a starting place for the reader of any discipline who wishes to
become acquainted with key works in other disciplines. (The remainder of
the article gives special attention to how the rise of Western capitalism
has shaped the family and sketches the general outline of a model for
the historical study of this relationship, in which class relations are
a central variable.)

For the reader seeking a detailed introduction to the American sociological
literature (including many of the "classics") as it relates to the history
of the family, ELDER (1978 or 1980) is suggested. Special attention is
given to theories of social change and to age and the life course. These
articles are described in more detail under IV.A.3. and IV.A.4. An older
survey article on the U.S. family is LASLETT (1973). See also IX.B.1.

C

I.C. BROAD SURVEYS: _BY ANTHROPOLOGISTS_

(I.C.1.) Yanagisako, Sylvia Junko
                1979 "Family and Household: The Analysis of Domestic
                      Groups." Annual Review of Anthropology 8: 161-205.

For a brief, selective discussion of historical and anthropological studies
on changes-over-time in domestic groups--an anthropological term for
families and households--YANIGISAKO 1979 (pages 176-184) is suggested.
This article assumes a moderately knowledgeable professional reader and
would be appropriate for non-anthropologists seeking an overview of anthropological theory and of contemporary and historical anthropological
research. Although much of the essay deals with the structure and
organization of the domestic group, Yanagisako (pages 190-193) feels that
a fully cultural understanding of kinship also requires attention to
symbolic meanings and introduces the reader to the literature on symbolic
analysis.

(I.D.1.) Lee, W.R.
1981 "Past Legacies and Future Prospects: Recent Research on the History of the Family in Germany." <u>The Journal of Family History</u> 6 (Summer): 156-176.

(I.D.2.) Evans, Richard J., and W.R. Lee, editors
1981 <u>The German Family</u>. London, England: Croom Helm.

(I.D.3.) Soliday, Gerald L.
1982 "Some Recent Studies in German Family History." <u>Journal of Family History</u> 7 (Winter): 425-434.

Review of:

Richard J. Evans and W.R. Lee, editors, 1981, <u>The German Family: Essays on the Social History of the Family in Nineteenth- and Twentieth-Century Germany</u>. London, England: Croom Helm. Totowa, New Jersey: Barnes and Noble.

Arthur E. Imhof, 1981, <u>Die gewonnen Jahre: Von der Zunahme unserer Lebensspanne seit dreihundert Jahren oder von der Notwendigkeit einer neuen Einstellung zu Leben und Sterben</u>. Munich, Germany: C.H. Beck.

Michael Mitterauer and Reinhard Sieder, 1982, <u>The European Family: Patriarchy to Partnership from the Middle Ages to the Present</u>. Oxford, England: Basil Blackwell. German original: 1977, <u>Vom Patriarchat zur Partnerschaft: Zum Strukturwandel der Familie</u>. Munich, Germany: C.H. Beck.

Ingeborg Weber-Kellermann, 1978, <u>Die deutsche Familie: Versuch einer Sozialgeschichte</u>, 4th edition, Frankfurt am Main, Germany: Suhrkamp.

(I.D.4.) Rippley, La Vern J.
1976 <u>The German Americans</u>, Boston, Massachusetts: Twayne Publishers.

Perhaps the most comprehensive brief English-language survey of research on the German family's history is the LEE article. He critiques and discusses the literature on family and household analysis, historical demography, the function of the family within the economy, and finally research relating to folklore, legal history, and related non-quantifiable fields. Foreign initiative, Lee states, has been predominant; German scholars are criticized as having gotten a late start and having made only limited progress in certain areas. An extensive bibliography is provided. (For an expanded version of this article, but without the convenient bibliography, see his chapter in the Evans and Lee anthology.)

The SOLIDAY article provides a detailed introduction to four books, each of which in its own way provides the reader with an overview of the history of the German family. Published in both English and German, the Mitterauer and Seider book is said to be probably the best general introduction to European family history available in the English language. It covers six centuries of family history, primarily in German-speaking Europe. Written for the general educated public, this book would also be suitable for classroom use. Available only in English, the Evans and Lee volume is an interdisciplinary collection of articles on the German family. Contributors are primarily British and German scholars and the focus tends toward the working-class family. (The major German-language collection on the European family is: Werner Conze, editor, Sozialgeschichte der Familie in der Neuzeit Europas. Industrielle Welt, Band 21. Stuttgart, Germany: Klett-Cotta Verlag. 1977.)

Also reviewed by Soliday are two books available only in the German language. Imhof's treatment of life expectancy from the 17th century to the present, written for the general educated public, is said to show how profoundly human and lively historical demography can be. The social history of the German family by ethnologist Weber-Kellermann includes a treatment of domestic space, clothing styles, and popular customs as indicators of changes in family life, as well as such topics as the persistence of patriarchy, the changing roles of women, the discovery of childhood, etc.
For those interested in German immigrants in America (German-Americans), a good starting point is the RIPPLEY book. It gives a broad overview of many facets of the German experience in the U.S. from pre-revolutionary times to the present, including emigration motives and adjustment strate-gies. However, there is no chapter devoted specifically to the family.
(On German-Americans, see also VI.I.4.)

INTRODUCTIONS TO RELATED BODIES OF LITERATURE

I.E. RELATED LITERATURE: ECONOMICS

(I.E.1.) Sawhill, Isabel V.
    1977 "Economic Perspectives on the Family." Daedalus
    106 (Spring): 115-125.

(I.E.2.) Ferber, Marianne A., and Bonnie Birnbaum
    1981 "The Impact of Parental Work on the Family as an
    Economic System." Unpublished paper, prepared for
    the Panel on Work, Family, and Community, sponsored
    by the Committee on Child Development, Research and
    Public Policy. (February, 1981). The authors are
    at the University of Illinois.

(I.E.3.) Liston, Margaret I.
    1980 A Century of Family Economics Research 1862-1962:
    A Bibliographical, Historical, and Analytical
    Reference Book. Forthcoming 1985. To be distributed
    by: Department of Family Economics, University of
    Missouri--Columbia, Columbia, Missouri.

The historical study of the family as an economic unit has been dominated
by non-economists, primarily historians (see I.A.2. for an overview of
this literature). There are, however, bodies of literature by economists
and by family economists.

There are perhaps two major "schools" in U.S. economics: the institutional (M.I.T. and Berkeley) and the neoclassical (Chicago and Columbia
on the one hand and Pennsylvania, with a somewhat different approach, on
the other hand.) The institutional approach includes a concern for the
evolution and impact of social rule and custom and focuses more on change
than do many neoclassical economists. (See V.E.5. for one non-technical
example.)

Within the neoclassical approach, the so-called Chicago school is well
known for its "new home economics"; heavily influenced by human capital
theory and the theory of the allocation of time, it employs a cost-benefit
model of family decision-making to explain fertility rates, marriage and
divorce rates, rates of wives' employment, and other aspects of the allocation of goods and time by the household. A good, if somewhat critical,
introduction for the non-economist is found in SAWHILL and also in
FERBER and BIRNBAUM. The most recent major book is Becker's A Treatise
on the Family (see III.A.4. and III.A.5.) and the older classic is
Theodore Schultz, editor, Economics of the Family: Marriage, Children,
and Human Capital (University of Chicago Press, 1974). Critics of the
"new home economics" claim that it cannot handle change very well and that,
while potentially applicable to historical data, its models have been
primarily applied to contemporary data so far. (See also Section III.A.)

Also neoclassical in approach is the Pennsylvania group. Compared to the

Chicago school, it puts more stress on the family as a unit of analysis, often employs transactions-cost analysis, and relies more on household utility functions than on household production functions. The "transactional approach" being developed (Robert Pollak) is said to both provide a theoretical alternative to Becker's framework and to generalize that framework, taking into account internal structure and organization. (For examples of work by members of this school, see IX.A.1.)

A quite different body of literature is that of family economics. Long before most economists "discovered" the family, family economists--often associated with university departments of home economics or with government agencies--were carrying out research on the economic circumstances of U.S. families. Family economists usually have studied the contemporary family of their time, but their accumulated research findings provide a wealth of information on American families, especially from about 1910 onward. The single best resource for locating this widely scattered literature is the LISTON book. She provides a history of family economics in the U.S. from 1862 to 1962--key events in the history of the discipline, how changing environmental circumstances shaped the directions of research, and trends-over-time in research topics, aims, methodologies, and institutional contexts. Part VII provides a concise summary of the book. The selective bibliography in Part VI (organized chronologically within subtopics) is invaluable for family historians who want to explore this literature.

I.F. RELATED LITERATURE: *WOMEN'S HISTORY AND FEMINIST THEORY*

(I.F.1.) Bell, Susan Groag
            1979 (Untitled Book Review.) Signs 5 (Winter):
            348-349.

            Review of: Renate Bridenthal and Claudia Koonz,
            editors, 1977, Becoming Visible: Women in European
            History. Boston, Massachusetts: Houghton Mifflin.

(I.F.2.) Cott, Nancy F., and Elizabeth H. Pleck, editors
            1979 A Heritage of Her Own: Toward a New Social History
            of American Women. New York: Simon and Schuster.

(I.F.3.) Lerner, Gerda
            1979 The Majority Finds Its Past: Placing Women in
            History. New York: Oxford University Press.

(I.F.4.) Lerner, Gerda
            1969 "New Approaches to the Study of Women in History."
            Journal of Social History 3 (Fall): 53-62.

(I.F.5.) Sicherman, Barbara
            1975 "Review Essay: American History." Signs (Winter):
            461-485.

(I.F.6.) Norton, Mary Beth
            1979 "Review Essay: American History." Signs 5 (Winter):
            324-337.

(I.F.7.) Lougee, Carolyn C.
            1977 "Review Essay: Modern European History." Signs 2
            (Spring): 628-650.

(I.F.8.) Shanley, Mary Lyndon
            1979 "Review Essay: The History of the Family in Modern
            England." Signs 4 (Summer): 740-750.

(I.F.9.) Rapp, Rayna, Ellen Ross, and Renate Bridenthal
            1979 "Examining Family History." Feminist Studies 5
            (Spring): 174-200.

(I.F.10.) Bridenthal, Renate
            1982 "The Family: The View From a Room of Her Own."
            In Barrie Thorne with Marilyn Yalom, editors,
            Rethinking the Family: Some Feminist Questions,
            225-239. New York: Longman.

(I.F.11.) Thorne, Barrie
            1982 "Feminist Rethinking of the Family: An Overview."
            In Barrie Thorne with Marilyn Yalom, editors,
            Rethinking the Family: Some Feminist Questions,
            1-24. New York: Longman.

(I.F.12.) Eisenstein, Zillah, editor
          1979 Capitalist Patriarchy and the Case for Socialist
                Feminism. New York and London: Monthly Review
                Press.

(I.F.13.) Rubin, Gayle
          1975 "The Traffic in Women: Notes on the 'Political
                Economy'of Sex." In Raynd R. Reiter, editor,
                Toward an Anthropology of Women, 157-210. New
                York: Monthly Review Press.

(I.F.14.) Kelly, Joan
          1979 "The Doubled Vision of Feminist Theory." Feminist
                Studies 5: 216-227.

(I.F.15.) MacKinnon, Catharine A.
          1982 "Feminism, Marxism, Method, and the State: An
                Agenda for Theory." Signs 7 (Spring): 515-544.

(I.F.16.) Benjamin, Jessica
          1978 "Authority and the Family Revisited: or, A World
                Without Fathers?" New German Critique, Number 13
                (Winter): 35-56.

For recent collections of key articles, Bridenthal and Koonz (see Bell
review) on women in European history and COTT and PLECK on women in
American history are recommended.

An important book-length treatment of U.S. women's history is the collected
essays of Gerda LERNER (1979). Via the footnotes, the history of the
field in the U.S. can also be traced.

An early example of her numerous articles which have influenced the subsequent directions of women's history in the U.S. is LERNER (1969).
Lerner has been instrumental in the establishment of women's history as
a field in its own right, not to be confused with family history.

For an integration of women's history with family history, for the U.S.,
see the Degler book (V.B.8., V.B.9., IX.D.2.) and his chapter in Kammen (I.A.4.).

Excellent review essays on the new historical scholarship, as it relates
to women, appear occasionally in Signs. For women in American history,
see SICHERMAN (1975) and NORTON (1979). See LOUGEE (1977) on Western
Europe and SHANLEY (1979) on modern England.

Recent attempts to bring some of the feminist insights from women's
history and other disciplines to bear upon the study of the family--
and to redefine our thinking about "the family"--include RAPP, ROSS,
and BRIDENTHAL (1979), BRIDENTHAL (1982), and THORNE (1982). Readers
wanting an introduction to recent U.S. feminist theory per se should
refer to the social-feminist anthology by EISENSTEIN (especially the
Hartmann article) and the articles by RUBIN (on Levy-Strauss and Freud),
KELLY (the public-private debate), and MACKINNON. The BENJAMIN critique

of Horkheimer may also be useful (the British counterpart to the Eisenstein anthology is Kuhn and Wolpe, 1978, Feminism and Materialism, Routledge and Kegan Paul). For a course syllabus on feminist theory, see X.M.6. On feminist theory, see also Section V.C.

(I.F.17) Roth, Darlene R.
1983 "Review Essay/Growing Like Topsy: Research Guides to Women's History." Journal of American History 70 (June): 95-100.

Review of:

Hinding, Andrea, Ames Sheldon Bower, and Clarke A. Chambers, editors, 1979, Women's History Sources: A Guide to Archives and Manuscript Collections in the United States. Volume I: Collections. Volume II: Index. New York: Bowker.

Harrison, Cynthia E., editor, 1979, Women in American History: A Bibliography. Santa Barbara, California: ABC-Clio.

Haber, Barbara, editor, 1978, Women in America: A Guide to Books, 1963-1975. Boston, Massachusetts: Hall.

Terris, Virginia R., editor, 1980, Woman in America: A Guide to Information Sources. Detroit, Michigan: Gale.

Tingley, Elizabeth, and Donald F. Tingley, editors, 1981, Women and Feminism in American History: A Guide to Information Sources. Detroit, Michigan: Gale.

Lerner, Gerda, 1981, Teaching Women's History. Washington, D.C.: American Historical Association.

Summer Institute on Women in American History Faculty, Staff and Participants, 1981, A Woman's Place Is in the History Books, HER STORY: 1620-1980: A Curriculum Guide for American History Teachers. Princeton, New Jersey: Woodrow Wilson National Fellowship Foundation.

For a discussion of recent bibliographies, guides to information and archival sources, and teaching guides on women in U.S. history, see ROTH.

I.G.   RELATED LITERATURE: *PSYCHOHISTORY*

(I.G.1.)   Skolnick, Arlene
          1975   "The Family Revisited: Themes in Recent Social
                 Science Research." Journal of Interdisciplinary
                 History 4 (Spring): 703-719.

(I.G.2.)   Sinofsky, Faye, John J. Fitzpatrick, Louis W. Potts, and
          Lloyd deMause
          1975   "A Bibliography of Psychohistory." History of
                 Childhood Quarterly 2 (Spring): 517-562.

(I.G.3.)   Schoenwald, Richard L.
          1973   "Using Psychology in History: A Review Essay."
                 Historical Methods Newsletter 7 (December):
                 9-24.

                 Review of: Fred Weinstein and Gerald M. Platt,
                 1973, Psychoanalytic Sociology: An Essay on the
                 Interpretation of Historical Data and the
                 Phenomena of Collective Behavior. Baltimore,
                 Maryland, and London, England: Johns Hopkins
                 University Press.

(I.G.4.)   Quitt, Martin H.
          1976   "The Contemporary 'Crisis' of the American Family:
                 The Perspective of a Family Historian and
                 Psychohistorian." History of Childhood Quarterly
                 4 (Summer): 101-110.

(I.G.5.)   Cavallo, Dominick
          1981   (Untitled Book Review.) Social Science History 5
                 (Fall): 492-495.

                 Review of: David E. Stannard, 1980, Shrinking
                 History: On Freud and the Failure of Psychohistory.
                 New York: Oxford University Press.

Applications of psychological interpretations and theories to family
history are seldom done by psychologists but rather by historians and
others. (However, for a review by a psychologist of social science
works relevant to family history, including a treatment of psychological
theories of child socialization, see the SKOLNICK article.)

An extensive bibliography on "psychohistory" is SINOFSKY, FITZPATRICK,
POTTS and deMAUSE (1975). Included are English, French, and German-
language works, divided into six categories: methodology and general;
history of childhood; ancient; medieval and renaissance; modern; and
Asia. (For another bibliography, see IV.D.1.)

Useful early statements on approaches to applying psychology to family
history include Demos (VI.B.4.) and also SCHOENWALD. Demo's Little
Commonwealth book (VI.A.9.), applying Erik Erikson's developmental theory

to the Puritan family, is still considered by many as a model of how
psychology can inform history. For a discussion of psychohistory versus
family history, as approaches to interpreting contemporary crises of the
American family, see QUITT.

We did not attempt a systematic coverage of psychohistory-proper; suffice
it to say that there are opposing "camps" (represented by Lloyd deMause's
Journal of Psychohistory and Charles Strozier's more-mainstream Psychohistory
Review) and ongoing criticisms against psychoanalytic psychohistory (most
recently by Stannard, reviewed in the CAVALLO article) in this controversy-
ridden field.

For additional literature, see also VI.A.2. and Section IV.D.

On Weinstein and Platt, see also VI.A.10.

H

I.H.   *THE HISTORY OF FAMILY HISTORY*

(I.H.1.) Ryan, Mary P.
            1982 "The Explosion of Family History." Reviews
            in American History 10 (December): 181-195.

(I.H.2.) Hareven, Tamara K.
            1972 "The History of the Family as an Interdisciplinary
            Field." The Journal of Interdisciplinary History
            2: 399-414.

(I.H.3.) Hareven, Tamara K.
            1975 "Introduction: The Historical Study of the Family
            in Urban Society." Journal of Urban History 1
            (May): 259-267.

(I.H.4.) Farber, Bernard
            1979 "Family History as a Moral Science." Sociology
            and Social Research 63 (Number 3): 603-612.

(I.H.5.) May, Dean L.
            1979 "In Search of a Family History: Where Do We Go
            From Here?" Sociology and Social Research 63
            (Number 3): 596-601.

(I.H.6.) Smith, James E., and Barbara Laslett
            1979 "Introduction." Sociology and Social Research
            63 (Number 3): 425-431.

(I.H.7.) Hill, Reuben
            1979 "Historical Change in Marriage and the Family:
            Where Do We Go From Here?" Sociology and Social
            Research 63 (Number 3): 590-602.

The "History of the Family" as a field of study has a history of its own.
Several accounts of how it grew, and the issues with which it grappled
at different stages, are available.

For the United States, the introductions in the Gordon readers (I.J.1.)
sketch key events in the growth of the field. RYAN chronicles this
development in a different way, tracing how scholars approached the American
family over the past decade. Research began with colonial history and
gradually, if meanderingly, proceeded into the 19th century and then--
sociological contributions aside--practically stopped in the early 20th
century. Questions shifted with historical period, from themes of patriarchal
authority in the 17th century to domesticity in the 19th century. This
article also presents an overview of major findings about the family in
American history. Smith (I.A.3.) is also recommended.

For an account which includes also Britain and France, Stone (I.A.1.) is
useful.

Then there are older articles which simultaneously present an interpretation of the state-of-the-field at earlier points in time and influenced its later development by identifying problems, questions, and approaches which need more attention. A key example of such an early, influential article is HAREVEN (1972). She gave special impetus to the interdisciplinary development of the field, calling attention to the promise of welding the tools of demography to the conceptual models of anthropology, psychology, and sociology. See also HAREVEN (1975). A more-recent attempt, primarily by sociologists, to grapple with the state-of-the-field and where it should go from here can be found in the 1979 special issue of Sociology and Social Research (statements by FARBER, MAY, SMITH and LASLETT, and HILL).

OTHER GENERAL REFERENCES AND RESOURCES

I.I. RESOURCES: *BIBLIOGRAPHIES*

(I.I.1.)   Soliday, Gerald, with Tamara K. Hareven, Richard T. Vann, and
           Robert Wheaton, editors
                    1980 History of the Family and Kinship: A Select
                          International Bibliography. Millwood, New York:
                          Kraus International.

(I.I.2.)   Milden, James W.
                    1977 The Family in Past Time: A Guide to Literature.
                          Library of Social Science Series, Volume 32. New
                          York: Garland.

(I.I.3.)   Skinner, G. William, and Arthur P. Wolf
                    1980 Unpublished bibliography on "Family and Demography."
                          Course handout for Anthropology 271-272, Winter
                          Quarter 1980, Stanford University.

The SOLIDAY volume is the definitive bibliography in the field and covers
over 6,000 secondary works, mostly published before 1977. It is not
limited to English language publications and spans all geographic areas
and time periods. Organized according to geographic area (the German
family, the Baltic family, etc.), it includes key works selected by
specialists in the various geographic regions.

The MILDEN volume is a less-selective bibliography which covers literature
from about 1910 up to early 1975 and provides a one- or two-sentence
description of each item. Each chapter focuses on a different geographic
area, subdivided first by historical period and then by content-topic
(general, children, demography, divorce, etc.). It includes some dissertations and unpublished papers as well as books and journal articles.

Anthropologists may find especially useful the 49-page SKINNER and WOLF
bibliography, created for an anthropology course in family and demography.
It covers a broad range from population and social biology to history and
sociology, but with a strong enthnological component often missing in
other bibliographies. Included are English-language books and articles
published between about 1957 and 1979, listed alphabetically by author.

J

(I.J.1.)   Gordon, Michael, editor
     1973   The American Family in Social-Historical
        Perspective. New York: St. Martin's Press: 1st edition.
        1978 (2nd edition); 1983 (3rd edition).

(I.J.2.)   Rosenberg, Charles, editor
     1975   The Family in History. Philadelphia, Pennsylvania:
        University of Pennsylvania Press.

(I.J.3.)   Rabb, Theodore K., and Robert I. Rotberg, editors
     1973   The Family in History: Interdisciplinary
        Essays. New York: Harper and Row.

(I.J.4.)   Demos, John, and Sarane Boocock, editors
     1978   Turning Points: Historical and Sociological
        Essays on the Family. Chicago, Illinois:
        University of Chicago Press. (Supplement to
        Volume 84 of the American Journal of Sociology.)

There are a number of books containing collections of major articles in
the field. Among the best for purposes of students and others who want
a broad introduction to key works on the American family are the GORDON
anthologies (1973, 1978, 1983); each edition includes a good proportion
of articles not in the others. The organization varies but is by content-
topics rather than historical period. For example, the 1983 edition
includes sections on perspectives on the social history of the family,
the domestic environment, the stages of life, relations between the sexes,
and ethnic diversity. Each subsection has a list of suggested readings.
The development of family history in the U.S., and the impetus it got from
French and English scholars, is chronicled in the Introduction.

Other well-known but older general anthologies include ROSENBERG (1975)
and RABB and ROTBERG (1973), neither of which is limited to American
history.

For a volume of essays representing a working interchange between historians
and sociologists, see DEMOS and BOOCOCK.

Some other anthologies on sub-areas of family history are mentioned in
Section X.N.

I.K. RESOURCES: BRIEF SURVEY ARTICLES FOR STUDENTS

(I.K.1.) Hareven, Tamara K.
    1983 "American Familes in Transition: Historical
    Perspectives on Change." In Arlene J. Skolnick
    and Jerome H. Skolnick, editors, <u>Family in
    Transition: Rethinking Marriage, Sexuality,
    Child Rearing, and Family Organization</u>, 4th
    edition, 73-91. Boston, Massachusetts, and
    Toronto, Canada: Little, Brown and Company.

(I.K.2.) Laslett, Barbara
    1983 "Family Membership: Past and Present." In
    Arlene S. Skolnick and Jerome H. Skolnick,
    editors, <u>Family in Transition: Rethinking
    Marriage, Sexuality, Child Rearing, and Family
    Organization</u>, 4th edition, 53-72. Boston,
    Massachusetts, and Toronto, Canada: Little,
    Brown and Company. Also in: <u>Social Problems</u>
    25 (June 1978): 476-490.

(I.K.3.) Kelly, Joan
    1981 "Family Life--An Historical Perspective."
    In Amy Swerdlow, Renate Bridenthal, and Phyllis
    Vine, 1981, <u>Household and Kin</u>, 1-45. New York:
    The Feminist Press.

Teachers who wish to add an historical perspective to undergraduate
courses in sociology, psychology, social psychology, anthropology, or
family studies may wish to assign one of the following short articles
summarizing how the family has changed historically. The first two
provide a bibliography for further reading.

The HAREVEN article focuses on the American family. Nostalgic myths are
shattered and replaced with facts about changes in the structure and
composition of families, in family functions and values, in the stages of
the life cycle, and the implications all of this has for understanding
contemporary families and their strengths and problems.

LASLETT's article also deals with U.S. history, with more stress on
sociological literature and on understanding the historical roots of such
contemporary "social problems" as the mid-life crisis, divorce, and family
violence. Changes in household composition, demographic factors (mortality,
age-at-marriage, fertility), the ideology of family life, and the
relationship of the family to other social institutions have affected
socialization in ways that increase the family's salience to personal-
identity formation.

The KELLY chapter differs from the preceding two in several ways: it is
broadly cross-cultural, spans a much longer time period, and is explicitly
geared to anthropology students,beginning with an analysis of family forms
and kinship in contemporary tribal societies. Against this backdrop, family

life is traced from feudal Europe, through pre-industrial Europe, to industrializing Europe and America (the separation of work and home, the division of family labor, women's work in the home) and, finally, to the striking changes of the last 20 years.

See also Sections X.M. to X.O. on teaching.

I.L. <u>*DISSERTATIONS*</u>

(I.L.1.) Howard, Ronald Lee
     1975 <u>A Social History of American Family</u>
       <u>Sociology, 1865-1970</u>. Unpublished
       Ph.D. dissertation, University of
       Missouri, Columbia, Missouri.

I.M. *PUBLICATIONS*

(I.M.1.) Anderson, M.
               1979 "The Relevance of Family History."
                     Sociological Review Monograph, Monograph
                     Number 28: 49-73.

(I.M.2.) Demos, J.
               1974 "American Family in Past Time." American
                     Scholar 43 (Number 3): 422-446.

(I.M.3.) Jeffrey, K.
               1975 "Varieties of Family History." American
                     Archivist 38 (Number 4): 521-532.

(I.M.4.) Lantz, H. R., J. Keyes, and M. Schultz
               1975 "American Family in Preindustrial Period--
                     From Base Lines in History to Change."
                     American Sociological Review 40 (Number 1):
                     21-36.

(I.M.5.) Valentin, J. H.
               1974 "Alienation and Family History." American
                     Journal of Psychotherapy 28 (Number 4):
                     592-598.

II. FAMILY/HOUSEHOLD
STRUCTURE AND COMPOSITION

A

II.A. *CONCEPTUAL AND THEORETICAL APPROACHES*

(II.A.1.) Verdon, Michel
          1979 "The Stem Family: Toward a General Theory."
                Journal of Interdisciplinary History 10 (Summer):
                87-105.

VERDON develops the beginnings of a new theoretical model of family structure.
He first reviews the treatment of the stem family in sociological theories
and in demographic-economic models as they pertain to Western Europe, in
order to demonstrate why three widespread assumptions are "highly questionable
if not implausible." These assumptions are that the stem family is: (1) a
transitional phase in the nuclearization of the family; (2) a common
Western European phenomenon; and (3) goes hand-in-hand with impartible
inheritance (all land passed on to one son, rather than being divided up).

Verdon attacks these assumptions by introducing a limit of growth concept,
defining the stem family as a limit of growth of a residential group,
suggesting conditions that give rise to stem families, and presenting
evidence that invalidates the basic assumptions contained in most other
theories about the stem family. Although a residential group changes
its composition over time, its composition rarely surpasses a certain
level, maintains Verdon. Beyond that level, it creates new groups--
this is the group's limit of growth. Also, there are numerous ways in
which three-generation residential groups can be formed without ever
having reached the stem family level. Lastly, ethnographic evidence
from Western Europe is used to systematically underscore the weaknesses
of the above assumptions.

The theoretical ideas contained in this paper are referred to, and put
into a larger conceptual model, in his 1980 paper (II.A.2.) discussed
below.

(II.A.2.) Verdon, Michel
          1980 "Shaking Off the Domestic Yoke, or the Sociological
                Significance of Residence." Comparative Studies
                in Society and History 22 (January): 109-132.

VERDON explores the problems confronted by researchers in the study of
the histoy of the family, specifically as these problems relate to the
subject-matter and types of evidence investigators must rely upon. He
describes and evaluates the anthropological models which have been used
in the study of residential or domestic groups and concludes that these
paradigms are inadequate for "the proper task" of social anthropology
or comparative sociology. Verdon then offers a new paradigm intended
to shift the focus of study onto residence as a process via which
individuals form groups, a process which should be kept analytically

separate from those regulating the formation of groups of production and reproduction. He claims that this "operational paradigm" is superior to both descriptive and comparative analyses.

For other conceptual and theoretical treatments, see also I.C.1., II.F.3., and IV.A.7.

II.B. *REVIEWS OF MAJOR BOOKS*

(II.B.1.) Burr, Wesley R.
　　　　　　 1979 "An Economic Theory of Familial Organization."
　　　　　　 Contemporary Sociology 8 (May): 351-352.

　　　　　　 Review of: Robert F. Winch, with the collaboration
　　　　　　 of Rae Lesser Blumberg, Maria-Pilar Garcia,
　　　　　　 Margaret Gordon, and Gay C. Kitson, 1977, Familial
　　　　　　 Organization: A Quest for Determinants. New York:
　　　　　　 Free Press.

(II.B.2.) Farber, Bernard
　　　　　　 1979 "...and Ogburn and Murdock Begat Winch."
　　　　　　 Contemporary Sociology 8 (May): 352-355.

　　　　　　 Review of: Robert F. Winch, with the collaboration
　　　　　　 of Rae Lesser Blumberg, Maria-Pilar Garcia, Margaret Gordon,
　　　　　　 Gay C. Kitson, 1977, Familial Organization: A Quest
　　　　　　 for Determinants. New York: Free Press.

Wesley R. BURR reviews this volume in two major ways: one, by stating its
importance as a contribution to the cumulative study of the ways in which
societal forces influence the family; two, by citing its usefulness as a
"working" volume for macrosociology of the family. Winch's book begins
by bringing new data to light through its review of previous essays and
research. Chapter six contains Winch's tentative theoretical model of
economic determinants of family complexity. The last half of the book
reports data having implications for the model's accuracy and utility.
Burr considers this volume to be a basis for theory construction as well
as a foundation upon which other researchers can build.

Bernard FARBER focuses on a comparison between Winch's volume and
Jack Goody's, Production and Reproduction: A Comparative Study of the
Domestic Domain (New York: Cambridge University Press, 1976). After
noting the methodological differences between these researchers, Farber
writes of the compatibility in their results on the study of influences
on family organization using the Ethnographic Atlas data base--with one
major exception, namely their differing interpretations of the role of the
economy in molding family organization. Winch gives primary emphasis to
economic factors that put stress on institutions (including the family)
to adapt while Goody attributes change to non-economic variables.
According to Farber, these differences stem from their differing conceptions
of the family as a social institution.

(II.B.3.) Hareven, Tamara K.
　　　　　　 1975 (Untitled book review.) History and Theory 14:
　　　　　　 242-251.

　　　　　　 Review of: Peter Laslett and Richard Wall, editors,
　　　　　　 1972, Household and Family in Past Time. Cambridge,
　　　　　　 England, and New York: Cambridge University Press.

(II.B.4.) Vann, Richard T.
                1974 (Untitled book review.) <u>Journal of Social History</u>
                      18: 105-118.

                      Review of: Peter Laslett with Richard Wall, editors,
                      1972, <u>Household and Family in Past Time</u>. Cambridge,
                      England: Cambridge University Press.

<u>Laslett</u> and <u>Wall</u>'s book, HAREVEN states, provides a definitive collection
of studies on the comparative structure of households over the past 400
years. The recurring dominant form of familial organization--be it in
16th century England, 18th century U.S., 19th century Japan, or Serbia
from the middle ages onward--is that of the nuclear ("simple") household.
The extended family of Western nostalgia never was the norm and hence could
not have been "destroyed" by industrialization. Yet, as the reviewer
observes, important variations in internal familial and household
organization are obscured by Laslett's classification system, and especially
by his failure to distinguish among families at different stages of the
life cycle. Family and household complexity varied over different
stages of the family cycle and depended upon a variety of internal conditions
and external circumstances. Also, Laslett's approach does not take into
account kin interaction outside the household. The major historical
transition occurred not in changing size or composition of the household,
but rather in the changing functions of the family and the role of relationships within it. Such internal family processes should be the focus of
study in family history.

The book review by VANN gives a more-detailed picture of the 22 essays
which comprise this edited volume. Many are based upon evidence from
census-type community listings. Vann begins with the history of these
sources and their utilization, to set the various studies in context.
Unanswered questions are identified. Laslett's "analytic introduction" is
said to be the chief conceptual contribution of this book.

(II.B.5.) Litchfield, R. Burr
                1979 "Broadening the Social Explanation of Demographic
                      History." <u>Journal of Interdisciplinary History</u>
                      9 (Spring): 717-722.

                      Review of: Peter Laslett, 1977, <u>Family Life and</u>
                      <u>Illicit Love in Earlier Generations: Essays in</u>
                      <u>Historical Sociology</u>. New York: Cambridge
                      University Press.

                      David Levine, 1977, <u>Family Formation in an Age of</u>
                      <u>Nascent Capitalism</u>. New York: Academic Press.

The <u>Laslett</u> and the <u>Levine</u> books reviewed here are both products of the
Cambridge Group for the History of Population and Social Structure. Both
go somewhat beyond purely demographic explanations to broader questions
of social history--Levine to a greater extent than Laslett--according to
reviewer LITCHFIELD. Laslett incorporates household structure and Levine
includes economic aspects of the larger social context, in addition to

purely demographic variables such as marital fertility, marriage age, mortality, illegitimacy ratios, etc., in their analyses of (primarily British) parish registers and household listings. A brief sketch of the content of both books is provided.

(II.B.6.) Laslett, Barbara
                        1973 "Family Structure and Social History: A
                              Methodological Review Essay." Historical
                              Methods Newsletter 7: 2-8.

                              Review of: Michael Anderson, 1970, Family
                              Structure in Nineteenth Century Lancashire.
                              Cambridge, England: Cambridge University Press.

Anderson's study of family structure in 19th century England, Barbara LASLETT says, is one of the first attempts to develop and apply a sociological (exchange theory) framework to explain variations in household organization during the transition to an industrial economy. This attempt is not entirely successful, however, since his interpretations are plausible but not proven. The book is said to be valuable as a model of inventive ways for working with census data on household organization, including the construction of a local life table and the use of an intensive sample. Several methodological shortcomings in this study are pointed out and alternative approaches suggested.

(II.B.7.) Engerman, Stanley L.
                        1978 "Studying the Black Family." Journal of Family
                              History 3 (Spring): 78-101.

                              Review of: Herbert G. Gutman, 1976, The Black
                              Family in Slavery and Freedom, 1750-1925. New
                              York: Pantheon.

In this extended review essay, Stanley L. ENGERMAN discusses the development of slave family patterns and sexual morés, particularly as offered in Herbert Gutman's volume, The Black Family in Slavery and Freedom, 1750-1925. With a focus on the new insights and questions raised by Gutman's work, Engerman presents a brief but comprehensive review of relevant literature-- past and present--representing both traditional and current views concerning the black family. Engerman examines many of the book's central themes by placing them in historical and historiographic content. Engerman praises the book highly, stating that his review "cannot convey the richness of Gutman's studies and the many areas which he has illuminated." On Gutman (1976), see also VI.A.12.

II.C. STUDIES OF: EUROPEAN POPULATIONS

(II.C.1.) Parming, Tönu
1979 "Long-Term Trends in Family Structure in a Soviet Republic." Sociology and Social Research 63 (Number 3): 443-475.

From an historical demography perspective, PARMING examines developments in Estonian family formation, with primary attention to patterns of family dissolution, and family size, covering a period of two centuries. The Estonians have the U.S.S.R.'s highest average age of marriage, highest divorce rate, and lowest fertility. Parming draws conclusions at two separate levels: one regarding the Estonians, the other regarding the understanding of the general fertility decline. For example, Parming finds that all major Estonian demographic characteristics (except divorce) predate the Soviet period and the industrial/urban transformation of society which occurred after the Second World War. As for the general fertility decline, it occurred prior to significant urbanization or industrialization; important socio-economic and cultural realities affected Estonia's fertility rate through family variables, before those factors which are associated with modernization came about to keep fertility low.

(II.C.2.) Schmidtbauer, Peter
1980 "Household and Household Forms of Viennese Jews in 1857." Journal of Family History 5 (Winter): 375-389.

SCHMIDTBAUER uses the Viennese census of October 31, 1857, to compare Jewish and non-Jewish (Christian) populations in four different areas of a Jewish settlement. Using the number of servants, the professions of household heads, and the presence of aristocratic families as criteria for the social stratification of these groups, he notes few similarities, but a great number of differences between the Jewish and Christian Viennese populations. Differences exist in patterns of immigration, frequencies of different household types, kinship ties and domestic arrangements, numbers of children and the patterns of marriage and children leaving home. Factors affecting the differences between Jewish and Christian populations are reviewed including the city's employment structure, the traditional values of East European Jewish society, and the strong extended kinship and community relations found in the East European ghetto. In sum, this study reveals the persistence of traditional patterns among Jewish immigrants in 19th century Vienna.

(II.C.3.) Anderson, Michael
1978 "Family, Household, and the Industrial Revolution." In Michael Gordon, editor, The American Family in Social-Historical Perspective, 38-50. New York: St. Martin's Press.

Michael ANDERSON explores, for the 19th century urban-industrial English community of Preston, the increase in coresidence of married couples with their parents, its origins, and its time of emergence. He first presents selective historical data on household and family structure in Preston and compares these data (a 10% sample of houses drawn from 1851 census books) to other scholars' data on British family structure. Anderson views the urban-industrial revolution as associated with a significant increase in the coresidence of parents and married children. In order to understand the changes in patterns of kin relationships, especially in that of coresidence, Anderson states, a special set of hypotheses focusing on economic advantages and disadvantages is needed. Such a set of hypotheses are presented (see page 44) and used as a conceptual framework for understanding the patterns of coresidence.

> Mitterauer, Michael (guest editor)
> 1982   Special Issue: The Family in Eastern Europe.
> <u>Journal of Family History</u> 7 (Spring).
> Contents:

(II.C.4.)   Peter Czap, Jr., "The Perennial Multiple Family Household, Mishino, Russia 1782-1858": 5-26.

(II.C.5.)   Erik Fügedi, "Some Characteristics of the Medieval Hungarian Noble Family.": 27-39.

(II.C.6.)   Béla Gunda, "The Ethno-Sociological Structure of the Hungarian Extended Family": 40-51. See Andrejs Plankans, "Ties of Kinship and Kinship Roles in an Historical Eastern European Peasant Community: A Synchronic Analysis": 52-75. (X.A.3.)

(II.C.7.)   Juhan Kahk, Heldur Palli, and Halliki Uibu, "Peasant Family and Household in Estonia in the Eighteenth and the First Half of the Nineteenth Centuries": 76-88.

(II.C.8.)   Milovan Gavazzi, "The Extended Family in Southeastern Europe": 89-102.

(II.C.9.)   Michael Mitterauer and Alexander Kagan, "Russian and Central European Family Structures: A Comparative View": 103-131.

CZAP examines developments in Russian family history by focusing on the means by which peasant family/households preserved and continually renewed themselves over a period of generations, thus sustaining the individuals and the small families existing within them. In this system of "perennial multiple family households," the family was dependent upon early male and female marriage and required extended coresidence of married brothers, in order to produce and to preserve domestic units. These factors then fulfilled the demands of the landlord and met the expectations of the commune. In addition, his analysis of changes in the composition and structure of individual households reveals a pattern designed to mute the effects of cyclic change and to prevent radical fluctuations in the size, structure, and capability of the household. This system is interpreted as reflecting a social strategy consistent with the Russian concept of serfdom (abolished in 1861), which deprived bonded peasants of civic identity, and regarded them as units of tribute and taxation.

FÜGEDI's essay is a preliminary report on research which examines certain characteristics of the medieval Hungarian noble family. The research was planned in two phases: (1) to establish the nature of the social system; and (2) to analyze the main variables of the system in order to describe typical behavior. This article focuses upon phase 1. Genealogies and the property histories of the selected descent groups form the foundation of the quantitative investigation. The system was analyzed by comparing the scattered records with the legal norm (the Tripartitum, a codification of Hungarian customary law, written in 1514 by Stefan Werböczy). Some of the major characteristics examined include patrilineages and kin positions, naming practices, women's roles and status, marriage forms, and also the aristocracy and nobility, including their acquisitions of land, title, and power.

GUNDA's examination and reconstruction of the Hungarian extended family system indicates that these families grew horizontally as well as vertically, and changed almost yearly. Gunda finds that, as an economic unit character-ized by patriarchal-patrilocal organization, the power of the extended family was extremely varied but clearly patriarchal in character. In addition, other evidence shows that certain matrilineal features were preserved in this family form. Factors examined include the property possessed by the extended family as well as how architecture and customs expressed the extended family system. The origin of the extended family is discussed briefly, as is the final decline of the extended families. This decline, which began toward the end of the nineteenth century, was primarily caused by the drive for personal independence as encouraged by economic, social, and intellectual conditions. The author concludes that the Hungarian extended family system of the 17th and 18th centuries and later is more closely connected with the social organization of the neighboring Slavs than with that of the hypothetical Finno-Ugric extended family system of thousands of years ago.

KAHK, PALLI, and UIBU describe the results of their work on the historical development of Estonian families in the 17th and 18th centuries. Various social and demographic characteristics are examined in detail. The forms of peasant households are shown to depend more on social than on demographic factors. The number of inhabitants living in a peasant household and their functions in it were ruled by the same principal laws that regulated socio-economic development in a feudal village. These are the major conclusions about the nature of socio-economic changes from feudalism to capitalism and the simultaneous development of the modern family in Estonia.

GAVAZZI, in part one, presents a brief explanation and description of the Zadruga (extended family) in Southeastern Europe, with particular emphasis on incorrect conceptions about this family form. Attention is given to the essential features of these families, the process of dissolution of the extended family, and the history of these families. In part two, Gavazzi offers a discussion of the literature on the South Slavic extended family and reviews the hypotheses contained therein (concerning the emergence, origin, and age of the South Slavic family). Two major, contradictory hypotheses are noted: one, a romantic view of popular tradition that

29

maintains that this extended family form was a heritage from old Slavic patterns of the middle ages; the other, that the emergence of South European extended familes can be traced to the Byzantine system of tax collection.

On the Zadruga, see also X.C.1., X.C.2., and X.C.3.

MITTERAUER and KAGAN discuss Russian family structure by contrasting special features of Russian family form to Central European ones. The sources used are from the third soul revision of the Russian Empire (1762-1763), and the Seelenbeschreibungen and similar sources for the Austrian area, both analyzed in terms of family structures. This article focuses on five urban and rural populations from the Russian province of Jaroslav'. Topics include: family size and complexity, the seniority principle in authority hierarchies, the problem of remarriage, marrige age, generation gaps, kinship structure of families, non-blood-related coresidents, and patrilineality as the basic structural principle.

(II.C.10) Mitterauer, Michael
        1981 "Marriage Without Co-residence: A Special Type
              of Historic Family Forms in Rural Carinthia."
              Journal of Family History 6 (Summer): 177-181.

Michael MITTERAUER is the director of the Institut für Wirtschafts- und Sozialgeschichte at the University of Vienna, Austria, where "soul registers" (population lists) are being processed as a part of a research project exploring changes in the Austrian family since the 17th century. Through the examination of relevant social, economic, legal and cultural factors, Mitterauer analyzes the changes in family constellations in rural Carinthia. Recent material from the parish archives of Zweinitz as well as twenty listings (1757, 1759) from thirteen parishes in the Carinthian diocese of Gurk were analyzed, subsequently revealing approximately 370 persons not coresiding with their spouses.

It is this non-coresidential family form which is discussed in this essay, with particular emphasis on the relationship between its structure and the organization of labor. Marriages without coresidence occurred primarily among servants, with farmhands being the largest group living apart from their spouses. For example, of the 190 married farmhands found in the registers only 18 lived with their wives at the time of the recording; among the married maids, only 6 of 90 lived with their spouses. In addition, he finds marriage without coresidence among the peasant populations. Mitterauer then expands his discussion to include these "servant marriages" in disciplinary perspectives. In sociological perspective (specifically Charles H. Cooley) the household which the maid and her children join (but not the servant couple) is a "primary group." In family sociology terms, this group does not meet the established criteria for either "family" or "incomplete family." From a functionalist perspective, the familial functions are divided between two primary groups, said to be--the peasant household where the mother works and the (separated) servant couple with their children.

On family and household structure in Europe, see also VIII.A.3., V.D.1., and X.C.1-3.

II.D. STUDIES OF: U.S. POPULATIONS, GENERAL

(II.D.1.) Kobrin, Frances
1976 "The Fall in Household Size and the Rise of the
Primary Individual in the United States." In
Michael Gordon, editor, 1978, The American Family
in Social-Historical Perspective, 69-80. New
York: St. Martin's Press.

Frances E. KOBRIN examines the decline in household size and the rise of
the primary individual (in the United States) through a discussion of the
concepts and data related to living arrangements, the influence of demographic
changes, and the emergence of the "primary individual." Her findings and
interpretations show that a process of "nuclearization" has occurred, which
then interacted with certain demographic changes to produce a significant
decline in household size. When combined with increases in the rates of
separation and divorce, and in the proportion of never-married young,
these changes account for the most recent increases in the proportion of one-
person households, she states. Additionally, there are effects on the family
that extend beyond the fertility and "empty nest" effects, including a
process of age-segregation and a decreasing tolerance for family forms which
include nonnuclear members. Family membership is predicted to occur over
a more restricted portion of the life-cycle, with (perhaps) less than a
majority of adults living in families, and that the rest will live alone
if current trends continue.

(II.D.2.) Modell, John, and Tamara K. Hareven
1978 "Urbanization and the Malleable Household: An
Examination of Boarding and Lodging in American
Families." In Michael Gordon, editor, 1978, The
American Family in Social-Historical Perspective,
51-68. New York: St. Martin's Press.

MODELL and HAREVEN examine the institution of boarding in 19th and early
20th century America, with special focus on the social and economic significance
of its increasingly negative evaluation among the population. The pressures
of rapid urbanization threatened traditional values; middle class fears of
family breakdown led to the perception of lodging practices as indicative
of social and familial disorganization.

However, Modell and Hareven interpret boarding as part of a process of
"family equalization," a constructive response by urban Americans to
gain control of their environment. They ask why it persisted so long and why
it eventually declined around the 1930s. Some of the findings supported by
the data in this study indicate that boarding was: a migrant rather than
immigrant practice; an alternative to the nuclear or extended family for
native Americans; that boarders were often unmarried individuals; and that
the practices of boarding and of taking in boarders were a function of the
life cycle, with one-third to one-half of all individuals boarding in their
early adulthood and also taking in boarders at a later stage. The frequency
of boarding declined as housing became less scarce, as the state began to
provide some financial assistance for the unemployed and sick and elderly,

as increasing prosperity allowed the unmarried young adult to afford a private apartment.

(II.D.3.) Michael, Robert T., Victor R. Fuchs, and Sharon R. Scott
                  1980 "Changes in the Propensity to Live Alone: 1950-
                        1976." Demography 17 (February): 39-56.

MICHAEL, FUCHS, and SCOTT focus on the remarkable growth in single-person households in post-war America. Such households included 3.9% of all adults in 1950 and rose to 10.2% by 1972. The authors investigate determinants of the "propensity to live alone," using 1970 data across states for single men and women ages 25 to 34 and for elderly widows. The estimated cross-state equations track about three-quarters of the increase in the propensity to live alone between 1950-1976 and suggest that income growth has been the principal determinant. Other variables positively related to the propensity to live alone were geographic mobility, level of schooling, and for young people a liberal social climate.

(II.D.4.) Zuckerman, Michael
                  ca. 1981 "The Colonial Southern Family." Unpublished
                            paper.

ZUCKERMAN describes his currently in-progress study as an "unconventional interpretation" of colonial southern family life meant to explore a differing cultural configuration than that previously thought to typify the great planter and slave societies of South Carolina and the Chesapeake. He believes that these households were neither lovingly nuclear nor patriarchal in the current "traditional" family sense, being more a peerage of siblings than a patriarchy. This study attempts to show that the pattern of parental neglect and indifference was not atypical of planter parents, and also explores the consequences for later family life and social relations of such early unconcern. Zuckerman anticipates the construction of a model of the developmental dynamic of the colonial southern family which will illuminate southern life, and subsequent American life as well.

On U.S. family/household structure, see also VII.I.1.

(II.E.1.) Shifflett, Crandall A.
              1975 "The Household Composition of Rural Black
                    Families: Louisa County, Virginia, 1880."
                    Journal of Interdisciplinary History 6 (Autumn):
                    235-260.

In this essay SHIFFLETT discusses the relationship between economic factors
and family structure by measuring the extent to which economic and social
forces have conditioned family residence choices. A U.S. sample of black
and white families from the 1880 manuscript census for Louisa County,
Virginia, was used. To construct a model showing household composition
of families as a dynamic process, rather than a static institution, the
sample households were divided into four family-cycle stages: newlyweds
and young, mid-stage and mature families. Changes in household composition
over the family cycle, and among the varying family types within each
developmental stage, are examined. On a general level, some of this
study's findings include: the solidarity of strong black kinship networks;
the inadequacy of internal economic need as an explanation of household
composition; and, that families of both racial groups with limited means
of production sometimes met economic need with greater exploitation of
family labor.

(II.E.2.) Gutman, Herbert G.
              1975 "Persistent Myths About the Afro-American
                    Family." Journal of Interdisciplinary History
                    6 (Autumn): 181-210.

In this paper on Afro-American History, GUTMAN explores two central arguments
found in E. Franklin Frazier's The Negro Family in the United States (New
York, 1949) and presents new evidence relating to the family and household
composition of Afro-Americans especially in the South between 1860 and
1880, and in Buffalo, New York, between 1855 and 1925. In so doing, Gutman
refutes Frazier's contention that "two streams" of Afro-American family
life developed from the slave experience, of which the "matriarchy" was
the more important in the 19th century, and that "class" affected family
structure in a direct way. Since the two-parent household was viewed by
Frazier as a minority who owned property, enjoyed middle-class occupations,
or had independent artisan skills, writes Gutman, Frazier directly linked the
two-parent, Afro-American household to property ownership, and linked skill
to "class." According to Gutman's own research findings, female-headed
households were common but not typical; occupation, income, and property
ownership data indicate that "class" factors alone did not determine the
presence of a two-parent household; and that 50%-80% of black households
were nuclear in composition and headed by two parents.

(II.E.3.) Furstenberg, Frank F., Jr., Theodore Hershberg, and John
              Modell
              1975 "The Origins of the Female-Headed Black Family:
                    The Impact of the Urban Experience." Journal of
                    Interdisciplinary History 6 (Autumn): 211-233.

FURSTENBERG, HERSHBERG, and MODELL examine the family structure and composition of various American ethnic groups in the city of Philadelphia, via an analysis of samples taken from the decennial federal population manuscript schedules from 1850 through 1880. Each sample includes at least 2,000 households for each census year, with white ethnic samples including immigrants from Ireland and Germany as well as native Americans and with black samples including all black households.

At issue in this paper is what the authors consider the "monolithic interpretation of the black experience," that is, the destructive impact of slavery upon the current status of black Americans. The authors assert that this interpretation requires further historical data to correct what they term "...misconceptions about the past that have resulted in certain erroneous interpretations of the present." Contrary to popular belief, they find much similarity in household structure among each of the ethnic groups, with black families just as likely to be organized in nuclear households as others. Also, black female-headed families emerged as a result of economic discrimination, poverty, and disease--not as a consequence of the institution of slavery.

(II.E.4.) Harris, William
                 1976 "Work and the Family in Black Atlanta, 1880."
                      Journal of Social History 9 (Spring): 319-330.

William HARRIS examines the adjustment of newly-freed black American slaves to urban life in Atlanta, Georgia, via samples drawn from census manuscripts for 1870 and 1880, and compares these findings with those of the Irish in Boston for the year 1850. His findings suggest that: in the economic sense, blacks in slavery were as well prepared for 19th century urban life as were the Irish; slavery itself was not the cause of the lack of social mobility among blacks; and, that the higher frequency of fatherless households among blacks may have been caused by differences in sex ratios, or economic and class distinctions between blacks and whites. Three related conclusions of this research are that: most black families in 1880 were not "matriarchal" or "matrilocal" in a structural way; the evidence is inconclusive about whether slavery resulted in a somewhat higher incidence of fatherless households among blacks; and, the differences in proportions of fatherless households between blacks and whites was far less one hundred years ago than today. The author concludes "that it is not where they (blacks) started, but what happened along the way that left blacks behind on the road to economic security and social stability."

On family and household structure of U.S. blacks, see also VII.I.1., VI.A.11., and VII.G.2.

II.F. STUDIES OF: OTHER REGIONS OR CROSS-CULTURAL COMPARISONS

(II.F.1.) Wells, Robert V.
                1974 "Household Size and Composition in the British
                       Colonies in America, 1675-1775." The Journal of
                       Interdisciplinary History 4 (Spring): 543-570.

In acknowledging the complexity and diversity of New World families,
WELLS discusses the composition of families and households in order to
describe the differences within and between colonies, as well as those over
time. The wide variation in family size from one colony to another showed
certain patterns; for example, household size was almost always larger in the
islands, and household size in the islands tended to increase between
1675 and 1775. As for family composition, much of the difference in the
average size of the household was largely dependent upon the number of
slaves or servants present. More whites per household were found in the
mainland colonies than were found in island colonies, with this number
seeming to remain constant over time in both cases. Several other factors,
as they relate to household size and composition, are discussed in this
essay. These include the number of children in a family, the proportion
of female-headed households, patterns of slaveholding, and the racial or
ethnic background of the head of household. Although much of this paper's
emphasis relies on the explanation of household size and composition by
physical characteristics, a brief section includes the socio-economic
status and property of the household head.

(II.F.2.) Wheaton, Robert
                1975 "Family and Kinship in Western Europe: The
                       Problem of the Joint Family Household." The
                       Journal of Interdisciplinary History 4 (Spring):
                       601-628.

WHEATON discusses some of the problems and questions raised by the strong
focus on the family household, without the consideration of kinship ties
as they extend beyond it, in recent studies of family history. Drawing
on material from comparative ethnography, he examines the joint family
household in European history.

First, the concepts of family and household are discussed, particularly
the inherent difficulties in their definition and in their analysis.
Then the argument is broadened to include the reduction in visibility of
the joint household system, and the minimizing of its impact on the
historical record. In the absence of certain preconditions, joint family
households could not operate. Finally, he examines five cultures with
"patrilineal tendencies" (Italy, Latvia, Serbia, India, and China) in
order to consider cross-cultural evidence on kinship systems as they
extend beyond the household of the joint family.

(II.F.3.) Sanjek, Roger
          1982 "The Organization of Households in Adabraka:
                Toward a Wider Comparative Perspective."
                Comparative Studies in Society and History
                24 (January): 57-103.

According to SANJEK, this study of the organization of households in
Adabraka, Ghana, reveals three basic orientations: that the analysis of
household composition is only one part of the study of households; that
households should not be studied (and then compared) as bounded units of
analysis; and that households always exist within a political-economic
context of employment structures, relations to the control of production,
and class. It is upon these premises that Sanjek conducts the examination
of Adabraka households. This essay includes what households do or do not
do in historical and ethnographic settings within a world system framework,
as well as questions raised about the role of households in performance
of the universal activities and about households in their political-
economic contexts. The conclusion includes an assessment of the political
implications of Adabraka household organization, with emphasis on the
wider comparative perspective of households.

For research methodology relevant to family/household structure, see
Sections X.A. through X.D.

II.G. <u>*DISSERTATIONS*</u>

(II.G.1.) Pi-Sunyer, Mary Jane Richards
             1973 <u>Households in a Nineteenth-Century Town:</u>
                   <u>A Historical Demographic Study of Household</u>
                   <u>and Family Size and Composition in Amherst,</u>
                   <u>Massachusetts, 1850-1880</u>. Unpublished
                   Ph.D. dissertation, University of Massachusetts.

II.H. _PUBLICATIONS_

(II.H.1.) Kertzer, D. I.
        1977 "European Peasant Household Structure--
        Some Implications From a 19th-Century
        Italian Community." Journal of Family
        History 2 (Number 4): 333-349.

(II.H.2.) Krech, S.
        1982 "Black-Family Organization in the 19th-
        Century--An Ethnological Perspective."
        Journal of Interdisciplinary History 12
        (Number 3): 429-452.

(II.H.3.) Lammerme, P. J.
        1973 "Urban Black Family of Nineteenth Century--
        Study of Black Family Structure in Ohio-Valley,
        1850-1880." Journal of Marriage and the
        Family 35 (Number 3): 440-456.

(II.H.4.) Mendels, F. F.
        1978 "Notes on Age of Maternity: Population-Growth
        and Family-Structure in Past." Journal of
        Family History 3 (Number 3): 236-250.

(II.H.5.) Netting, R. M.
        1979 "Household Dynamics in a 19th-Century Swiss
        Village." Journal of Family History 4 (Number 1):
        39-58.

(II.H.6.) Seward, R. R.
        1973 "Colonial Family in America--Toward A Socio-
        Historical Restoration of its Structure."
        Journal of Marriage and the Family 35 (Number 1):
        58-70.

III. MARRIAGE: BEGINNINGS AND ENDINGS

III.A.   *CONCEPTUAL AND THEORETICAL APPROACHES: GARY BECKER AND THE*
         "NEW HOME ECONOMICS"

(III.A.1.)   Becker, Gary S.
             1973 "A Theory of Marriage: Part I." Journal
                   of Political Economy 81 (July/August):
                   813-846.

(III.A.2.)   Becker, Gary S.
             1974 "A Theory of Marriage: Part II." Journal
                   of Political Economy 82 (March, Part 2):
                   S34-S56.

(III.A.3.)   Freiden, Alan
             1974 "The United States Marriage Market." Journal
                   of Political Economy 82 (March, Part 2):
                   S34-S56.

BECKER's theory of marriage is one key component of the "new home economics"
school of economists. Now fully elaborated in A Treatise on the Family
(see III.A.4. and III.A.5.) the basic notions were first published in the
following two-part paper. (Non-economists are referred to I.E.1. for help
in interpretation).

Part I sketches the skeleton of a theory--based on the assumption that
marriage is voluntary--which focuses on the "marriage market" of potential
mates. It is assumed that this "market" is in equilibrium (no mate switching)
and that each person tries to find a mate who maximizes his or her well-
being (best possible mate). The gain ("utility") from marrying (versus from
remaining single) for any two persons is positively related to their
incomes, human capital (non-market-productivity-augmenting variables
such as education or beauty), and the relative difference between their
wage rates. Except for such traits as wage rates, the matings of "likes"
is usually optimal (similar race, education, ability, height, etc.). The
division of output between mates, however, is determined by marginal
productivities which change as the supply of and demand for different kinds
of mates changes.

Part II extends and modifies the theory. The assumption of complete
information about all possible mates is dropped. It includes explanations
dealing with "love" (why persons who care for each other are more likely
to marry), polygyny (why it has been more common among successful men
and why the sex ratio and inequality-among-men have influenced the incidence
of polygyny), natural selection over time and assortive mating (e.g., why
differences in incomes between different families can persist over several
generations), and life-cycle marital patterns (which marriages are more likely
to terminate in separation and divorce and how the assortive mating of those
remarrying differs from the assortive mating in their first marriage).

The FREIDEN article is an early attempt to provide "empirics" for part of
Becker's theory, i.e., to estimate the reduced-form equation explaining

variation in the proportion of females married. Using U.S. data, primarily from the 1960 census, three factors--the ratio of the sexes, the potential returns to marriage, and the cost of divorce--are shown to explain many of the real differences in marital behavior in the U.S. Indirect effects of the marriage market on the reproduction rate are also shown. Results of this cross-sectional study imply that long-term economic growth may result in more people desiring to remain single.

(III.A.4.) Ben-Porath, Yoram
1982 "Economics and the Family--Match or Mismatch? A Review of Becker's A Treatise on the Family." Journal of Economic Literature 20 (March): 52-64.

Review of: Gary S. Becker, 1981, A Treatise on the Family. Cambridge, Massachusetts: Harvard University Press.

(III.A.5.) Hannan, Michael T.
1982 "Families, Markets, and Social Structures: An Essay on Becker's A Treatise on the Family." Journal of Economic Literature 20 (March): 65-72.

Review of: Gary S. Becker, 1981, A Treatise on the Family. Cambridge, Massachusetts: Harvard University Press.

Both BEN-PORATH and HANNAN provide detailed summaries of the content of Becker's new book. This book employs the precepts of neoclassical micro-economic analysis (assuming fixed preferences, maximizing behavior, and equilibrium) to construct a starkly economic theory of how a series of "optimizing decisions" will be made regarding: (a) the allocation of roles and resources and the distribution of income within families; (b) the formation, dissolution, growth, and structure of families; and (c) the implications of these analyses for inequality and social mobility. The wide range of topics encompassed are reflected in the chapter titles: single-person households; division of labor in households and families; polygamy and monogamy in marriage markets; the demand for children; family background and the opportunities of children; the equilibrium distribution of income and intergenerational mobility; altruism and the family; families in nonhuman species; imperfect information; marriage and divorce; and the evolution of the family. Much of the analysis used models of the allocation of time and human capital.

Something of the flavor of Becker's approach is conveyed by the following exerpt from Ben-Porath (page 53): "The mechanisms that regulate both the sorting of people into couples and the roles of the spouses are derived from the process in which individual utility, family income, and aggregate income are maximized, where income is a broad concept that also covers the value of nonmarket activities. Thus the questions of whether to marry at all and who is going to marry whom, are related to what happens within marriage--what the gains are and how they are distributed, and what division of labor they rest on."

Given the high degree of abstraction and the unobservability of most of the crucial variables (utility functions, endowments, efficiencies, heritabilities, prices of children, etc.), both reviewers question whether this theory is really amenable to empirical verification or falsification. A number of other limitations are also noted.

(III.A.6.) Huber, Joan and Glenna Spitze
            1980 "Considering Divorce: An Expansion of Becker's
                  Theory of Marital Instability." American Journal
                  of Sociology 86 (1): 75-89.

Using a national probability sample (N=1,360) of husbands and wives married to one another in 1978, sociologists HUBER and SPITZE explore the correlates of thinking about divorce in order to extend Becker's theory of marital instability. These authors add sociological variables and measure individual utilities in an attempt to discover why spouses decide to divorce, why particular events will increase the probability of dissolution, and how sex-role attitudes influence both spouses in thinking about divorce. The findings show that wives' thoughts of divorce increase with their work experience, having a youngest child aged six to eleven, and egalitarian housework attitudes, and decrease with age at marriage, marital duration, and husband's housework contribution. Husbands' thoughts of divorce increase with wife's work experience and wife's egalitarian housework attitudes and decrease with the presence of children under six, marital duration, and age differences. Their findings imply that the husband's earnings and the presence of children may deter divorce less now than they have in the past.

III.B. MARRIAGE

(III.B.1.) Steckel, Richard H.
             1980 "Slave Marriage and the Family." Journal
                   of Family History 5 (Winter): 406-421.

The importance, strength, and viability of marriage as an institution
among southern U.S. black slaves is underscored by STECKEL's new findings
from plantation records and Civil War pension files. Analysis of the
seasonal patterns of marriage and first birth indicates that reproduction
was influenced by marriage. A sizeable group of slave couples made family
formation decisions in the context of marriage or in anticipation of
marriage. Study of birth lists (primarily 1820-1865) which also enumerate
the father indicates that slave unions were highly stable, particularly
those that survived the first one or two years. The women on these lists
changed partners so infrequently that an important portion of women in
their late twenties and thirties lived as widows and had no more children.

(III.B.2.) Safley, Tomas Max
             1982 "To Preserve the Marital State: The Basler
                   Ehegericht, 1550-1592." Journal of Family
                   History 7 (Summer): 162-179.

According to SAFLEY, the Protestant magistrates of early modern Europe
sought to control marriage as a primary element of social control via
educating and disciplining their subjects in a reformed definition of
marriage and its purpose in the community. The records of the marriage
court (Ehegericht) of Basel, Switzerland, from 1550 to 1592 demonstrate
two fundamental theses: (1) enforcement of the reformed marital code
sharpened and reinforced a specific model of marriage which reflected
the values and concerns of the Basel magistracy; and (2) the Protestant
tribunal of Basel in the last half of the 16th century, assumed an
increasingly activist posture in enforcing marital discipline and public
morality. The exposure and correction of marital deviance by the authorities
played an important role in defining the group experience of the community.

(III.B.3.) Taylor, Michael D.
             1982 "Gentile da Fabriano, St. Nicholas, and an
                   Iconography of Shame." Journal of Family
                   History 7 (Winter): 321-332.

TAYLOR relates the iconography of Gentile da Fabriano's 1425 painting of
St. Nicholas Providing Dowries for the Three Daughters to the historical
conditions of this time period. It is argued that the activities, gestures,
and behaviors of the daughters signify the social incompetence and dishonor
of the father because of his inability to provide dowries for the daughters.
The analytical interpretations are based on the premise that these actions
are not functional, but rather signs of the family's character which indicate
a moral and social degradation complicated by an emphasis on honor--an

integral part of marital contracts in late medieval and early modern Florence. In addition to the assumption that Gentile has radically altered the traditional iconography of St. Nicholas, Taylor concludes that the painting's insistence on the shame of being unendowed may be understood as part of the intensified debate and the manifold threats to honor raised by dowry fund legislation.

On marriage, see also VI.C.1. and X.I.4.

III.C. _DIVORCE_

(III.C.1.) Cott, Nancy F.
                1976 "Eighteenth-Century Family and Social Life
                       Revealed in Massachusetts Divorce Records."
                       Journal of Social History 10 (Fall): 20-41.

COTT examines issues of family and social life, privacy and community,
and relations among family members through a critical analysis of
Massachusetts divorce records. Used with scholarly reservation, but as
valid assets in illuminating intimate aspects of domestic life and social
surroundings, these divorce records tend to confirm the view that the
mid- to late-18th century was a period of important transition in family
life--not by sudden transformation, but through the gradual emergence
of modern patterns. For example, the predominately non-emotional definition
of marriage (a pattern of traditional society) was greatly influenced by
the concept of romantic love in marriage (a pattern of modern society).
These and other findings suggest that the contrast between traditional and
modern is a less schematic one than previously thought.

(III.C.2.) Schultz, Martin
                1976 "Marital Disruption in Early America."
                       Unpublished Ph.D. dissertation prospectus.
                       (Dissertation completed June, 1980.)

Including both incompatability and divorce, SCHULTZ describes, compares,
and analyzes the incidence of marital disruption in the United States for
the years 1790-1867. The data include court records, demographic information,
and relevant legislation, and serve three principal roles: (1) as a basis
for a description of the incidence of marital incompatibility and dissolution
from 1790 to 1867; (2) as a baseline for comparison with earlier and later
data on marital disruption; (3) and as a framework for the analysis of the
relationship between family life, marital stability, and social change.
Other objectives include a wider understanding of the historical foundations
of marital disruption and of the contributions of important theoretical
insights regarding family processes and social change.

(III.C.3.) Preston, Samuel H., and John McDonald
                1979 "The Incidence of Divorce Within Cohorts of
                       American Marriages Contracted Since the Civil
                       War." Demography 16 (February): 1-26.

PRESTON and McDONALD present a new cohort divorce series, combining vital
registration and census data sources, for annual marriage cohorts back to
1867 in order to examine the incidence of divorce. Actual experience to 1970
is traced and a projection beyond that point is made for cohorts with incomplete
divorce histories. The authors state that the cohort divorce series moves
steadily upwards and shows much less variability than an equivalent series of
period divorce rates. Factors related to high divorce within a cohort are armed
service mobilization and high unemployment rates in the year of marriage, and slow
national economic growth between pre- and post-war marital periods.

(III.D.1.) Diefendorf, Barbara B.
　　　　　　1982 "Widowhood and Remarriage in Sixteenth-Century
　　　　　　　　　 Paris." <u>Journal of Family History</u> 7 (Winter):
　　　　　　　　　 379-395.

(III.D.2.) Wyntjes, Sherrin Marshall
　　　　　　1982 "Survivors and Status: Widowhood and Family in
　　　　　　　　　 the Early Modern Netherlands." <u>Journal of Family
　　　　　　　　　 History</u> 7 (Winter): 396-405.

(III.D.3.) Brown, Irene Q.
　　　　　　1982 "Domesticity, Feminism, and Friendship: Female
　　　　　　　　　 Aristocratic Culture and Marriage in England,
　　　　　　　　　 1660-1760." <u>Journal of Family History</u> 7
　　　　　　　　　 (Winter): 406-424.

The following three articles grew out of a Berkshire Conference Session on "Widowhood in Early Modern Europe," which focused on the opportunity widowhood gave women to develop personal and psychological (as well as economic) independence.

DIEFENDORF analyzes the social, economic, and legal position of Parisian widows in the second half of the sixteenth century, including the situation of the widow who remarried. She argues that 16th century notions of feminine frailty and the legal incapacity of Paris married women at the time must be understood within the context of a traditional concern for the protection of family line and property, and that there is an ironic contrast between the presumed frailty of women and the important responsibilities actually entrusted to widows for the management of family affairs and property.

WYNTJES' study of the early modern north Netherlands, based on approximately 1,000 widows from noble, gentry, and propertied middle-class families, demonstrates that widows' legal rights, exercised within and outside the family sphere, were the basis of their visible authority and power.

The last article, by BROWN, introduces a different mode of independence which includes married and never-married women and men, as well as widows. Domesticity, the careful, self-conscious cultivation of affection and mutuality in the family, has usually been recognized only in its Victorian or later forms. This essay identifies an earlier Enlightenment form of domesticity, based on rational friendship, the equal capacity for reason in both sexes, and a distinctive view of death and Christian spirituality. It flourished in a network of English aristocratic and gentry families after the Restoration. The essential relationship was that of <u>friend</u> (which could be kin or non-kin and of either sex).

Focusing upon English aristocratic widows, especially the correspondence of Mary Granville, she explores rational friendship and its corollaries (the legitimacy of marriage refusal, socially unequal intermarriage, and the single life) and concludes that rational domesticity promoted emotional interdependence beyond the nuclear family, helped legitimate intermarriage between unequals, and provided one way to deal with the increasing inequality among kin.

III.E. *DISSERTATIONS*

(III.E.1.) Alter, George Charles
1978 The Influence of Social Stratification on
Marriage in Nineteenth Century Europe:
Verviers, Belgium, 1844-1845. Unpublished
Ph.D. dissertation, University of Pennsylvania.

(III.E.2.) Gottlieb, Beatrice
1974 Getting Married in Pre-Reformation Europe:
The Doctrine of Clandestine Marriage and
Court Cases in Fifteenth-Century Champagne.
Unpublished Ph.D. dissertation, Columbia
University.

(III.E.3.) Helmholz, Richard Henry
1970 Marriage Litigation in Medieval England.
Unpublished Ph.D. dissertation, University
of California, Berkeley.

III.F. <u>*PUBLICATIONS*</u>

(III.F.1.) Knodel, J.
            1972 "Malthus Amiss: Marriage Restrictions in 19th Century
                  Germany." <u>Social Science</u> 47 (Number 1):
                  40-45.

(III.F.2.) Brennan, E. R.
            1981 "Kinship, Demographic, Social, and Geographic
                  Characteristics of Mate Choice in Sanday,
                  Orkney Islands, Scotland." <u>American Journal
                  of Physical Anthroplogy</u> 55 (Number 1): 129-138.

(III.F.3.) Cott, N. F.
            1976 "Divorce and Changing Status of Women in
                  18th-Century Massachusetts." <u>William and
                  Mary Quarterly</u> 33 (Number 4): 586-614.

(III.F.4.) Pickens, K. A.
            1980 "Marriage Patterns in a 19th-Century British
                  Colonial Population." <u>Journal of Family History</u>
                  5 (Number 2): 180-196.

(III.F.5.) Scammell, J.
            1974 "Freedom and Marriage in Medieval England."
                  <u>Economic History Review</u> 27 (Number 4): 523-537.

(III.F.6.) Searle, E.
            1976 "Freedom and Marriage in Medieval England--
                  Alternate Hypothesis." <u>Economic History
                  Review</u> 29 (Number 3): 482-486.

(III.F.7.) Weisbrod, C., and P. Sheingorn
            1978 "Reynolds v. United States--19th-Century Forms
                  of Marriage and Status of Women." <u>Connecticut
                  Law Review</u> 10 (Number 4): 828-858.

(III.F.8.) Hall, P. D.
            1974 "Marital Selection and Business in Massachusetts
                  Merchant Families, 1800-1900," in Rose Laub Coser,
                  editor, 1974, <u>The Family and Its Structure and
                  Functions</u>, 226-242. New York: St. Martin's Press.

(III.F.9.) May, Elaine Tyler
            1978 "The Pressure to Provide: Class, Consumerism, and
                  Divorce in Urban America, 1880-1920." <u>Journal of
                  Social History</u> 12 (December): 180-193.

(III.F.10.) O'Neill, William L.
            1965 "Divorce in the Progressive Era." _American
                  Quarterly_ (Summer): 205-217.

(III.F.11.) Smith, Daniel Scott
            1973 "Parental Power and Marriage Patterns: An Analysis
                  of Historical Trends in Hingham, Massachusetts."
                  Journal of Marriage and the Family 35 (August):
                  419-428.

IV. THE LIFE CYCLE

IV.A. CONCEPTUAL AND THEORETICAL APPROACHES

(IV.A.1.) Hareven, Tamara K.
1978 "Cycles, Courses, and Cohorts: Reflections on
Theoretical and Methodological Approaches to the
Historical Study of Family Development." Journal
of Social History 12 (Number 1): 97-107.

There are two distinct approaches to studying the family "developmentally,"
i.e., as a changing entity over the life of its members: (1) the family
cycle, and (2) the life course approach.

Family cycle refers to role changes or stages of the family as a group, e.g.,
marriage, the various stages of parenthood, and so on until the death of the
family head. According to HAREVEN, life course analysis focuses on the
"transition" or major changes in individuals' lives: their timing, which
entails the synchronization of individual with family transitions; their
interaction with larger historical change; and the cumulative impact of
earlier life course transitions upon subsequent ones.

Life course analysis is most meaningful with longitudinal data (individuals'
entire lives and families over several generations). Examples of how such
longitudinal data sets have been created via record linkage, and of how to
infer a good deal about longitudinal pattern from cross-sectional data, are
given.

Cohort analysis, often used by demographers, is but one of a variety of
methodologies which can be employed in life course analysis. It isolates
specific age groups and measures their interaction with historical conditions
either longitudinally or cross-sectionally.

(IV.A.2.) Vinovskis, Maris A.
1977 "From Household Size to the Life Course: Some
Observations on Recent Trends in Family History."
American Behavioral Scientist 21 (November/December):
263-287.

This essay reviews efforts of the last ten years to develop a comprehensive
framework for the analysis of family history, with particular attention
given four alternative approaches for studying the family: the analysis of
household size and composition; the study of generations; the use of a
family-cycle model; and the development of a life course perspective.
Contrasting these four approaches allows VINOVSKIS to pinpoint key current
conceptual and methodological issues in the field of family history.

The article begins by noting the bifurcation of approaches to family life
in the past: one group of historians analyzed vital events using parish
registers while another group analyzed household size and composition using
the censuses. The merging of these differing perspectives would provide a

more balanced and dynamic analysis of family life in the past. The life-course approach suggests the need, as well as the means, for linking information about family processes with that of family size and composition within the context of historical changes in society as a whole. The result, notes Vinovskis, is a significant conceptual improvement that will facilitate further analysis of the family.

(IV.A.3.) Elder, Glen H., Jr.
                    1980 "History and the Life Course." Unpublished
                            paper available from author. (Forthcoming in:
                            D. Bertaux, editor, Biography and Society.
                            Sage Publications, 1980.)

The life course perspective is based on the premise that aging involves several interacting processes (social, psychological, and biological) from birth to death, and that life-course variations among individuals and cohorts are shaped in part by historical conditions. Within this framework, ELDER introduces "social structure and personality" as a field of inquiry and then indicates the utility of a life course approach through two applications: (1) at the macro level, the relation between cohorts and mentalitiés, and (2) a study of social change and life-course differences within cohorts. The first application draws upon the literature, using an historical perspective that locates social structure, personality, and actors in specific temporal contexts and adds a processual dynamic to their interrelationship. The second application draws upon empirical research on two birth cohorts and identifies an approach to social structure and personality that is comparative, contextual, longitudinal, and explanatory through an under-standing of life course variations in historical settings.

(IV.A.4.) Elder, Glen H., Jr.
                    1978 "Approaches to Social Change and the Family."
                            American Journal of Sociology 84 (Supplement):
                            S1-S38.

The 1960s marked a turning point in sociological and historical inquiry in archival studies of family, kinship, and the life course. Empirical research on the family underwent a shift in direction, away from the general-theory and research of the postwar era. Such developments in the field of family history are discussed by ELDER, with sections on: (1) critical appraisals of theory, research, and speculation on matters of family change; (2) social theory and its relation to the historical record; and (3) age--its temporal properties and social-historical implications.

The critical reappraisal of knowledge, theory, and evidence that emerged in the 1960s led to a greater awareness of the limits of sociological knowledge about the family in past time, but the family was still depicted as a generalized structural form, not as a domestic group that undergoes developmental change in specific historical settings. Yet a second turning point toward historical research is reflected in the development of analytical concerns whose common objective was to construct theories that explicate the process by which families change within and across generations, that specify the antecedents and consequences of change as well as conditions that alter the casual process. Lastly, the development of the concept of age provided a tool for locating families in historical context and representing their life course by the timing and arrangement of events and social roles, allowing examination of how life stages affected their adaptation to broader historical changes.

(IV.A.5.) Hareven, Tamara K.
1977 "Family Time and Historical Time." <u>Daedalus</u> 106 (Spring): 57-70.

How individuals time their transitions into and out of various family roles and how these patterns of timing relate to the family as a collective unit are examined in this essay. Several concepts of time--individual time, family time, and historical time--are considered with regard to their interaction over the past two centuries in the United States.

The discovery of complexity in family behavior in the past can provide a new perspective on the problems families face in contemporary society. HAREVEN's picture of family behavior in the past is one of diversity and flexibility that varied with certain social and economic needs. Modern society requires even greater family diversity, because of the complexities, role conflicts, and variations imposed upon the individual. History offers evidence that families are able to display variety and diversity in their organization and timing and to handle conflicts between the needs of individuals and the collective demands of the family under changing historical conditions. Yet further expansion and diverstiy can be expected from the contemporary family, as it adapts to new social conditions.

(IV.A.6.) Elder, Glen H., Jr.
1975 "Age Differentiation and the Life Course." <u>Annual Review of Sociology</u> 1, Palo Alto, California; Annual Reviews, Inc.: 165-190.

From the cohort-historical and sociocultural perspective, ELDER examines issues and research on the relation between social change and the life course. The chapter begins with a preliminary overview of theoretical perspectives and issues on age differentiation in the life course and then reviews selected studies of social change in the life patterns of cohorts and individuals.

Use of the <u>cohort-historical perspective</u> has led to a greater awareness of the dual function of age (as an index of birth year and of career stage), of methodological problems (in disentangling life stage, cohort, period or time of measurement effects), and of age as a surrogate for other variables which need to be specified in explanatory analysis. The <u>sociocultural perspective</u> on age--with regard to normative age divisions, prescribed transitions, age expectations and timetables, and temporal characterizations of age patterns in the life course--has generated assumptions and assertions far exceeding the empirical evidence. Thus a number of important questions on relations among social change, cohort differentiation, and normative age patterns remain as yet unanswered.

(IV.A.7.) Hareven, Tamara K.
                    1974 "The Family as Process: The Historical Study of
                          the Family Cycle." Journal of Social History 7
                          (Spring): 322-329.

The longitudinal analysis of the family cycle considers the family as a
process over time and assumes that individuals experience a variety of
patterns of family structure and household organization during different
stages of their life cycle. Rather than being static units, families evolve
stage-specific types of organization, structure, and relationships which are
not always evident from cross-sectional analysis. This perspective is
used by HAREVEN in the analysis of family patterns in 19th century society
because it allows for the differentiation of two types of historical time:
"family time" and "social time." Family time designates changes in the
family cycle (marriage, childbirth, maturation, and leaving home), while
social time designates changing institutional conditions in the larger
society (occupational structure, migration, settlement patterns, and changing
policies and legislation governing family behavior). Thus, the family cycle
approach could provide a framework for merging demographic and quantitative
data with social, cultural, and psychological information on family behavior
and on decisions affecting demographic behavior.

(IV.A.8.) Keniston, Kenneth
                    1971 "Psychological Development and Historical
                          Change." The Journal of Interdisciplinary
                          History 11 (Autumn): 329-346.

The concepts of developmental psychology include theories about sequences
of the stages of human development, the conditions that foster or inhibit
development in children, and the consequences of early development for later
adult roles, symbolizations, and values. That these concepts have been
ignored in the study of historical change--in favor of the concepts of
socialization, acculturation, and modal personality--is at issue in this
essay. In fact, KENISTON argues that developmental concepts will prove
more useful than such alternative concepts for explaining the relationship
between historical context and psychological development. Under discussion
are such topics as: current views on human development, the contingency
of human development, and life stages and developmental profiles. This
essay examines the psychological effects of wide-scale historical changes in
the developmental matrix, so that one may better understand the processes
by which socio-historical change produces psychological change and by which
psychological change on a mass scale may, in turn, generate social and political
transformations.

For other conceptual and theoretical approaches, see also IX.B.2.

IV.B. _REVIEWS OF MAJOR BOOKS_

(IV.B.1.) Cherlin, Andrew
           1979 "Following the Life Course." Contemporary
                 Sociology 8 (July): 531-533.

                 Review of: John Demos and Sarane Spence Boocock,
                 editors, 1978, Turning Points: Historical and
                 Sociological Essays on the Family. Chicago,
                 Illinois: University of Chicago Press.

                 Tamara K. Hareven, editor, 1978, Transitions: The
                 Family and the Life Course in Historical Perspective.
                 New York: Academic Press.

                 Tamara K. Hareven and Maris A. Vinovskis, editors,
                 1978, Family and Population in Nineteenth-Century
                 America. Princeton, New Jersey: Princeton University
                 Press.

The concern with individual lives and historical variation distinguishes
life course studies from older family life cycle studies, writes
CHERLIN, and it is this life course perspective which forms the common
bond among the three volumes reviewed here. As a set of concepts which
frequently are linked to the methods of historical demography and quantitative
sociology, this life course perspective emphasizes the transitions and
turning points of family life. A brief account of the inception of the life
course perspective and its basic "tenets" is followed by a review of the
contents and characteristics of each volume.

All three books emerged from conferences organized primarily by Tamara
Hareven. The 1974 conference which produced the HAREVEN and VINOVSKIS
volume, where scholars interested in the family life cycle applied historical
demography techniques to census records and other data, also produced
a consensus that the concept of family life cycle was too rigid and static.
The search for a more flexible organizing principle led them to the life
course perspective, which had been developed by Glen Elder. As a result,
Hareven organized a second conference in 1975 in which scholars applied
Elder's approach (the proceedings being published in Transitions) and a
third conference soon thereafter, resulting in Turning Points.   Of the
three volumes, Transitions is said to be the most cohesive because most
contributors analyzed the same data (on one Massachusetts county in 1880)
and because it is the only one of the three which is devoted completely to
the life course perspective.

The review concludes with a caution: the life course perspective is not a
theory of family life but rather a set of concepts frequently linked to the
methods of historical demography and quantitative sociology. As such, this
perspective can tell us how better to study families but it cannot tell us
what to study.

(IV.B.2.)   Watkins, Susan Cotts
          1980   "On Measuring Transitions and Turning Points."
                 Historical Methods 13 (Summer): 181-186.

                 Review of: John Demos and Sarane Spence Boocock,
                 editors, 1978, Turning Points: Historical and
                 Sociological Essays on the Family. Chicago,
                 Illinois: University of Chicago Press.

                 Tamara K. Hareven, editor, 1978, Transitions: The
                 Family and Life Course in Historical Perspective.
                 New York: Academic Press.

WATKINS reviews these two volumes together because of their common topic
and approach--the life course perspective. Admittedly narrow in approach,
this review focuses on certain methodological problems presented by the life
course perspective: (1) the choice of the family versus the individual as
the unit of analysis; (2) problems in the separation of the effects of
age, period, and cohort; and (3) the limitations imposed on the interpretation
of analyses that are longitudinal in intent but cross-sectional in execution.

(IV.B.3.)   Modell, John
          1975   "Level of Change Over Time." Historical Methods
                 8 (September): 116-127.

                 Review of: Glen H. Elder, Jr., 1974, Children of
                 the Great Depression: Social Change in Life
                 Experience. Chicago, Illinois: University of
                 Chicago Press.

MODELL's review appeared in 1975, just at the time when an influential group
of historians had discovered the potentials of sociologist Elder's life
course approach (see IV.B.1.). Reflecting the excitement of this new
"discovery," this review conveys both a sense of Elder's study (his approach,
data, measurement, and findings) and of the richness of insight it yields
about the implications of drastic socioeconomic (macro) change for family (micro)
changes, and about the link between social structure and personality.

Much attention is given to issues of analyzing time and social change, as
well as methodological shortcomings of this study. Plausible research
strategies for applying longitudinal analysis to available historical data
are also suggested.

(IV.B.4.)   Demos, John
          1973   "Reflections on the History of the Family: A
                 Review Essay." Comparative Studies in Society
                 and History 15 (October): 493-503.

                 Review of: Alan Macfarlane, 1970, The Family of
                 Ralph Josselin: A Seventeenth Century Clergyman.
                 New York: Cambrdige University Press.

David Hunt, 1970, <u>Parents and Children in History:</u>
<u>The Psychology of Family Life in Early Modern France.</u>
New York: Basic Books.

This 1973 review essay focuses on qualitative approaches to the study of
family history, specifically the works of <u>Macfarlane</u> and <u>Hunt</u>. While both
researchers are influenced by anthropology, DEMOS explains that Macfarlane
emphasizes kinship and community structures, while Hunt emphasizes the
"culture and personality" approach. Demos separately reviews the contents
of each volume, noting the merits and the limitations of each as well as
comparing their differences and similarities. It is these similarities,
or points of convergence, that may have the largest historiographic
significance. That the processes of development and change are absent in
the works of these authors is one such point. Another principle implicit
in these volumes is that of avoiding second-hand information--each historical
actor should be allowed to tell his own story. These researchers are said
to have sacrificed breadth for depth, in favor of what might be called a
greater "authenticity."

IV.C.   *THE LIFE CYCLE: EMPIRICAL WORKS*

(IV.C.1.)   Chudacoff, Howard P.
>   1980   "The Life Course of Women: Age and Age
>   Consciousness, 1865-1915." Journal of
>   Family History 5 (Fall): 274-292.

This essay examines early manifestations of certain demographic, social, and economic changes as they occurred among adolescent and adult women in Providence, Rhode Island, between 1865 and 1915. Using four Providence census samples as well as literary materials for information about norms and attitudes, CHUDACOFF describes six life course transitions of women: entry into the workforce; leaving the parental home; marriage; birth of first child; exit from the work force; and birth of last child. Some of the findings include these changes-over-time in women's life course timing: the experiences of certain events became increasingly more closely identified with a particular age or age interval; parental functions filled an ever-smaller proportion of adult careers; and the transition from youth to adulthood became more abrupt. The data also indicate that much of late 19th century and early 20th century American society became more age-conscious and age-differentiated, and that modern culture and institutions have roots in social and demographic trends emerging during that period or change. Two of the most notable features of this pattern are: (1) popular and academic social analysts were dividing life into more distinct stages and, concurrently, (2) institutions were being organized by finer age distinctions among men as well as women.

(IV.C.2.)   Elder, Glen H., Jr., and Jeffrey K. Liker
>   1981   "Hard Times in Women's Lives: Historical Influences
>   Across 40 Years." Unpublished manuscript, to
>   be published in the American Journal of Sociology.

Time-series analyses have empirically documented the link between economic change and changing health-states in populations and among individuals, but only for population aggregates. Longitudinal studies at the individual level are rare and most are too limited in time span to test duration hypotheses. One exception is this study by ELDER and LIKER. It examines the consequences of the Depression experiences of middle and working class American women for their health and well-being in old age, forty years later. The basic premise is that health is a product of the interaction between stressor and resources; the hypotheses under investigation are: that their well-being in old age is partially a function of how they dealt with problems of human and material loss during the 1930s; and that adaption-to-loss is contingent on both the severity of the deprivation and on the resources brought to the situation. The findings show that adaptations to human and material loss in the 1930s varied widely by social class, reflecting the greater severity of economic stress and the greater resource disadvantage of working class families. A longitudinal comparison of health measurements reveals consistently adverse effects of economic loss for working class women and benign outcomes among women of higher status.

(IV.C.3.) Elder, Glen H., Jr.
                   1981 "Scarcity and Prosperity in Postwar Childbearing:
                   Explorations From a Life Course Perspective."
                   Unpublished manuscript.

The basic premise of this study is that historical events may influence
subsequent times via their impact on lives and institutions, more specifically
that Depression experiences in postwar childbearing underscore the fundamental
interdependence of social change and the life course. ELDER undertakes the
conceptual task of linking Depression experiences with adult status and
childbearing in the postwar era and then conducts an empirical test of such
linkages.

The fertility implications of different "pathways" between the Depression
years and postwar America are examined. This model is then compared with
longitudinal data on the actual completed fertility of women and men who
grew up in the Great Depression. Within the two birth cohorts under study,
the experience of men and women in the 1930s varied widely, as did their
adult status or accomplishments in a period of economic growth and unparalleled
affluence. The analysis identifies circumstances associated with the bearing
of more children than average among the deprived who in adulthood lived in
affluent circumstances and also circumstances associated with fertility
control among the deprived who encountered relative hardships during their
adult years.

(IV.C.4.) Runck, Bette
                   1980 "Families in Hard Times--A Legacy." In Eunice
                   Corfman, editor, Families Today: 29-63. National
                   Institute of Mental Health, Science Monographs,
                   Number 1. U.S. Government Printing Office,
                   Washington, D.C. 20402.

This article provides the general educated reader with an excellent,
comprehensive description of Glen Elder's research on the effect of the
Depression on the lives of individuals and families. For those unfamiliar
with this research, RUNCK offers a description of Elder's data which include:
a set of archival records from the University of California's Institute of
Human Development on several generations of California families who lived
through the Depression; an explanation of the life-course approach used by
Elder in organizing records, constructing life histories, and conducting
analyses (both cohort analysis and linkage); and a discussion of similarities
and differences between the Oakland and Berkeley subjects under study.
The second half of this chapter considers history and the family--how the
reorientations in theory and methods of studying historical changes in the
family and also the clarification of "the bond between age and time" have
influenced contemporary research on the family. Finally, Runck notes that
Elder's work has been instrumental in moving other researchers away from an
ahistorical bias and promoting the construction of theories that explicate
the family as a domestic group undergoing change in specific historical
settings.

(IV.C.5.) Wells, Robert V.
              1971 "Demographic Change and the Life Cycle of
                    American Families." Journal of Interdisciplinary
                    History 2 (Autumn): 272-282.

This analysis of change in family life cycles is based upon data from two
studies; the data for 18th century families is taken from WELL's own
study on 276 Quaker families from New York, New Jersey, and Pennsylvania,
while the data for American families in general in the 19th and 20th
centuries is taken from a 1965 study by Glick and Parke. The evidence suggests
that marriages were typically formed at much the same point in life throughout
the last two centuries and that the birth of the first child followed within
a year or two. However, in the 19th and 20th centuries the median length
of time between marriage and the end of childbearing stage of life was only
9.7 years, compared to 17.4 years for 18th century Quaker women. Hence the
parents of the 18th century spent a larger portion of their lives rearing
children than did parents in later centuries. Parents in the 20th century
also experienced a more stable family situation, in part because families
of the late 18th century were subjected to growth and the continual threat
of a high mortality for a much longer time-span. Among other findings,
Wells notes that the life cycle of most American families over the last
two centuries has become more complex; from the almost-exclusive concern
with childbearing and childrearing before 1800, there has been a gradual
shift toward emphasis on the parents' lives after their children have left
home. Changes in mortality conditions and the effects of long-term fertility
decline only partially explain this change in the family cycle.

For other empirical works on the life cycle, see also II.D.2. and X.I.4.

(IV.D.1.) Lopez, Manuel D.
            1974 "A Guide to the Interdisciplinary Literature
            of the History of Childhood." History of
            Childhood Quarterly 1 (Winter): 463-494.

Written by a reference librarian, this is a 30-page annotated listing of
bibliograpic aids--abstracts, indexes, handbooks, library catalogs, directories,
etc.--useful for locating literature on the history of childhood (including
books, newspapers, journals, theses and dissertations, diaries and letters,
autobiography and biography, etiquette and character-books, manuscript and
subject collections, book reviews, government publications, graphics, etc.).
There is also a subsection on aids specifically useful for the history of
pediatrics. Within each of the 11 major categories, the sequence is from
the general or comprehensive to the specific or particular, or from the
current to the retrospective. For a bibliography of the literature itself,
see I.G.2.

(IV.D.2.) Lyman, Richard
            1980 "A Draft Code-Book for the Analysis of Children
            in Medieval Literature." Unpublished manuscript.
            A revised version is in preparation.

For content analysis of medieval literature as it pertains to family life,
interested scholars are referred to LYMAN's manuscript. Sixteen major
coding categories with over 100 subcategories are defined. Examples of two
such major categories and their subtopics are: (I) Nature of Material--didactic,
moralizing, fictional, historical, poetic, religious, problem with authorship
or dating, other (specify); (XVI) Indicators of Ambivalence--parent explicitly
describes child as important to self, parent overtly expresses love for the
child, parent expresses concern that the child will displace him/her, parent
rejects child by formal act of disavowal, disinheritence, etc., and other.

(IV.D.3.) Stewart, Abigail J., David G. Winter, and A. David Jones
            1975 "Coding Categories for the Study of Child-
            Rearing from Historical Sources." Journal of
            Interdisciplinary History 4 (Spring): 687-701.

This paper aims to present an objective and reliable set of categories for
coding one important source of historical evidence on child development, namely
child-rearing manuals, and also to illustrate how this coding system can be
used in actual research. The manuals are said to provide an accurate
measure of the important issues relating to children and their development
(as viewed by elite groups within society as a whole). The coding system
presented by STWEART, WINTER, and JONES has several features: (1) it can be
readily used by previously untrained coders with reliability sufficiently
high for research purposes; (2) it is based on the kinds of statements that
actually occur in child-rearing manuals, so that it can be applied with a
minimun of inference; and (3) although based in a general way on psychoanalysis,

it lends itself to a variety of frameworks. As an illustration of the kinds
of findings that can be obtained through this coding system, a brief summary
of Stewart's research on trends in English child-rearing is provided.

(IV.D.4.) Demos, John
             1971 "Developmental Perspectives on the History
                   of Childhood." Journal of Interdisciplinary
                   History 11 (Autumn): 315-327.

DEMOS' developmental approach to the study of childhood makes an effort to
find certain underlying themes, in the experience of children in a given
culture and period, in order to illuminate the formation of later personality.
This approach assumes that "the child is father to man" and that each culture
fosters the development of certain dominant character traits or styles. Two
different but interrelated ways of utilizing this approach are explained:
(1) vertical—which examines the child's development through time; and (2)
horizontal—which separates the different areas of the child's experience. Demos
exemplifies this approach with materials on 17th century American Puritans,
presenting tentative conclusions about particular aspects of Puritan practice
in the treatment of infants and very young children. The conclusion notes
methodological and theoretical problems arising in this type of analysis and
reiterates the premise on which this approach is based, i.e., the child as the
creator of culture—a dynamic force in his or her own right.

(IV.D.5.) deMause, Lloyd
             1974 "The Evolution of Childhood." History of
                   Childhood Quarterly 1 (Spring): 503-606.
                   Also in Lloyd deMause, editor, 1974, The
                   History of Childhood. New York: Psychohistory
                   Press.

DeMAUSE's book is the result of a project that sought to uncover the major
stages of childhood in the West since antiquity; this introductory chapter to
that volume explains the project's inception and, more importantly, outlines
the "psychogenic theory of history" as used in the project. This evolutionary
theory of historical change in parent-child relations assumes that the central
force for change in history is neither technology nor economics but rather
the "psychogenic" changes in personality occurring because of successive
generations of parent-child interactions. He begins by reviewing selected
previous works on children in history and expands his discussion to include
examples of psychological principles that apply to adult-child relations of
the past. The last three sections of this chapter include overviews of
the history of infanticide, abandonment, nursing, swaddling, beating, and
sexual abuse and an examination of how widespread these practices were in
each historical period.

(IV.D.6.) Ebel, Henry
             1977 "The Evolution of Childhood Reconsidered."
                   The Journal of Psychohistory: History of Childhood
                   Quarterly 5 (Summer): 67-80.

EBEL offers a critical analysis of deMause's "The Evolution of Childhood" (see IV.D.5.) in an attempt to strengthen it by first pointing out what he sees as its severest flaws and limitations. This critique is then followed by the proposal of a variant interpretation of the history of childhood in which conventional assumptions about the nature of our species and of its awesome pilgrimage through time, geography, and "inner space" are challenged. Ebel uses several core passages from deMause's work and allows his argument to develop in the form of an extended commentary on the contents of these passages.

(IV.D.7.) Kozak, Conrad M.
             1978 "Economic Systems, Child Rearing Practices and
                  Personality Development." American Journal of
                  Economics and Sociology 37 (January): 9-24.

This essay begins by presenting Max Weber's view that the values inherent in particular religious ideologies (such as Calvanistic Protestantism) give rise to attitudes predisposing individuals toward a particular type of economic organization (such as capitalism). Then came McClelland's reformulations, with socialization practices as the intervening variable. As KOZAK states, it now became the socialization practices which supposedly meditated and inculcated religious values in such a way that certain economic attitudes (e.g. need for achievement) and behavior patterns emerged in adulthood. However, the relevant research literature contains no reported relationship between religious affiliation and entrepreneurialism, independence training or need achievement. Recent research indicates that, in evolving societies, the economic-ecological variables strongly influence both the types of child-rearing practices and the parentally-instilled values depend largely upon the economic structure and occupational roles of the society. As technological complexity increases, the direct effect of technology upon personality becomes greater.

(IV.D.8.) Lindemann, Mary
             1981 "Love for Hire: The Regulation of the Wet-Nursing
                  Business in Eighteenth-Century Hamburg." Journal
                  of Family History 6 (Winter): 379-395.

Under examination in this essay is the wet-nursing system as it existed in eighteenth-century Hamburg, particularly as wet-nursing was criticized by influential writers, pediatricians, and authorities. Some critics attacked wet-nurses as indolent creatures filled with superstitions and more often than not capable of sly scheming, and others attacked mothers who allowed their children to be nursed by "mercenaries" who offered "love for hire." Although there existed some opposition to the preference for maternal milk, authorities were nevertheless united in their condemnation of baby-farming. Widely accepted humoral doctrines (the influence of bodily fluids, particularly milk, on the formation of mind, soul, and disposition in addition to physical well-being) and moral arguments, as well as medical and hygenic ones, at once espoused mother's milk as the ideal and brought about increased regulation in wet-nursing practices. LINDEMANN attempts to clarify some of the practical problems and the population issues involved in regulating

the "business" of wet-nursing in Hamburg, in light of the medical opinions
and moral convictions discussed in the first part of this essay.

(IV.D.9.) Friedberger, Mark
              1981 "The Decision to Institutionalize: Families
                    With Exceptional Children in 1900." Journal
                    of Family History 6 (Winter): 396-409.

FRIEDBERGER examines the impact of the birth of the metally handicapped
child upon the family and the subsequent decision made by the parents to
institutionalize such a child. The material used is from a linked sample
of U.S. institutional and census data drawn from six state schools for the
mentally handicapped between the years 1895 and 1905. The development over
time of American institutions is also traced, from the eugenic hereditary
approach of the past to the "exceptional children" concept of the present.
Although the evidence shows that some middle-class parents were concerned
about the quality of care their children would receive in institutions, the
majority of parents (in 1900) chose this option to free themselves from
bearing full responsibility for the care of their mentally handicapped
child. Parents were also led to believe that surrender of their son or
daughter would eventually benefit society as a whole, ridding society of
a troublesome and extraneous member.

(IV.D.10) Minge-Kalman, Wanda
              1978 "The Industrial Revolution and the European
                    Family: The Institutionalization of 'Childhood'
                    as a Market for Family Labor." Comparative
                    Studies in Society and History 20 (July): 454-468.

The treatment of children in Europe (mostly Britain, France, Germany) before
the industrial revolution is briefly described (child labor in peasant
agriculture, cottage industries, and mills; domestic service and apprenticeship;
neglect of infants). The rise of educational systems in the 19th century
extended childhood from age 5 or 6 to, eventually, 15 or 16 or longer.
During the transition from peasant to industrial wage-labor society, the
family changed from a food-producer to a socializer and educator of
laborers for an industrial labor market. The concept of childhood changed
drastically. "Adolescence" was born and, with its lengthening, the burden
of parents to support children grew greatly, only a small part of this burden
being direct educational costs. Contemporary investments of family money
and time in their children are detailed (for time, 1972 figures are cited
for nine European countries plus the U.S.). Home-based family labor is now
a multimillion "cottage industry." The home as the scene of labor has not
been lost, but the product has changed: children have become a labor-
intensive, capital-intensive product of the family in industrial society.

On the history of childhood, see also IX.E.1.

(IV.D.11.) Hiner, N. Ray
          1975 "Adolescence in Eighteenth-Century
                America." The Journal of Psychohistory:
                History of Childhood Quarterly 3 (Fall):
                253-280.

HINER advocates a revision of the standard view that nothing resembling
modern adolescence emerged before the late 19th century. He believes
that an investigation informed by modern psychology and the new social
history will allow the youth of the past to be "heard," if we learn how to
listen. His own analysis of essays on youth published in New England
during the first three decades of the 18th century finds an unprecedented
quantity of, and remarkable sophistication in, sermons and essays concerning
youth, their behavior, their social and psychological characteristics, and
their spiritual needs. Hence the belief that adolescence either did not
exist or was little noticed or understood in America before the late 19th
century appears invalid. The youth of early 18th century New England had
a great deal in common with today's adolescents—in the unstable social
conditions that they faced, in their prolonged dependence and marginality,
psychological characteristics, relations with their elders, and in the
specific adjustments they made as individuals.

(IV.D.12.) Elder, Glen H., Jr.
          1980 "Adolescence in Historical Perspective."
                In Joseph Adelson, editor, Handbook of
                Adolescent Psychology: 3-46. New York:
                John Wiley and Sons.

The study of adolescence has included two dominant perspectives which have
shaped perceptions of adolescence, theoretical concerns, and research—the
developmental and the social perspectives. During the 1960s, a third
perspective developed, viewing the developmental and social timetables of
adolescence according to historical time and change. This shift toward
historical consideration brought about the two advances which constitute
the central themes of this chapter: (1) the integration of three traditions
of research and theory (developmental, social, and historical) in a life-course
framework, and (2) its application to the studies of youth. Studies that
illustrate the use of archival resources for tracing the effects of historical
setting and change on the life course of youth are discussed, as are
comprehensive studies that have applied a life-course perspective to such
aspects of social change as early industrialization and institutional change,
institutional changes between late-19th century America and 1970, and the
Great Depression. The purpose of this article is not to survey all
available literature on the study of youth, notes ELDER, but rather to
suggest the possibilities which the life-course perspective brings to the
study of adolescence.

On the history of adolescence, see also VII.I.2.

IV.E.   *LIFE STAGES: OLD AGE*

(IV.E.1.)   Uhlenberg, Peter
    1980   "Death and the Family." Journal of Family
           History 5 (Fall): 313-320.

This article focuses on the impact of declining mortality in the 20th
century upon the American family, i.e., on the role of mortality as an
independent variable producing change. UHLENBERG constructs relatively
simple measures of how different mortality levels affect important aspects
of the family, using three dates (1900, 1940, and 1976) to provide a
perspective on historical change, and using four stages of the life course
(childhood, young adulthood, middle age, and old age) to provide a perspective
of individual change. The calculations use period life tables for each
date, revealing the implications of mortality conditions at specific
points in time, in answer to the basic question: how would mortality at
the 1900, 1940, or 1976 levels impinge on the family experience of individuals?
The findings imply that the decrease in mortality led to a deepening of
emotional bonds between family members (childhood), a downward pressure
exerted upon fertility (young adulthood), the "empty nest" being refilled by
responsibilities for one's aging parents (middle age), and an increase in
the significance of the final stages of life for widows (old age).

(IV.E.2.)   Spicker, Stuart, Kathleen Woodward and David Van Tassel, editors,
    1978   The Aging and the Elderly. Atlantic Highlands,
           New Jersey: Humanities Press.

(IV.E.3.)   Van Tassel, David
    1979   Aging, Death and the Completion of Being.
           Philadelphia, Pennsylvania: University of
           Pennsylvania Press.

There is a small but growing body of literature--both contemporary and
historical--focusing on old age and the elderly. For a sense of the
field as it emerged, see David Van Tassel's commentaries in SPICKER et.al.
(1978) and also in VAN TASSEL (1979).

(IV.E.4.)   Clark, Elaine
    1982   "Some Aspects of Social Security in Medieval
           England." Journal of Family History 7 (Winter):
           307-320.

CLARK investigates one system of support that was available to the elderly
in the villages and small market towns of late medieval England: a highly
personalized strategy which afforded the elderly the means to surrender the
use of their lands and resources to family members or nonkin in exchange for
individually arranged pension benefits. It is argued that pensions represented
a calculated response to problems of change induced by a configuration of
factors such as the onset of physical infirmity, the coming of age of

children wanting land in order to marry, and a peasant's sudden weariness of years of hard labor. An examination of the evidence (primarily maintenance contracts) reveals three ways in which pensions were arranged: (1) support was court ordered and served the interests of the elderly and the demands of the manor lord; (2) voluntary arrangements, planned by two parties on behalf of a third; and (3) the majority of support cases on record, the bargains which pensioners themselves negotiated. In general, the immediate needs of the old were balanced against the long-term interests of the young; a private system of support defined by shared resources was implemented as a compact between fathers and sons and as a negotiated agreement between the retired and the employable.

On old age, see also III.D.1., III.D.2., and X.I.2.

IV.F. *METHODOLOGICAL APPROACHES TO THE LIFE CYCLE*

(IV.F.1.) Boocock, Sarane Spence
1978 "Historical and Sociological Research on the
Family and the Life Cycle: Methodological
Alternatives." In John Demos and Sarane
Spence Boocock, editors, Turning Points:
Historical and Sociological Essays on the
Family, S366-S394. Chicago, Illinois: University
of Chicago Press. (Supplement to American
Journal of Sociology, Volume 84.)

Some of the specific methodological issues raised by the historical papers
presented in Parts II and III of Turning Points are examined by Boocock.
The three sections of her essay examine: (1) the types of data sources represented
including their strengths and weaknesses; (2) the selection of the research
case and the modes of sampling used; and (3) some of the modes of data
analysis used. This brief but comprehensive treatment is meant to identify
alternative methods in which historical materials can be further analyzed
in a context of specifically sociological concerns and concepts. The focus
on methodology also points to numerous ways in which the joint contributions
of historians and sociologists can further understanding of the processes of
change that concern both disciplines. The studies under discussion range
from intensive case studies of a single place and historical period to attempts
to chart trends in life cycles and family cycles over long intervals,
identifying the factors that differentiated family and life-course experiences
for individuals in different places or settings.

On methodological approaches to the life cycle, see also IV.B.3.

IV.G. <u>DISSERTATIONS</u>

(IV.G.1.) Mechling, Jay Edmund
            1971 <u>A Role-Learning Model for the Study of</u>
                  <u>Historical Change in Parent Behavior; With</u>
                  <u>a Test of the Model on the Behavior of</u>
                  <u>American Parents in the Great Depression.</u>
                  Unpublished Ph.D. dissertation, University
                  of Pennsylvania.

IV.H. *PUBLICATIONS*

(IV.H.1.) Clement, P. F.
1979 "Families and Foster Care--Philadelphia in the Late 19th-Century." Social Service Review 53 (Number 3): 406-420.

(IV.H.2.) Elder, G. H.
1977 "Family History and Life Course." Journal of Family History 2 (Number 4): 279-304.

(IV.H.3.) Litchfield, R. B., and D. Gordon
1980 "Closing the Tour--A Close Look at the Marriage Market, Unwed Mothers, and Abandoned Children in Mid-Nineteenth Century Amiens." Journal of Social History 13 (Number 3): 458-472.

(IV.H.4.) Rodgers, R. H., and G. Witney
1981 "The Family Cycle in 20th-Century Canada." Journal of Marriage and the Family 43 (Number 3): 727-740.

(IV.H.5.) Hanawalt, B. A.
1977 "Child-Rearing Among Lower Classes of Late Medieval England." Journal of Interdisciplinary History 8 (Number 1): 1-22.

(IV.H.6.) Hendricks, C. D., and J. Hendricks
1975 "Historical Development of Multiplicity of Times and Implications for Analysis of Aging." Human Context 7 (Number 1): 117-129.

(IV.H.7.) Neugarten, B. L.
1973 "Patterns of Aging--Past, Present, and Future." Social Service Review 47 (Number 4): 571-580.

(IV.H.8.) Weiss, N. P.
1978 "Mother-Child Dyad Revisited--Perceptions of Mothers and Children in 20th-Century Child-Rearing Manuals." Journal of Social Issues 34 (Number 2): 29-45.

(IV.H.9.) Demos, John
1975 "Old Age in Early New England." In Michael Gordon, editor, 1983, The American Family in Social-Historical Perspective, Third Edition, 269-305. New York: St. Martin's Press.

(IV.H.10.) Greven, Philip
1977 "Patterns for the Past." In Philip Greven, 1977, The Protestant Temperament: Patterns of Child Rearing, Religious Experience, and the Self in Early America. New York: Alfred A. Knopf.

(IV.H.11.) Kett, Joseph F.
            1977 "The Stages of Life, 1790-1840." In Joseph F. Kett,
                  1977, Rites of Passage: Adolescence in America,
                  1790 to the Present. New York: Basic Books.

(IV.H.12.) Modell, John, Frank F. Furstenberg, Jr., and Theodore Hershberg
            1976 "Social Change and Transitions to Adulthood in
                  Historical Perspective." Journal of Family History
                  (Autumn): 7-32.

V.A.   CONCEPTUAL AND THEORETICAL APPROACHES

(V.A.1.)   Hareven, Tamara K.
                1976 "Modernization and Family History: Perspectives
                      on Social Change." Signs 2 (Autumn): 190-206.

This paper examines the validity of the concept of modernization as
an explanation for the history of the family in general and more specifically,
for major changes in family behavior in America over the past century.
Major weaknesses of current modernization theory are its simplistic model
of change and of a mechanical concept of timing. However, modernization
theory is shown to provide a useful analytical framework for the study
of changes in society, demographic behavior, and family organization
preceeding industrialization and urbanization. Moreover, HAREVEN assesses
the contribution that the historical study of the family can make to
the understanding of the process of modernization as a description of
social change, especially as it relates to the changing social roles
of women. This perspective argues for the acceptance of a complex
model of behavior (in which men and women clearly modernize at different
rates and in which individuals may adopt modern patterns in one area of
their lives and hold onto traditional patterns in other areas), a model
which allows for the critical variables of class and ethnicity in the
historical study of the family. What becomes critical, then, is not
determining whether certain families at a certain point in time are
traditional or modern, but rather how families balance traditional and
modern attitudes and how the process of change takes place.

On modernization, see also I.A.7.

For other conceptual and theoretical approaches, see Section I.F. and
Section V.C.

V.B. REVIEWS OF MAJOR BOOKS

(V.B.1.) Lerner, Gerda
　　　　　　1978 "Review Essay: Motherhood in Historical
　　　　　　　　　 Perspective." Journal of Family History 3
　　　　　　　　　 (Fall): 297-300.

　　　　　　　　　 Review of:

　　　　　　　　　 Adrienne Rich, 1976, Of Woman Born: Motherhood
　　　　　　　　　 as Experience and Institution. New York:
　　　　　　　　　 W.W. Norton.

　　　　　　　　　 Linda Gordon, 1976, Woman's Body, Woman's Right:
　　　　　　　　　 A Social History of Birth Control in America.
　　　　　　　　　 New York: Grossman Publishers, Viking Press.

The two books reviewed here, on motherhood and reproductive control, are
both highly praised by LERNER as original, well written, and representing
significant advances in theory and scholarship about the separate historical
experience of women.

Rich is a writer/poet with a radical-feminist stance on motherhood, while
historian Gordon writes a social history of the birth control movement
in the U.S. and an intellectual history of attitudes toward sexual
regulation from a Marxist-feminist perspective. Gordon focuses more on
race/class differences and Rich more on the universality of the female
experience. Both books focus attention on the maternal potential of
women as a crucial causative factor of her subordinate status in society,
and the regulation by men—in modern societies, via the state and medical
establishment—of female reproduction as a key element in continuing that
subordination. Gordon's study is the more scholarly of the two and uses
primary sources. Rich's secondary sources offer somewhat antiquated
historical interpretations, yet her basic argument would probably not
have been different had she used better sources.

(V.B.2.) Interrante, Joseph, and Carol Lasser
　　　　　　1979 "Victims of the Very Songs they Sing: A
　　　　　　　　　 Critique of Recent Work on Patriarchal Culture
　　　　　　　　　 and the Social Construction of Gender."
　　　　　　　　　 Radical History Review 20 (Spring/Summer):
　　　　　　　　　 25-40.

　　　　　　　　　 Review of:

　　　　　　　　　 Nancy Cott, 1977, The Bonds of Womanhood:
　　　　　　　　　 "Woman's Sphere" in New England, 1780-1835. New
　　　　　　　　　 Haven, Connecticut: Yale University Press.

　　　　　　　　　 Ann Douglas, 1977, The Feminization of American
　　　　　　　　　 Culture. New York: Knopf (Avon paperback, 1978).

Stuart Ewen, 1976, <u>Captains of Consciousness:</u>
<u>Advertising and the Roots of Consumer Culture.</u>
New York: McGraw-Hill.

Barbara Ehrenreich and Deidre English, 1979, <u>For</u>
<u>Her Own Good: 150 Years of Experts' Advice to</u>
<u>Women</u>. Garden City, New York: Doubleday.

The authors examine four books that address themes of patriarchy, capitalism, and culture. All but the Cott volume is said to have fallen into the trap of "victimization"--that is, exaggerating the power and social control exerted on the masses by patriarchal ideology. INTERRANTE and LASSER, nevertheless, believe that all of these works make a substantial contribution to the theoretical elaboration of the concept of patriarchy and deepen the understanding of the historical context of sexual spheres and gender identities. Some comments on each of these works are as follows.

<u>Cott</u>, drawing on the personal papers of over 100 New England women, celebrates their ability to shape their own lives and develop a strong and important subculture which both accommodated parts of the dominant national culture and resisted certain aspects of an increasingly market-oriented, industrializing society. The ways in which women made use of the ideology of domesticity for their own purposes are stressed.

<u>Douglas</u> discusses the general changes in women's positions, along with the responses of some women to those changes. However, the failure to examine different class responses forces Douglas's retreat into an explanantion based on victimization of the general category "women."

<u>Ewen</u>'s study of the growth of advertising and "consumer consciousness" is a version of victimization which sees American society as being enslaved by the machinations of those who manipulate people's "needs" and as such reveals most clearly the weaknesses of victimization as an explanation.

<u>Ehrenreich</u> and <u>English</u> study the changes in some of those household activities which shape consumerism. They chronicle the change from a nebulous desire for guidance to a perceived need for direction in women's domestic roles. While the authors are at their best when they detail how advice and perscription were transformed in their passage from the bourgeoisie to the working class, their restricted orientation in emphasizing victimization and the general category of "women" as an explanation often lacks class specificity; this failure to maintain a class analysis hampers the author's ability to locate women's experience in the larger process of change.

(V.B.3.) Stage, Sarah
        1980 "Women's History and 'Women's Sphere': Major
             Works of the 1970s." <u>Socialist Review</u> 10
             (March/June): 245-254.

Review of:

Caroll Smith-Rosenberg, 1975, "The Female World
of Love and Ritual: Relations Between Women in
Nineteenth-Century America," Signs 1 (1): 1-29.

Nancy F. Cott, 1977, The Bonds of Womanhood:
"Women's Sphere" in New England, 1780-1835.
New Haven, Connecticut: Yale University Press.

Barbara Ehrenreich and Deidre English, 1979,
For Her Own Good: 150 Years of Experts' Advice
to Women. Garden City, New York: Doubleday.

Ann Douglas, 1977, The Feminization of American
Culture. New York: Alfred A. Knopf (also, Avon
paperback).

Linda Gordon, 1976, Woman's Body, Woman's Right:
A Social History of Birth Control in America.
New York: Grossman (also, Penguin paperback).

Five major works of the mid-1970s on women's history are reviewed by
STAGE in terms of their contrasting positions on such issues as a distinct
"women's sphere" in the 19th century, (to what extent it existed, whether
it served more to oppress women or to strengthen them by fostering
supportive female subcultures or by being a prerequisite for a feminist
movement) and the ideology or culture of domesticity (its importance in
making tolerable the shift to industrial capitalism and whether it served
more to hamper or help 19th-century feminism).

In general, the works by Smith-Rosenberg, Cott, and Gordon are judged to
be much stronger than those of Douglas and of Ehrenreich and English. The
Gordon book is given special attention. It views the struggle of women
to control their reproductive lives as a women's issue (not just as a
"reform movement") and focuses on the extent to which birth control is
social and political, not merely medical or technological. (Much of
birth control technology had been available for centuries.) She describes
how 19th century women were able to fight for greater sexual autonomy
without directly challenging the dominant Victorian ideologies. Gordon
paints "with a wide brush" the broad outlines of the social history of
birth control from the initial radical, feminist struggle into a liberal
reform that has divided women along class lines and blurred larger
feminist issues.

(V.B.4.) Remy, Dorothy
        1980 (Untitled book review.) The Review of Political
              Economics 12 (Summer): 97-99.

Review of:

Karen Sacks, 1979, Sisters and Wives: The
Past and Future of Equality. Westport,
Connecticut: Greenwood.

Meredith Turshen, 1980, Women, Food and Health
in Tanzania: The Political Economy of Disease.
London, England: Onyx Press.

According to REMY, the position that women have always been subordinate
to men primarily because of innate physical (or psychological) qualities
can lead to despair, for such an analysis contains no mechanism for
change. When the idea of innate inferiority (or superiority) is abandoned,
subordination can be seen as an aspect of identifiable social relations
and, once identified, oppressive social relations can be challenged and
transformed.

The two volumes reviewed here both reject the "innatist" view in favor
of a closely reasoned analysis of the social origins of inequality.
Both focus on the transition from nonclass to class society. Anthropologist
Sacks locates the inequality of women in the systematic destruction by
a capitalist ruling class of a political economy based on kinship.
Turshen examines the abrupt incorporation of nonclass societies in the
capitalist mode of production and argues that the mode of production
(i.e., the social system by which work is organized to provide the means
of subsistence) defines the boundaries and conditions under which disease
occurs.

Both volumes are said to significantly contribute to the theoretical
discussion about the historical basis of women's subordination, and both
agree that the key issue is women gaining (collective) control of the
means of production.

(V.B.5.)   Cobb, Richard
          1981   "The Discreet Charm of the Bourgeoisie." The
                 New York Review of Books 28 (December 17): 57-59.

                 Review of: Bonnie G. Smith, 1981, Ladies of
                 the Leisure Class: The Bourgeoises of Northern
                 France in the Nineteenth Century. Princeton,
                 New Jersey: Princeton University Press.

A study of the ladies of the upper-middle class of Roubaix-Tourcoing
and of Lille (France) between 1800 and 1914, Smith's book explores the
history of the family and the home as measured in the private calendar
of female domestic and biological cycles. Woman's reproductive function,
her domestic power, and her fragility and imprisonment are stressed.
Reviewer COBB provides a sense of the "narrow clannishness and parochialism"
of this subculture, both from his own experiences and from the book, and
notes that among the bourgeoise du Nord we are dealing with family
structures that are unique. Smith is praised for making the most of an
excellent subject and for making a major contribution to the history of
leisure and of private life and criticized for excessive use of sociological
jargon.

(V.B.6.) Anderson, Barbara A.
              1982 (Untitled book review.) <u>American Journal</u>
              <u>of Sociology</u> 87, number 6, (May): 1431-1433.

              Review of: Louise A. Tilly and Joan W. Scott,
              1978, <u>Women, Work, and Family</u>. New York:
              Holt, Reinhart and Winston.

This volume is written in three parts: (1) "The Family Economy in Early
Modern England and France," (2) "Industrialization and the Family Wage
Economy," and (3) "Toward the Family Consumer Economy." In the first
part, <u>Tilly</u> and <u>Scott</u> discuss to what extent the work of both married and
single women (in or out of the household) was a part of family strategy
in the late 17th and early 18th centuries. The second part deals
with industrialization as it influenced the change from the household
as a subsistence unit to the household surviving through accumulation
of money, especially through the wages of women. In the third part,
the authors discuss the factors that led to decreased paid work by
women for several decades after 1910.

ANDERSON recommends this work to anyone interested in changing roles
of women with industrialization, in female labor force participation,
in family power, or in family decision-making. As an introduction to
the changing status and roles of women in England and France from the
late 17th century to the present, it would also be useful as a supplementary
text in undergraduate college courses on women, modernization, social
change, work and occupations, or social history. <u>Women, Work, and Family</u>
is not a piece of primary research but rather summarizes and interprets
a large body of literature.

(V.B.7.) Lindemann, Barbara S.
              1982 (Untitled book review.) <u>The Journal of</u>
              <u>American History</u> 69 (June): 139-140.

              Review of: Mary Beth Norton, 1980, <u>Liberty's</u>
              <u>Daughters: The Revolutionary Experience of</u>
              <u>American Women, 1750-1800</u>. Boston, Massachusetts:
              Little, Brown, and Co.

<u>Norton</u> presents evidence which challenges the widely accepted view of
colonial America as a "golden age" when women enjoyed a higher status
than their contemporaries in Europe or their 19th-century descendants.
Primarily a study of attitudes revealed in the private writings of women,
<u>Liberty's Daughters</u> describes mid-18th century conventional wisdom
about female capabilities, courtship, marriage, housework, motherhood, and
wifely roles. It also offers a detailed examination of work, family, and
kinship among 18th-century slave women. LINDEMANN considers this volume
to be a significant contribution to the reinterpretation of the position
of women in preindustrial North America.

(V.B.8.) Kerber, Linda K.
              1982 (Untitled book review.) <u>Signs</u> 8 (1): 138-143.

Review of: Carl N. Degler, 1980, At Odds: Women
and the Family in America from the Revolution
to the Present. New York and Oxford, England:
Oxford University Press.

Much of what is known about the history of the family in the United
States, with special emphasis upon women, is for the first time
integrated and summarized in one book. The uniting theme is that of
autonomy, more specifically, that men and women encounter different
obstacles in their quest for individualism and that the family has
been (and still is) in conflict with women's search for autonomy.

Degler follows four themes (ways in which power relations between
patriarch and subordinates have been mediated) throughout American
history: (1) affection and mutual respect between partners; (2)
separate spheres for women, which permitted limited autonomy; (3)
an increasingly child-centered focus; and (4) a marked decline in
family size. The rise of the "modern family" is dated from about the
second half of the 18th century.

Topics include contraception, sexuality, the female suffrage movement,
and women's work, to name a few. Over time, the tension between the
competing claims of women and of the family has become increasingly more
intense--a dilemma for which Degler sees no resolution.

In addition to an overview and critique of key ideas of the book, reviewer
KERBER seems to suggest that the conflict between women and family is--to
a greater degree than Degler states--really a conflict between men and
women. The separation of child rearing (which could be shared) from
child bearing is suggested as one starting point for a social-change
agenda which would not necessarily pit women's claims for autonomy
against the needs of the family. For other reviews of the Degler book,
see V.B.9. and IX.D.2.

(V.B.9.) Riegelhaupt, Joyce
          1982 "Women, Work, War, and Family: Some Recent
                Works in Women's History. A Review Article."
                Comparative Studies in Society and History
                24 (October): 660-672.

          Review of:

          Darlene Gay Levy, Harriet Branson Apple White,
          and Mary Durham Johnson, 1979, Women in
          Revolutionary Paris 1789-1795. Urbana:
          Illinois University Press.

          Thomas Dublin, 1979, Women at Work: The
          Transformation of Work and Community in
          Lowell, Massachusetts, 1826-1860. New York:
          Columbia University Press.

Susan Estabrook Kennedy, 1979, _If All We Did
Was To Weep at Home_. Bloomington: Indiana
University Press.

Carol R. Berkin and Clara M. Lovett, 1980,
Women, War and Revolution. New York: Holmes
and Meier.

Carl N. Degler, 1980, _At Odds: Women and the
Family in America from the Revolution to the
Present_. New York and Oxford, England: Oxford
University Press.

Three books on U.S. women (mainly in the 19th century) and two on
women in wartime situations (a document collection from Paris 1789-1795
and a collection of articles on Germany, the U.S., France, China, Cuba,
and the Soviet Union) are discussed in this review article by RIEGELHAUPT.

Most relevant to the family is the book by Degler. His focus is primarily
on middle- and upper-class native-born American white women, with a heavy
focus on the 19th century. This book is an attempt to synthesize the
results of two separate fields--women's history and family history--for
the educated nonspecialist reader. A comprehensive bibliography is
lacking. Degler is said to argue that it is structurally impossible to
achieve equality for women while also maintaining the institution of
the family. Since marriage is always a power relationship, the family
could never be organized on egalitarian principles. He is criticized
for studying "the family" as an ideal type rather than as a changing
historical process. The success of the 19th century, for Degler, was
the emergence of a family in which men were permitted to be individuals.
But this "family"--and hence men's rights--was (and are) built upon the
subordination of women. For other reviews of the Degler book, see also
V.B.8. and IX.D.2.

For additional books, see also XI.B.2.

V.C. *STATUS/POWER*

(V.C.1.) Easton, Barbara
         1978 "Feminism and the Contemporary Family."
         Socialist Review 8 (3): 11-36.

EASTON argues that, at each stage, the U.S. women's movement has wisely
chosen to attack the weakest and not the strongest areas of male
dominance. Patriarchy has changed historically and, with it, the response
of (white) feminist women. She details the nature and ideological/
structural bases of patriarchy (male dominance and female dependence) and
the responses of the women's movement from the 19th century to the
present time--first fighting patriarchy in the public sphere and only
since the 1960s attacking it within the family as well. However, as
"legitimate" forms of male dominance are undermined, illegitimate
forms become more prominent.

(V.C.2.) Cooper, Sandi E.
         1979 "Feminism and Family Revivalism." Chrysalis
         8 (Summer): 58-65.

Nowadays, the questions of family, marriage and divorce, and child-
rearing come close to being a national obsession, writes COOPER;
simultaneously, ethnic consciousness is on the rise. Throughout this
essay, the implications of these "twin rivals" are discussed in terms
of their academic, social, and political relationships to feminism
and the feminist perspective. Much scholarly literature has shifted
its focus from women to appeals on behalf of children, youth, and society,
reflecting a developing assault on feminism. Of particular interest
is the extensive critique of Lasch's Haven in a Heartless World (1977),
which Cooper says is a thinly disguised attack on feminism and an open
assault on social-science experts concerned with the family. The
article concludes with suggestions for a renewed feminist agenda.

(V.C.3.) Folbre, Nancy
         1980 "Patriarchy in Colonial New England." The
         Review of Political Economics 12 (Summer):
         4-13.

Based upon a critical review of the historical literature and specific
research on the history of Hampshire County, Massachusetts, FOLBRE
challanges conventional assumptions regarding family relations in
colonial New England (e.g., that family relations are relatively
egalitarian when all family members contribute to production), and,
by implication, assumptions regarding the precapitalist family in similar
historical contexts. For example, while the work of women and children
may have been important, it did not guarantee them any significant
power within the family. It is argued that, in fact, production within
the colonial household took place in the context of patriarchal social

relations which gave the male head of household control over his family
and power to benefit from their labor. In addition, a description
of the relations of domination between fathers and sons as well as
between men and women suggests a fundamental relationship between
these two aspects of patriarchy. If women's most important productive
contribution did not lie in household tasks, but in bearing and
rearing children who would become direct producers, then decline in
patriarchal control over children might decrease the incentives for
high fertility and might mitigate or modify the motives for patriarchal
control over women.

(V.C.4.) Sokoloff, Natalie J.
                    1981 "Motherwork and Working Mothers." Quest
                          5 (3): 41-52. Adapted from Natalie J. Sokoloff,
                          1980, Between Money and Love: The Dialectics
                          of Women's Home and Market Work. New York:
                          Praeger.

"It is neither the bearing nor the rearing of children that is oppressive
to women; rather, it is the institution of motherhood as organized
by and for patriarchy in U.S. capitalism..." So begins SOKOLOFF's
discussion of the historical development of motherhood as an institution
and of the relation of motherhood to waged labor. She traces the
growth of the 20th century ideology of individual and isolated motherhood
in the context of larger economic changes, social class differences,
and the reduction of child labor.

Full-time motherhood becmae the ideal, strangely enough, at a time
when women were increasingly employed in the labor market, when modern
technology of birth control and bottle feeding were becoming available,
and when family size was declining. Even today, women who go into waged
labor do so as mothers (they buy goods, and services for their families,
they are treated on the labor market as former, actual, or potential
mothers, and they continue to do "mothering" of men on the job).
The linkages between patriarchy and capitalism, between "motherwork" at
home and "motherwork" in the market, can and will be broken.

(V.C.5.) Fox-Genovese, Elizabeth
                    1982 "Gender, Class and Power: Some Theoretical
                          Considerations." The History Teacher 15
                          (February): 255-276.

Gender is social, not biological, and is not merely social but a relation
that interacts with class relations. FOX-GENOVESE uses a critique
of the "wonderfully provacative if wrong-headed" book by Michel Foucault,
(A History of Sexuality, New York, 1980) as the springboard for her
discussion of the complex historical interrelations among--and the conceptual
distinctions between--gender and sexuality, gender and class, and gender
and class and power, with emphasis upon U.S. and Western European history.
The obsessive concealment of sexuality in bourgeoise society discussed
by Foucault cannot be understood in terms of sexuality alone. It

testifies to the centrality of the gender system in the elaboration
of the social, economic, and political relations of capitalist society.
Capitalism, with its inherent impulse to generalize and standardize
social/economic relations and institutions, places a disproportionate
weight upon the gender system, both as custodian of hierarchical and
religious values and as agent in forging a viable social and political
order.

On status and power of women, see also VI.B.3. and Section I.F. On
Foucault, see also IX.D.2.

(V.D.1.) McLaughlin, Virginia Yans
        1971 "Patterns of Work and Family Organization:
             Buffalo's Italians." Journal of Interdisciplinary
             History 11 (Autumn): 299-314.

Seeking additional knowledge on the family as it relates to industrialization and urbanization, McLAUGHLIN examines the relationship between
female occupational patterns and family organization among south Italians
in Buffalo, New York, from about 1900 to 1930. The assumption that
the family should be viewed simply as a dependent variable is challenged;
instead, it is demonstrated that female assumption of new economic
functions did not necessarly alter family power arrangements or disrupt
the "traditional" family. In fact, the findings show that family
disorganization was minimal and female-headed families rare among Italian-
Americans. From the narrower focus of women's history, this discussion
then broadens to include the wider realm of women, the family, and
working-class culture. The traditional assumptions concerning the
impact of industrialization and employment upon the family and
women's role are questioned, and the need for careful examination of
women within the context of family life by class, ethnic group, region,
city, and religious background is established.

(V.D.2.) Walkowitz, Daniel J.
        1972 "Working-Class Women in the Gilded Age:
             Factory, Community and Family Life among
             Cohoes, New York, Cotton Workers." Journal
             of Social History 5 (Summer): 464-490.

In much of the work characterized as the "New Urban History," sociologists
and historians have focused on the relationship between social mobility
and behavior within the 19th-century working class. This scholarship
offers two alternative arguments concerning working-class oppression
and their efforts towards social amelioration. In the first argument,
the oppressed working class organized and struggled (even violently)
to gain some affluence and security through the labor movement. In
the second argument, workers individually achieved some mobility, and
consequently little or no united effort was made to win a social revolution.

WALKOWITZ finds parts of both these views to be correct. Although
workers lived and worked under oppressive conditions, they did achieve
some measure of social mobility. And considerable violence did
occur in labor struggles, but no social revolution took place. While
violence marked the struggle to control the conditions of industrial
life, the equation between poverty and violent social behavior is
not precise, as the history of the Cohoes, New York, cotton-worker
community shows.

He reconsiders the impact of the factory and the city on the lives of
the cotton worker and her family. The factory and community helped

both to sustain the mill operatives and to secure some social mobility
for them. Yet the modest gains in status and security did not liberate
them from economic and social worries, but rather restricted their
field of vision and alienated them from their own social reality. It
is within this context that the labor violence which erupted in Cohoes
during the early 1880s is interpreted.

The impact of the factory and the "company town" on the working class
family are also examined, in comparison to other communities.
Except for child labor, few structural differences existed between
working and middle class families. Variations in age of marriage,
family size, etc., seem mostly due to ethnic differences. However,
cotton-worker families, especially those of Irish descent, were more
often nuclear and more often single-parent families, than were
working class families in other industries and from other ethnic
groups.

(V.D.3.) Scott, Joan W., and Louise A. Tilly
              1976 "Women's Work and the Family in Nineteenth-
                    Century Europe." Comparative Studies in
                    Society and History 17 (January): 36-64.

This essay on women's work and women's place in the family argues
against an evolutionary social-change model that assumes a singular
and similar experience for all women, an experience in which political
and cultural and economic factors are closely interrelated and hence
change together. This assumption is tested against historical data
by TILLY and COHEN and found to be invalid. The changes that affected
women's work and women's place in the family in 19th and 20th century
Europe were to be anything but uniform. They were differentiated
geographically, ethnically, and temporally and they involved complex
patterns of family dynamics and family decision making. The first
contacts with structural changes in all cases, however, involved
adjustments of traditional strategies and were informed by values
rooted in the family economy. Behavior is less the product of new
ideas then of old ideas operating in new or changing contexts. Studying
the work of the vast majority of women in the 19th century requires
understanding their experience in light of their familial values, not
our own individualistic ones.

(V.D.4.) Tilly, Louise A., Joan Scott, and Miriam Cohen
              1976 "Women's Work and European Fertility Patterns."
                    Journal of Interdisciplinary History 6 (Winter):
                    447-476.

Although this article acknowledges Edward Shorter's contributions to
women's history and demographic history, its primary purpose is to
critically examine his hypothesis concerning the relationship between
"female emancipation" and increased rates of legitimate and illegitimate
fertility in Western Europe at the end of the 18th century. Shorter's
model asserted that sexual relationships and marriage patterns (hence,

fertility rates) were extremely sensitive to changes in social and economic
realities, and that the correlation of a number of events (industrialization, migration, changes in women's roles, changes in fertility rates)
all involve fertility; hence, a change in fertility rates can only mean
a change in sexual practices, which means a change in attitudes--
particularly of women.

Believing that this interpretaion, which relies on a single causal
sequence, is based on a chain of reasoning, not on evidence, TILLY, SCOTT,
and COHEN present the historical evidence about women's work experiences
before and during industrialization (evidence they believe ignored by
Shorter). These authors do not claim new and dramatic findings, but
seriously question both Shorter's premise about the position of pre-
industrial women and his central assertion that a change in popular
attitudes led to increased illegitimate, and possibly, legitimate
fertility. Finally, an alternative model is offered to explain fertility
changes, which is based on the evidence examined in this essay.

(V.D.5.) Brown, Bruce W.
            1978 "Wife-Employment and the Emergence of
                  Egalitarian Marital Role Prescriptions:
                  1900-1974." Journal of Comparative Family
                  Studies 9 (Spring): 5-17.

BROWN's investigation sought to determine whether or not wife-employment
is correlated with the emergence of egalitarian marital role prescriptions,
and if so, which variable causally influences the other and with what time-
lag. Changes in marital role prescriptions are studied via an analysis
of marriage advice articles published in U.S. women's magazines between
1900 and 1974. Marital role prescriptions did become more egalitarian
but were--as of 1974--still far from advocating complete husband-wife
equality.

A series of lagged correlations show that, with one exception, neither
marital role norms nor wife employment is necessarily causally prior;
most role prescriptions became more egalitarian at about the same
time as the proportion of employed wives was increasing. However, in
one case a possible causal priority could be identified: wife-employment
preceeded the emergence of egalitarian role prescriptions regarding
power-sharing (as indexed by norms that marital decisions should be
made jointly). This is said to provide support, at the macrosociological
level, for Blood and Wolfe's resource theory of marital power.

(V.D.6.) Bolin, Winfred D. Wandersee
            1978 "The Economics of Middle-Income Family Life:
                  Working Women During the Great Depression."
                  The Journal of American History 65 (June):
                  60-74.

BOLIN's examination of the labor force participation of U.S. women
during the 1930s shows that the number of married women in the workforce

increased by nearly 50 per cent, while their numbers in the population increased by only 15 per cent. Thus, despite the oversupply of labor and underemployment of the population as a whole, married women workers made substantial numerical gains at a time when women were under a great deal of public pressure to leave the labor market in order to avoid competing with men for the short supply of jobs.

By 1940, over 40 per cent of these working wives were of middle-income families. This is interpreted in relation to several factors: social, demographic, and technological developments; changes in the economic functions of the family as it became town-based rather than rural; and--the primary factor explored in this essay--the changing definition of economic need. She concludes that many, if not most, married women worked because of economic need, but "economic need" is a relative concept and it becomes a reality for different families at different levels of experience. In addition, the life-styles of working women continued to be based on traditional family values, and the work of the married woman usually reflected the primacy of her home life. In that sense, the relationship between home, self, and job remained constant.

(V.D.7.) Brownlee, W. Elliot
           1979 "Household Values, Women's Work, and
                 Economic Growth, 1800-1930." Journal
                 of Economic History 39 (March): 199-209.

This essay examines the state of economic knowledge about the development of the household in the United States since the 19th century. Several explanations for the low labor force participation of middle class (white) women in the period between early industrialization and the Great Depression are examined. These expalantions, including those emerging from fertility studies and resting on market forces, specify the domestic roles of housewives only imprecisely, i.e., they are imprecise about the way in which families in general, and mothers in particular, spend their time at home. Yet the assumptions made on this point play a central role in the above-mentioned explanations, according to BROWNLEE. Current theory would clearly benefit from an interdisciplinary effort (by economic historians as well as social and cultural historians) to replace these assumptions with measurements of the changing allocation of time spent on domestic work among family members and of the changing level and disposition of women's time within the household. Such time studies, made in conjunction with a wider examination of the devlopments of households as economic units and giving particular attention to the development of women's roles, would provide a fuller understanding of the sources of modern economic life.

(V.D.8.) Franzoi, Barbara
           1981 "Women and Industrial Work in the German
                 Reich, 1871-1914." Paper presented at the
                 Berkshire Conference on the History of Women.
                 (The author is located at College of St.
                 Elizabeth, Convent Station, New Jersey
                 07961.)

To understand the history of women and industrial work in pre-World War I
Germany, FRANZOI goes beyond the usual historical model for understanding
industrialization, a model that focuses on men's work in large factories
in heavy industry. She stresses two peculiarities of the German situation:
(1) the uneven nature of capitalist industrial development, in which
mechanization grew but so did handwork and homework; and (2) the strong
constraints that various political, social, and religious interest
groups placed upon industrial transformation. Both of these factors
helped channel women into very different kinds of work than that performed
by men. This investigation of a wider-than-usual range of occupations
in historical context alters the "German paradigm." For instance, the
customary picture of the millgirl fits only a small part of Germany's
industrial working women, even among young single women. Almost 50 per
cent of the industrial female labor force were employed in the clothing
industry and another third worked in foods and tobacco, both of these
industries being heavily home work. When women worked in a factory setting,
it was often seasonal and irregular. Most women were anchored to
family units, as wives or mothers or daughters. They changed jobs
often and, despite low wages, could exercise choice as to when and how
and what kind of work they did. Wives worked primarily when the husband's
income was insufficient for survival.

Working women add new dimensions to the understanding of capitalist
industrial development, and women's work in Germany has implications
that need to be evaluated in the broader context of European history
and the history of women.

On women and employment, see also Section III.A., IX.B.3., I.F.10.,
and X.G.6.

(V.D.9.) Milkman, Ruth
            1981   "Organizing the Sexual Division of Labor:
                   Historical Perspectives on 'Women's Work'
                   and the American Labor Movement." Socialist
                   Review 49 (January/February): 95-150.

The single most important change in the composition of the labor
force as a whole in the post-war period has been the dramatic rise
in female labor force participation. The failure of the labor movement
to come to terms with this development is an important part of the
explanation for the movement's present stagnation. To understand this
failure, writes MILKMAN, it is necessary to examine the historical
development of the relationship between working women and labor unions.
The relationship is examined for two formative historical periods--the
late 19th and early 20th centuries--when the labor movement experienced
its most rapid growth and became established in its present form. Topics
under discussion include: theories of occupational segregation by sex;
the working class family, deskilling, and women's employment; the AFL and
women workers; women in the years of the early CIO; and demobilizaiton,
women workers, and the postwar labor movement. Of special relevance to the
family is the brief discussion (pages 108-111) on the working class
family and how bourgeois family ideology led to the perception of wife-
employment as a capitalist assault on the working class family.

V.E. HOUSEWORK AND HOUSEHOLD PRODUCTION

(V.E.1.) Cowan, Ruth Schwartz
                1976 "The 'Industrial Revolution' in the Home:
                      Household Technology and Social Change in
                      the 20th Century." Technology and Culture
                      17 (June): 1-23.

The industrialization of the home, says historian COWAN, is a process
very different from the industrialization of other means of production.
Its impact is neither what we have been led to believe it was nor what
students of other industrial revolutions would have predicted.

The standard (functionalist) sociological model predicted that modern
technology would dissolve family life (it hasn't) and reduce the functions
of the wife (at least for middle-class non-rural U.S. families in the
20th century, her functions have increased rather than decreased).

Opposite to standard notions of how technological change affects the
market work force, the effect of household technology has been a
reduction of differentiation/specialization in the household work force.
As the middle class housewife's job became less specialized, it was
also proletarianized (decline in managerial functions and increase
in manual labor). Finally, instead of desensitizing the emotions
connected with household work, industrialization of the home seems
to have heightened the emotional context of the work--leading to free-
floating discontent (Betty Friedan's "the problem that has no name")
among workers who invested their (household) work with emotional weight
far out of proportion to its inherent value.

(V.E.2.) Hartmann, Heidi
                1981 "The Family as the Locus of Gender, Class,
                      and Political Struggle: The Example of
                      Housework." Signs 6 (Spring): 366-394.

The family should not be conceptualized, as family historians too often
have done, as an active agent with unified interests, but rather as a
locus of stuggle among individuals having different interests and
activities. The particular form familiar relations take largely
reflects and is shaped by patriarchy and capitalism, in HARTMANN's
Marxist-feminist perspective. Her essay has two parts. The first
explains the family's role as a location for production and redistribution
and speculates about the interaction between the family and the state
and how family-state relations have changed historically in Western
societies. The second part uses the example of housework to illustrate
the differences in material interests among family members caused
by their differing relations to patriarchy and capitalism; contemporary
U.S. data on who does how many hours of housework are interpreted in this
framework.

(V.E.3.) Swerdlow, Amy editor
                  1978 Feminist Perspective on Housework and
                        Child Care. Bronxville, New York: Sarah
                        Lawrence College.

For a comprehensive bibliography on housework, readers are referred to
the SWERDLOW volume.

(V.E.4.) Jensen, Joan M.
                  1980 "Cloth, Butter and Boarders: Women's
                        Household Production for the Market."
                        The Review of Political Economics 12
                        (Summer): 14-24.

An historical framework for analyzing American women's household
production for the market from the late 18th century to the early 20th
century is presented. JENSEN argues that women's household production--
particulary the making of cloth and butter and the taking in of boarders--
was a crucial economic factor in both urban and rural families, maintaining
within them a simple commodity mode of production. With the disappearance
of this type of household production, women moved from a household income
to a wage income and into the capitalist mode of production. Described
in this essay are types of work usually omitted from descriptions of
wage work and housework. A model of Marxist theory which incorporates
all types of women's work--including simple commodity production--
could more accurately describe the past and predict the future and
could illustrate how the development of capitalism has affected American
women. It is made clear that the women who sold cloth, sold butter,
and boarded lodgers were not so different in motivation from the women
who go out today as clerical or service workers; however, the political
implications of that process that are likely to be far different.
The fact that women are not only leaving the household but also leaving
a transitional mode of production may have an important impact on the
development of capitalism and on women's reaction to it.

(V.E.5.) Brown, Clair
                  1982 "Home Production for Use in a Market
                        Economy." In Barrie Thorne with Marilyn
                        Yalom, editors, Rethinking the Family:
                        Some Feminist Questions, 151-167. New
                        York: Longman.

Economist BROWN provides a critique of the neoclassical school's
"new home economics" approach to the home economy (pages 154-156)
and an alternative analysis of the home economy, with a focus on
home production/housework services. Topics include: the structural
characteristics of home production; two historical stages in the
relation of the home economy to the growing market economy (including
the decline on the relative importance of work done in the home to
the family's material standard of living); a documentation of how the
shift toward fewer people per household has increased the resources

needed per person to meet basic needs of shelter, transportation, and housework; the problems inherent in switching one's work effort between the home and market economies, because of the different work and value structures of the two economies, and how these differences hinder changes in the current division of labor between men and women in both economies.

On housework and household production, see also I.F.12 and IX.B.5.

V.F. *DISSERTATIONS*

(V.F.1.)   Bolin, Winifred Dorothy Wandersee
                  1976 Past Ideals and Present Pleasures: Women,
                        Work and the Family, 1920-1940. Unpublished
                        Ph.D. dissertation, University of Minnesota.

(V.F.2.)   Kittel, Margaret Ruth
                  1973 Married Women in Thirteenth-Century England:
                        A Study in Common Law. Unpublished Ph.D.
                        dissertation, University of California, Berkeley.

G V.G. *PUBLICATIONS*

(V.G.1.) Armitage, S. H.
1979 "Household Work and Childrearing on the
Frontier--Oral-History Record." Sociology
and Social Research 63 (Number 3): 467-474.

(V.G.2.) Bloch, R. H.
1978 "Untangling the Roots of Modern Sex-Roles--
Survey of 4 Centuries of Change." Signs 4
(Number 2): 237-252.

(V.G.3.) Boulding, E.
1976 "Historical Roots of Occupational Segregation--
Familial Constraints on Women's Work Roles."
Signs 1 (Number 3): 95-117.

(V.G.4.) Peal, E.
1975 "Normal Sex-Roles--Historical Analysis."
Family Process 14 (Number 3): 389-409.

(V.G.5.) Phillips, R.
1979 "Women's Emancipation, the Family and Social-
Change in 18th-Century France." Journal of
Social History 12 (Number 4): 553-567.

(V.G.6.) Shaffer, J. W.
1978 "Family, Class, and Young Women--Occupational
Expectations in 19th-Century Paris." Journal
of Family History 3 (Number 1): 62-77.

(V.G.7.) Volkov, A. G.
1981 "Changes in the Status of Women and the
Demographic Development of the Family."
Problems of Economics 24 (Numbers 5-7): 218-229.

(V.G.8.) Pleck, Elizabeth H.
1978 "A Mother's Wages: Income Earning Among Italian
and Black Women, 1896-1911." In Michael Gordon,
editor, 1978, The American Family in Social-Historical
Perspective, Second Edition, 490-510. New York:
St. Martin's Press.

90

VI. FAMILY LIFE: COMPREHENSIVE TREATMENTS

A

VI.A. *REVIEWS OF MAJOR BOOKS*

(VI.A.1) Breines, Wini
1981 (Untitled book review.) American Journal of Sociology 87 (July): 217-219.

Review of: Jean-Louis Flandrin, 1979, Families in Former Times: Kinship, Household and Sexuality. New York: Cambridge University Press.

Flandrin's book is an historical account of early domestic life which focuses on changing domestic ideology and behavior in France (and to a lesser extent in England) from the 16th to the 18th centuries. Through the use of diaries, notebooks, and confessional manuals, he studies the structure of kinship and households, particularly the accompanying customs, morality, and feelings.

Reviewer BREINES lists the topics included in this work and calls attention to information of special interest to sociologists of the family and everyday life. The first chapter is a technical discussion about kinship, especially the distinction between family and household and also historical kinship variations in France. The second major chapter considers the household and its structure and size, as well as the effects of conditions of agricultural production. The third chapter illuminates how the patriarchal Church and the dominant Christian morality shaped relationships among family members, including the development of the word "love" towards today's meaning. Finally the last chapter discusses the evolution of reproductive and sexual life, particularly the demographic realities (fertility, contraception, infant mortality, and wet-nursing). Breines also includes a brief review of Flandrin's scholarly disagreements with the Cambridge group, whom he feels ignore the census data on southern France and underestimate the actual extent of complex households, extended families, and the solidarity of kinfolk within the neighborhood.

(VI.A.2.) Ross, Ellen
1979 "Rethinking 'the Family.'" Radical History Review 20 (Spring/Summer): 76-84.

Review of: Mark Poster, 1978, Critical Theory of the Family. New York: Seabury Press.

The book under review is divided into two sections. The first discusses a number of major schools of psychological thought about the family (especially Freud, Reich and the Frankfurt School, Erikson and ego psychology, Laing and family therapy) and assesses their value for the

"critical theory" being sought. In the second section, Poster gives
us his own attempt at a definition and theory of the family, followed
by a brief sketch of family history in the modern West in which he
identifies four dominant family forms (modern bourgeois, modern working-
class, peasant, and aristocratic).

Poster details the unsuccessful attempts of a dozen or more psychological
schools to connect the psychic structure of individuals with the shape
of the wider society. Historians working with the family, women,
sexuality, etc., make rough assumptions about human personality at the
time and need an adequate "social psychology of consciousness" in place
of the current clumsy or even wrong concepts of human nature and
personality. The attempt to remedy this deficit, in the second part of
the book, is heavily criticized by ROSS as being partially invalid for
earlier times, dull, sensible but common-sense, failing to incorporate
gender and feminist analysis, and--by treating the family as an autonomous
separate sphere--making it difficult to theorize about this relation
between families and their social worlds.

(VI.A.3.)   Plumb, J.H.
            1977   "The Rise of Love." New York Review
                   of Books 24 (November 24): 30, 35-36.

                   Review of: Lawrence Stone, 1977, The
                   Family, Sex and Marriage in England:
                   1500-1800. New York: Harper and Row.

(VI.A.4.)   Hill, Christopher
            1978   "Sex, Marriage, and the Family in
                   England." Economic History Review
                   31 (August): 450-463.

                   Review of:

                   Lawrence Stone, 1977, The Family, Sex
                   and Marriage in England: 1500-1800. New
                   York: Harper and Row.

                   Peter Laslett, 1977, Family Life and
                   Illicit Love in Earlier Generations.
                   Cambridge, England: Cambridge University
                   Press.

These are two of a number of reviews which heralded the arrival, in 1977,
of Lawrence Stone's new book on the British family from 1500-1800.
The first is more of a general summary, while the latter is primarily
a critique. Both reviewers agree that Stone is on stronger ground when
discussing the well-to-do than the lower classes, because of the limitations
of available evidence.

PLUMB describes the sources--and their limitations--which can shed
light on the affective side of family life: people's hopes, aspirations,
satisfactions and frustrations and how family members felt about each

other. Then he summarizes the basic themes. By 1500, there were no
extended families in Britain. The well-to-do married in their late
20s and apparently used some form of fertility limitation. Marriages
were arranged according to family and property needs. Family atmosphere
was bleak--non-affectionate marriage, the overwhelming authority of the
husband, the constant death of infants, more discipline and beating of
children than love or tenderness for them. Then, toward the end of
the 17th century, a new world of family warmth began to slowly emerge.
Stone maintains that the "affective individualism" which grew up during
the 18th century was not caused by demographic changes or the Industrial
Revolution, since it preceded these.

The HILL review focuses primarily on Stone's work, with some comparisons
with another 1977 book by Peter Laslett. He details at length his
disagreement with some of Stone's interpretations. Stone's assumptions
that value-changes percolate downwards from upper to the lower classes,
about the harshness of Puritanism, and his statements about the culture
of sexual promiscuity among the very poor during the Industrial Revolution
are among those called into question.

For other reviews of Stone (1977), see also I.F.8.

(VI.A.5.) Tilly, Louise A.
                1978 "The Family and Change." Theory
                      and Society 5: 421-431.

                Review of:

                Eli Zaretsky, 1976, Capitalism, the
                Family, and Personal Life. New York:
                Harper and Row.

                Edward Shorter, 1975, The Making of the
                Modern Family. New York: Basic Books.

The historical trend toward privatization and individuation of personal
life is exemplified in the volumes under discussion: Zaretsky weighs the
positive and negative aspects of privatization while Shorter clearly
approves and welcomes this trend. More than a simple summary of these
works is provided by reviewer TILLY, who critically examines and elucidates
the numerous shortcomings of both volumes. For instance, Zaretsky's
concentration on ideology turns the reader away from the concrete
question of what happened to the working class family with the development
of industrial capitalism, to the abstract question of why. This lack of
evidence means that Zaretsky's historical argument remains an unproven
hypothesis. Although Shorter's work provides more historical evidence,
Tilly finds his work to be a culture-bound elitist interpretation of
change in family life. In addition, it shows contempt for ordinary
people of the past and for their culture because it embodies an ahistorical
refusal to understand such people on their own terms.

(VI.A.6.) Scott, Joan W.
  1977 (Untitled book review.) <u>Signs</u> 2 (Spring):
  692-696.

  Review of: Edward Shorter, 1975, <u>The Making
  of the Modern Family</u>. New York: Basic Books.

Although <u>Shorter</u>'s volume was readily accepted by the popular press, it
has received severe criticism from the scholarly community regarding its
validity as a characterization of the history of the family. This article
is no exception to that viewpoint. SCOTT views the book's language and
argument as ahistorical and presents specific examples and evidence to
support this. For instance, one of Shorter's major conclusions is his
interpretation of infant mortality, in which he suggests that parents
deliberately ignored information about infant diet, hygiene, etc., and
so contributed to high rates of infant death. Then he advances a theory
of pre-industrial lack of maternal love, based only upon comments made
by physicians and ignoring the evidence established by demographers and
historians about standard of living, ignorance about disease, etc. In
general, Scott believes that this work presents a distorted and inaccurate
picture of the lives of people in the past and misrepresents the process
by which their lives changed.

(VI.A.7.) Kaplow, Jeffry
  1977 (Untitled book review.) <u>Science
  and Society</u> 41 (Fall): 349-353.

  Review of: Edward Shorter, 1975, <u>The
  Making of a Modern Family</u>. New York:
  Basic Books.

Historians and sociologists opposed to a Marxist interpretation of
historical change have developed a theory about the process of transition
from traditional to modern society in which the industrial revolution,
bourgeois democracy, and the demographic revolution play major roles.
<u>Shorter</u> adds another building block to this convergence theory, writes
<u>KAPLOW</u>, when he states that "the changes in intimate life that modernization
fosters are essentially the same everywhere."

After criticizing Shorter's assumptions and evidence, Kaplow ultimately
offers an alternative approach to the history of the family which may
link it more satisfactorily to the emergence of capitalism than Shorter
has done and which is chronologically compatible with the general pattern
of change recognized by Shorter. It is better to see traditional society
as one in which community standards and pressures served more to reinforce
paternal authority than to contest it, instead of insisting on the opposition
of the individual or the family to the surrounding society and on the
oppressive action of community. Moreover, Kaplow's hypothesis takes
account of the development of the capitalist mode of production (passage
from simple to expanded reproduction), rather than merely relying on a
vaguely understood "capitalism" to explain the historic shift towards
individualism and affectionate familial relations.

(VI.A.8.)   Wells, Robert V.
            1977   (Untitled book review.) Journal of
                   Social History 10 (March): 361-364.

                   Review of: Edward Shorter, 1975, The Making
                   of a Modern Family. New York: Basic Books.

This review discusses both the contributions and limitations of Shorter's
attempt to describe and explain a major transformation in family
patterns which occurred between the late 18th century and the present.
WELLS briefly focuses on three problems: (1) the way the book is
organized, (2) the evidence and how it is interpreted, and (3) the causal
explanation. Shorter should have provided more explicit descriptions
of how he "mined" his sets of local reports and how his conclusions
were drawn from the data. In addition the role of market capitalism
in producing a revolution of sentiment needs to be more clearly
explicated. While these criticisms are important, Wells views the
descriptive materials on the revolution in sentiment as having lasting
value.

(VI.A.9.)   Dunn, Patrick
            1976   "Modernization and the Family." History
                   of Childhood Quarterly 4 (Fall): 203-208.

                   Review of: Edward Shorter, 1975, The Making
                   of the Modern Family. New York: Basic Books.

After a brief summary of the contents of Shorter's volume, DUNN presents
two major interrelated difficulties. One is the reliance on a concept
of "modernization" which is neither defined nor used rigorously, and the
second problem is a rather obvious reversal of the causal relationship
between economic or social change and psychological change (for instance,
he claims that "masturbation and polymorphous sexuality are creations
of modernization"). Also, several passages from the book are quoted
to illustrate that Shorter refuses to investigate what he acknowledges
throughout his book--the deeper, psychological origins of social and
economic change. In sum, it is not only Shorter's haughty attitude
which is at issue, but also his lack of empathy in the understanding
of the human predicament.

(VI.A.10)   Lasch, Christopher
            1975   "The Emotions of Family Life." New York
                   Review of Books 22 (November 27): 37-42.

                   Review of: Fred Weinstein and Gerald M.
                   Platt, 1969, The Wish to Be Free: Society
                   Psyche, and Value Change. Berkeley,
                   California: University of California Press.

From a perspective of Parsonian sociology, <u>Weinstein</u> and <u>Platt</u>'s volume analyzes the writings of the French Enlightenment, the theories of the French Revolution, and certain products of the "introspective revolution" (Freud and Kafka) in order to trace "the movement toward autonomy and inclusion." The history of the family is discussed under the assumption that changes in the family structure underlay these essential elements of "modernization." Reviewer LASCH discusses the author's extrapolation of Parsonian theory into the past, as well as their insufficient use of historical documents and secondary literature on the subject. This detailed review offers a comprehensive account of the contents of <u>The Wish to Be Free</u>, while citing both its limitations and contributions. Important questions are raised by this work; Weinstein and Platt have grasped the importance of large-scale value change in "modernization," despite the poverty of the conceptual scheme that underlies their argument. See also I.G.3.

(VI.A.11.) Burton, Orville Vernon
            1981 (Untitled book review.) <u>Social Science</u>
                  <u>History</u> 5 (Fall): 483-488.

                  Review of: Elizabeth Hafkin Pleck, 1979,
                  <u>Black Migration and Poverty: Boston, 1865-</u>
                  <u>1900</u>. New York: Academic Press.

This book is praised as being the single best historical monograph on urban blacks in the United States, a quantitative work which nevertheless emphasizes ideas over numbers.

<u>Pleck</u> investigates blacks in Boston, studying their economic mobility and family life between about 1870 and 1900. Racial discrimination, rather than slavery or last-immigrant-group explanations, was the critical factor in Afro-American urban poverty. New arrivals from the South had more stable marriages than did metropolitan black families. She identifies an interrelated system of sickness, poverty, sterility (from tuberculosis), urban birth, and long-time city residence, in which each variable correlated with marital instability.

Reviewer BURTON points out certain inconsistencies, shortcomings, and unanswered questions and suggests that explanatory models would have benefited by more knowledge of the rural southern life from which these black families originally came.

(VI.A.12.) Rury, John
            1978 "Towards a Working Class History of
                  Black American Culture." <u>Review of</u>
                  <u>Radical Political Economics</u> 10 (Spring):
                  71-73.

                  Review of: Herbert Gutman, 1976, <u>The</u>
                  <u>Black Family in Slavery and Freedom,</u>
                  <u>1750-1925</u>. New York: Pantheon.

Gutman's book is a full-scale history of the black family and of its
role in the formation of a distinctive American working class culture.
It succeeds in refuting the myth of an unstable black family structure,
as well as other "fallacies" in the slavery field. However, RURY finds
that important problems remain, with the study's greatest flaw being the
absence of a clear theoretical point of departure. Gutman argues against
the "isolation" thesis (Elkins), the prototypical "economic" slave (Fogel
and Engerman), and "organic" paternalism (Genovese). Instead, he argues
that the black family provided an outlet for expression and transmission
of a unique Afro-American culture. The book's underlying weakness is
said to be its failure to link the processes of conflict and of culture
dialectically. Despite this and other shortcomings, this volume
marks a major advance for black history, particularly because of its
longitudinal perspective which allows the identification of periods in
the development of the black family and of an "Afro-American" culture.
It is also important because of its finding that the black family was
able to build and maintain a stable family structure. Indeed, far from
weakening under slavery, the family provided the very means by which
blacks survived--and resisted--servitude. On Gutman (1976), see also
II.B.7.

Another major comprehensive treatment of family life is Degler (1980),
reviewed in IX.D.2., I.A.4., V.B.8., and V.B.9.

VI.B. *FOCUS ON MENTALITÉ, VALUES, EMOTIONS*

(VI.B.1.) Brobeck, Stephen
             1977 "Images of the Family: Portrait
                   Paintings as Indices of American
                   Family Culture, Structure and
                   Behavior, 1730-1860." The Journal
                   of Psychohistory: History of Childhood
                   Quarterly 5 (Summer): 81-106.

This exploration of portrait paintings, completed between 1730 and 1860,
has three purposes: (1) to assess their value as indices of family
structure, culture, and behavior, (2) to develop methods of investigation,
and (3) to formulate hypotheses about family character. They are useful
as supplements to other sources such as childrearing manuals (which
prescribe behaviors that may or may not have been adopted) or personal
papers (whose volume and preoccupation with economic matters limit
sample sizes). More importantly, these portraits represent valuable
artifacts that supply information about the norms and behaviors of
several hundred upper and upper middle class American families residing
mainly in New England and the Mid-Atlantic region. The portraits in
this investigation suggest some interesting hypotheses about family
type, inter-relations, and child-rearing practices writes BROBECK.
Examples of such hypotheses are that: the family conceived of itself as
those kinsmen living under the same roof; siblings demonstrated greater
affection for each other in the 19th century than in the 18th century;
and parents imposed fewer adult behaviors on children and tolerated
greater deviation from adult norms in the 19th century than in the 18th
century. Lastly, these images of the family may be usefully compared
to images of the European family.

(VI.B.2.) Davis, Natalie Zemon
             1977 "Ghosts, Kin, and Progeny: Some
                   Features of Family Life in Early
                   Modern France." Daedalus 106 (Spring):
                   87-114.

DAVIS characterizes the family in early modern France in terms of its
family strategies, identity, and order. These features of family life
were both aided by political, social, and religious developments and were
simultaneously in tension with them, with interesting long-range
consequences for attitudes toward social and corporate solidarity.

Topics covered include strategies of parsimony and inheritance, religion
and the relations of the living with the ghosts of the dead, oral and
written family histories handed down to children, kinship boundaries
and incest prohibitions, and control over the marriages of the young.

The material in this essay suggests two perspectives on historical change.
The first has to do with its source. Historians generally think of
change as emerging from the decisions of a small group, an elite; when
changes are perceived as emerging from the actions of large numbers of

people in the middle and lower levels of society, they are explained in terms of the forces acting upon them (e.g., urbanization) to which they react somewhat automatically. This investigation, however, shows historical change flowing from the decisions of myriad small groups, not all of whom were rich and powerful, sometimes even in defiance of canon law. The second perspective on historical change is that of the disjuncture between privatistic family values and the more corporate (often Catholic) values often accepted by these same families. Rather than being merely a cultural lag, such contradictory values may possibly be creative and keep little-used cultural options available for possible use in the future.

(VI.B.3.) Lantz, Herman, Martin Schultz, and Mary O'Hara
1977 "The Changing American Family From the Preindustrial to the Industrial Period: A Final Report." _American Sociological Review_ 42 (June): 406-421.

Changes in marital power patterns, the stress put on romantic love, and motivations for marriage are followed over four time periods between 1741 and 1865, as reflected in a content analysis of 6,559 issues of 36 U.S. magazines. For 1850-1865, family conflict patterns are also analyzed. Data was insufficient to allow a thorough analysis of sanctions for sexual deviance.

From 1741 to 1865, there was a decline in romantic-love themes. After 1825, the couples' motives for marriage assume more importance than those of their parents. There was a decline in themes of overt male power after 1794 and a corresponding increase, first in "mutual cooperation" (1794-1825) and then in overt-female-power themes (1825 onward, with a sharp rise after 1850). The time-period 1850-1865 seems to have been a period of significant family change, although earlier family changes probably set the stage and prepared the way. Family change proceeded first in those areas least antagonistic to the power structure of the traditional family.

(VI.B.4.) Demos, John
1972 "Demography and Psychology in the Historical Study of Family-Life: A Personal Report." In Peter Laslett and Richard Wall, editors, 1972, _Household and Family in Past Time_, 560-569. Cambridge, England: Cambridge University Press.

An informal and admittedly tentative examination of the relation between the demographic/quantitative approach and a psychological approach is offered here. Underlying the statistics about large families in small houses, extended vs. nuclear-family households, etc., are a radically different set of emotional arrangements and the issue of how people learn to handle their own feelings of anger and aggression. DEMOS calls for a more life-cycle-specific study of infancy and childhood-- for instance, at what age a shift from indulgence to strict discipline occurs--in order to better understand the fears, guilts, fixations and neuroses common among adults. Psychologist Erik Erikson's developmental theory is suggested as being very useful for such analyses.

Using examples from the Puritan family in colonial America, Demos underscores the potential complementarity of demographic and psychological approaches. Psychological theory cries out for solid evidence on the timing of certain crucial life-happenings, and demographic results are arid and sometimes quite meaningless without a leavening of qualitative insight.

For other works focusing on mentalité/value/emotions, see also VII.C.4., II.D.4., and I.B.4.

VI.C. OTHER EMPIRICAL STUDIES

(VI.C.1.) Pedlow, Gregory W.
                1982 "Marriage, Family Size, and Inheritance
                Among Hessian Nobles, 1650-1900." Journal
                of Family History 7 (Winter): 333-352.

European nobilities generally relied upon primogeniture (oldest son
inheriting most of his father's holdings) and often also developed
systems of family controls to limit the size of families and the number
of marriages--as strategies to keep land holdings intact and to limit
strain on the family fortune. But this practice was not universal.
The landed nobility (Ritterschaft) of Hesse-Kassel practiced neither
primogeniture nor strict family controls. This study, covering the
period from 1650 to 1900, reveals that less rigid systems of inheritance
and family controls could also be effective in preserving landholdings
while reducing the danger of family extinction.

PEDLOW provides a wide range of relevant demographic data and also
case examples of estate-transmission within specific families. Joint
ownership was one of several strategies employed. Compared to primogeniture
systems, Hessian nobles less often suffered indebtness, partial loss
of estates, and extinction of the family name; on the other hand, they
were seldom able to accumulate extreme wealth.

(VI.C.2.) Chrisman, Miriam
                ca. 1982 "Catholic Families, Protestant Families
                        in Early Modern France, England and the
                        Colonies." Unpublished manuscript.

In the course of the 16th century, fundamental theological differences
between Protestants and Catholics developed regarding marriage, and it
is these ideological differences which are examined in CHRISMAN's
unpublished draft. This study asks if it is possible to distinguish
between Protestant families and Catholic families. To this end, each
of four selected families (a Catholic and a Protestant noble family
and a Catholic and a Protestant middle-class family) is examined in
terms of its functions, division of responsibility, family activity
(in the marriage of the young), education, and particular religious
activities or behavior. One of the major findings for the noble families
is their similarities in such functions as the maintaining and preserving
of family property, status, and wealth from one generation to the next.
Yet major differences were also found, with education and religion playing
greater roles in the Protestant noble family. The control group--the
La Trémoille family, a French noble family whose members moved back and
forth between Catholicism and Protestantism--showed discernible religion-
related differences in marriage patterns and husband-wife relationships;
the religion of the intended partner played a significant role in the
marriage arrangements, while the relationship between husbands and wives
changed according to their religious persuasions.

Religion was far more important in the middle-class families than it was in the noble families. Religion was delegated a subordinate role in the noble family, with the primary functions focusing on the lineage and the name as well as the preservation of family property. The middle class placed more emphasis on an ideal because there was less at stake economically, and created Christian commonwealths within their own families.

(VI.C.3.) Douglass, William A.
          1980 "The South Italian Family: A Critique."
                Journal of Family History 5 (Winter):
                338-359.

(VI.C.4.) Douglass, William A.
          1975 "Issues in the Study of South Italian
                Society." Current Anthropology 16
                (December): 620-625.

                Review of:

                Jan Brøgger, 1971, Montevarese: A Study
                of Peasant Society and Culture in Southern
                Italy. Bergen-Oslo-Troms: Universitetsforlaget.

                J. Davis, 1973, Land and Family in Pisticci.
                London, England: University of London, Athlone
                Press. New York: Humanities Press.

DOUGLASS (1980) examines the image of the South Italian family found in the existing literature, specifically the co-residential patrilineal joint family household regarded as the ideal form of domestic group organization. The ethnographic and historical data are taken from the 1753 Onciario (household census) for the town of Agnone in the Molise and include domestic group organization, family forms in occupational groups, and economic statistics for peasant and day laborer households. Basically, this essay focuses on rationales underlying the prominence of the joint family ethos across social lines. By comparing Agnone's domestic group organization in 1753 and 1970, he shows that the incidence of joint family domestic group formation has decreased, even though the demographic feasibility of realizing such arrangements has improved. Familism is the key social organizational theme of the Italian South. Much of the existing literature on South Italian familism, with its focus on trust being limited to members of the nuclear family, is inapplicable to Agnone. Douglass concludes that the joint family group was (and to some extent, still is) the basic social unit of Agnone society.

For a related review of two contemporary anthropological studies of South Italian society, see DOUGLASS (1975).

(VI.C.5.) Brown, Keith
          1978 "Family History in a Japanese Town: 1872-
                1971." Paper presented at the Social Science
                Research Council's Conference on Historical
                Demography and Family History in East Asia,
                August 20-25.

This paper presents preliminary findings from a study aimed at understanding the history and changes of family organization in post-Meiji Japan. To compare rural and urban areas and to study the family and demographic history of each type of settlement, BROWN presents ethnographic and demographic data collected from three agricultural hamlets in a rural village, and from a merchant neighborhood, in a small castle town in northeastern Japan. The primary source of material on family size and composition is the Koseki vital registration system. These data cover a period of nearly 100 years, beginning in 1872. The findings suggest a variety of adaptive family types, with one viable organization in town families still being the stem family pattern usually associated with rural or traditional Japan. In addition, the comparison of rural and town populations reveals each as having its own internal diversity and following its own separate developmental path. Brown recognizes that these populations are becoming more alike, but notes that this is a function of similar responses to common conditions (convergence), rather than one population finally catching up with the so-called more modern attributes of the other.

This paper has a lengthy appendix consisting of 23 tables of demographic data.

For other empirical studies providing a comprehensive treatment of family life, see also X.K.2.

VI.D. <u>DISSERTATIONS</u>

(VI.D.1.) Berknre, Lutz Karl
        1973 <u>Family, Social Structure, and Rural Industry:</u>
            <u>A Comparative Study of the 'Waldviertel' and</u>
            <u>the 'Pays De Caux' in the Eighteenth-Century.</u>
            Unpublished Ph.D. dissertation, Harvard University.

(VI.D.2.) Bushman, Claudia Lauper
        1978 <u>Harriet Hanson Robinson and Her Family: A</u>
            <u>Chronicle of Nineteenth Century New England</u>
            <u>Life</u>. Unpublished Ph.D. dissertation, Boston
            University Graduate School.

(VI.D.3.) Jeffery, Kirk, Jr.
        1972 <u>Family History: The Middle-Class American Family</u>
            <u>in the Urban Context, 1830-1870</u>. Unpublished
            Ph.D. dissertation, Stanford University.

(VI.D.4.) Johnson, David George
        1970 <u>The **Medieval** Chinese Oligarchy: A Study of the</u>
            <u>Great Families in Their Social, Political, and</u>
            <u>Institutional Setting</u>. Unpublished Ph.D.
            dissertation, University of California, Berkeley.

(VI.D.5.) Johnson, Thomas Hoevet
        1975 <u>The Enos Family and Wind River Shoshone Society:</u>
            <u>A Historical Analysis</u>. Unpublished Ph.D. dissertation,
            University of Illinois, Urbana.

(VI.D.6.) Milden, James Wallace
        1974 <u>The Sacred Sanctuary: Family Life in Nineteenth-</u>
            <u>Century America</u>. Unpublished Ph.D. dissertation,
            University of Maryland.

(VI.D.7.) Mitchell, Albert Gibbs, Jr.
        1976 <u>Irish Family Patterns in Nineteenth-Century</u>
            <u>Ireland and Lowell, Massachusetts</u>. Unpublished
            Ph.D. dissertation, Boston University Graduate
            School.

(VI.D.8.) Nafziger, John Marvin
        1972 <u>The Development of the Twentieth Century</u>
            <u>American Mennonite Family as Reflected in</u>
            <u>Mennonite Writings</u>. Unpublished Ph.D. dissertation,
            New York University.

(VI.D.9.) Rishel, Joseph Francis
        1975 <u>The Founding Families of Allegheny County:</u>
            <u>An Examination of Nineteenth-Century Elite</u>
            <u>Continuity</u>. Unpublished Ph.D. dissertation,
            University of Pittsburgh.

(VI.D.10.)   Slater, Miriam
          1971   The Verney Family in the Seventeenth Century.
                 Unpublished Ph.D. dissertation, Princeton
                 University.

(VI.D.11.)   Wright, Raymond Sanford, III
          1977   Family and Community in Fifteenth-Century
                 Brunswick, Germany.   Unpublished Ph.D.
                 dissertation, University of Utah.

VI.E.   PUBLICATIONS

(VI.E.1.)   Gagen, D.
1976   "Prose of Life--Literary Reflections of Family,
Individual Experience and Social-Structure in
19th-Century Canada." Journal of Social History
9 (Number 3): 367-381.

(VI.E.2.)   Hareven, T. K.
1978   "Latin-American Essays in the Context of Family
History--Postscript." Journal of Family History
3 (Number 4): 454-457.

(VI.E.3.)   Jackson, K. A.
1976   "Family Entity and Famine Among 19th-Century
Akamba of Kenya--Social Responses to Environmental-
Stress." Journal of Family History 1 (Number 2):
193-216.

(VI.E.4.)   Lantz, H. R.
1975   "Research Note on Free Black Family In Our
Early History." Family Coordinator 24 (Number 3):
363-365.

(VI.E.5.)   Lomnitz, L. A., and M. P. Lizaur
1978   "History of a Mexican Urban Family." Journal
of Family History 3 (Number 4): 392ff.

(VI.E.6.)   McCarthy, J.
1979   "Age, Family, and Migration in 19th-Century
Black Sea Provinces of the Ottoman Empire."
International Journal of Middle East Studies
10 (Number 3): 309-323.

(VI.E.7.)   Plakans, A.
1975   "Seigneurial Authority and Peasant Family Life--
Baltic Area in Eighteenth Century." Journal
of Interdisciplinary History 5 (Number 4): 629-654.

(VI.E.8.)   Ring, R. R.
1979   "Early Medieval Peasant Households in Central
Italy." Journal of Family History 4 (Number 1):
2-25.

(VI.E.9.)   Strumingher, L. S.
1977   "Artisan Family--Traditions and Transition in
19th-Century Lyon." Journal of Family History
2 (Number 3): 211-222.

(VI.E.10.) Kulikoff, Allan
        1977 "The Beginnings of the Afro-American Family in
              Maryland." In A. C. Land, L. G. Carr, and
              E. C. Papenfuse, editors, 1977, Law, Society, and
              Politics in Early Maryland. Baltimore, Maryland:
              Johns Hopkins University Press.

(VI.E.11.) Pleck, Elizabeth H.
        1982 "Challenges to Traditional Authority in Immigrant
              Families." In Michael Gordon, editor, 1983, The
              American Family in Social-Historical Perspective,
              Third Edition, 504-517. New York: St. Martin's
              Press.

(VI.E.12.) Shammas, Carole
        1980 "The Domestic Enivronment in Early Modern England
              and America." Journal of Social History 14 (Fall):
              3-24.

VII. SEXUALITY, BIRTH, DEATH AND MIGRATION: DEMOGRAPHIC AND OTHER APPROACHES

A

VII.A. *THE FIELD OF HISTORICAL DEMOGRAPHY IN VARIOUS COUNTRIES: OVERVIEW*

(VII.A.1.) Maynes, Mary Jo
1981 "Demographic History in the United
States: The First Fifteen Years."
Historical Social Research/Historische
Sozialforschung Number 19 (July): 3-17.

This brief overview of demographic history in the United States provides
a particularly useful introduction to the major research centers, major
scholars, and their work. A selective bibliography of key studies and
of other review articles is included. Those wishing initial orientation
to the U.S. historical demography scene will find this article a valuable
starting place.

From the modest and recent beginning--a collection of articles on the
theme of "Historical Population Studies" in Daedalus in 1968--the study
of demographic history in the U.S. has expanded dramatically. MAYNES
examines the evolution of, and some current directions in, research on
a few clusters of central problems. These problem areas include: the
relationship between economic opportunity, especially in the form of
landholding, and demographic patterns; changing family and community
life under the impact of immigration and rapid population growth; changes
in demographic behavior and attitudes between first generation migrants
and their descendants; Afro-American history; the demographic transition
in Europe; and other topics.

(VII.A.2.) Roman, Louis
1981 "Rumanian Research in Historical
Demography: A Note." Journal of
Family History 6 (Summer): 231-233.

A brief overview and bibliography of historical-demographic studies in
Rumania since 1970 are provided by ROMAN. For the first time after World
War II, fundamental studies in historical demography have been done; the
works of Meteş, Ştefănescu, and Pascu are highlighted. Names of historians
in the field, as well as a few archaeologists and anthropologists, are also
mentioned.

(VII.B.1.) Anderson, Barbara A.
                1981 (Untitled Book Review.) Contemporary
                Sociology 10 (July): 532-533.

                Review of: Maris A. Vinovskis, 1979,
                Studies in American Historical Demography.
                New York: Academic Press.

Vinovskis has assembled in one volume, for convenient reference, a collection of 25 reprints of journal articles on the historical demography of the United States. This anthology is in some sense a "sampler" of work by major scholars in the field, including historians, sociologists, economists, and anthropologists. Among those represented are Daniel Scott Smith, John Demos, Russell R. Menard, Philip J. Greven, Jr., Richard Easterlin, and others. The introductory essay by Vinovskis (which also appeared in Annual Reviews in Sociology) gives an overview of the field. This would be a useful reader for students, ANDERSON states, if it were available in a less-costly paperback edition.

(VII.B.2.) Ewbank, Douglas C.
                1980 "The Implications of Recent Research in
                Historical Demography for Developing
                Countries." Journal of Family History.
                5 (Fall): 321-328.

                Review of:

                Charles Tilly, editor, 1978, Historical
                Studies of Changing Fertility. Princeton,
                New Jersey: Princeton University Press.

                Ron J. Lesthaeghe, 1977, The Decline of
                Belgian Fertility, 1800-1920. Princeton,
                New Jersey: Princeton University Press.

EWBANK reviews two books on historical demography, from the point of view of their implications for lowering fertility in today's LDCs (least developed countries). The book edited by Tilly, containing revised versions of 1972 papers by leading people in the field, is still very useful as an overview of the kinds of research that are being done and of the kinds of conclusions which are emerging. The Lesthaeghe book on the beginning of the fertility decline in Belgium successfully exploits the opportunities provided by the diversity of the Belgian case--having a variety of forms of industrialization and two distinct cultural heritages-- to gain insights into the causes of the fertility decline.

Following a quite detailed discussion of both books, Ewbank summarizes their implications for research on the determinants of fertility in LDCs. These include: (1) analysis must be based on units smaller than the nation; (2) research should simultaneously examine possibilities and benefits/costs of alternatives to fertility control (outmigration, agricultural change) together with fertility reduction, rather than focusing so narrowly on fertility decisions; (3) research should focus on the age group 12-25, since indications of coming population changes will probably show up first in this group.

(VII.B.3.) Hogan, Dennis P.
                    1982 (Untitled book review.) American Journal
                          of Sociology 87 (May): 1420-1421.

                          Review of: Ansley J. Coale, Barbara A. Anderson,
                          and Erna Härm, 1979, Human Fertility in Russia
                          Since the Nineteenth Century. Princeton,
                          New Jersey: Princeton University Press.

This book on geographic variations in nuptiality and marital fertility in Russia from 1897 to 1970 is the fifth volume in a series of monographs stemming from the European Fertility Project (initiated in 1963 by Ansley J. Coale of the Office of Population Research, Princeton University). The European Fertility Project documents for small geographic areas the declines in mortality and fertility that constitute the demographic transition, with special attention to the effects of marriage patterns on fertility. One long-range aim is the explanation of the demographic transition in Europe.

The volume on marital fertility in Russia is praised for its scholarly attention to detail. It provides indices of marital fertility (rural and urban), total fertility, and nuptiality for Russian provinces and republics around 1897, 1926, 1959, and 1970 (for European provinces, also for 1940). Some attempt is also made to identify social structural determinants of geographic variations in nuptiality and fertility at single points in time; for this task, the reviewer suggests that it would have been preferable to have used pooled cross-section techniques such as those used in: Toni Richards, "Fertility Decline in Germany: An Economic Appraisal," Population Studies 31 (November 1977): 537-553.

For reviews of other books, see also V.C.5., VIII.B.1., and IX.D.2.

(VII.C.1.)   Freedman, Estelle B.
    1982   "Sexuality in Nineteenth-Century
    America: Behavior, Ideology, and
    Politics." Reviews in American History
    10 (December): 196-215.

This is a review article, with an extensive bibliography, summarizing
what we do and do not yet know about sexuality in 19th century U.S.
society. Subtopics include sexual behavior (implications of changes in
fertility, premarital pregnancy, contraception, and abortion for sexual
behavior; prostitution; masturbation, lesbianism and male homosexuality;
qualitative aspects of how individuals experienced their sexuality, etc.),
sexual ideology (contrasting themes and views within various types of
literature at the time in utopian communities, etc.), and sexual politics
(in general, whose interests were served by ideological positions, which
social groups enforced sexual norms, by what means did notions of
sexual propriety come to predominate; more specifically, the role of
social class of parent-adolescent conflicts, and especially male versus
female control over reproduction and sexuality).

FREEDMAN suggests that, as the birth rate declined over the 19th century,
Americans began the process of struggling to come to terms with the potential
of an erotic, nonprocreative sexuality. This, plus the conservative
backlash which had emerged by the 1880s, provide the background for better
understanding sexual ideology, behavior, and politics of our own century.
More research is needed on working-class people, men, the urban sexual
underworld, medical problems such as venereal disease, and on sexual
politics in general.

(VII.C.2.)   Padgug, Robert A.
    1979   "Sexual Matters: On Conceptualizing
    Sexuality Matters in History." Radical
    History Review 20 (Spring/Summer): 3-23.
    (Special issue on "Sex in History.")

This is a special issue devoted to the study of sex in history with special
attention to conceptual issues in a political context. The first section,
critiquing key recent works, contains a series of review articles (by
E.P. Thompson, Ellen Ross, Joseph Interrante and Carol Lasser, Blanche Cook,
Burt Hansen, and Harry Liebersohn). Topics include homosexuality, sexual
ideology in Fascist Germany, capitalist patriarchy, and varying approaches
to and concepts of the family in history. There is a section on sources
(a survey by Nancy Sazhli of archival material available on 19th and 20th
century U.S. and a set of early 20th century Hopi documents edited by
Martin Duberman).

The third section includes four articles which use some of the new
theoretical perspectives on sexuality to guide their empirical research
(Ann Snitnow on romance novels, Jeffrey Weeks on homosexuality in Britain,
Louis Kern on a 19th century U.S. utopian community, and Donna Haraway on

sociobiology and "nature"). Finally, Liz Phillips introduces history teachers to new materials on sexuality aimed at high school students.

The editor's introduction by PADGUG stresses the hazards of using contemporary (conceptual) categories of sexuality for the study of the past. Subtopics include sexuality as ideology, biology and society, and sexuality as praxis. Both Freudian and Marxist approaches are criticized and a more adequate approach in the Marxist tradition is sought.

(VII.C.3.) Ross, Ellen, and Rayna Rapp
            1981 "Sex and Society: A Research Note From
                  Social History and Anthropology."
                  Comparative Studies in Society and History
                  23 (January): 51-72.

The seemingly most intimate details of private existence are actually structured by larger social relations: "the personal is political." Understanding sexuality requires attention to sex as a social experience; social definitions of sex may change rapidly and in the process transform the very experience of sex itself. The separations of industrial capitalism—of family life from work, of consumption from production, of personal from political life—have completely reorganized the context in which sexuality is experienced.

ROSS and RAPP bring the theories and methods of anthropology and social history to bear on the problem of how, specifically, society shapes sexuality. The aim is to provide some "guideposts" for future study.

The power and role of (1) family and kinship systems (including kin terminologies, inheritance practices, and marriage patterns), (2) communities (peer groups, transmission of sexual knowledge, ritual boundaries to permissible sexual relations, the involvement of Church regulations on sex etc.), and (3) large-scale institutional and informed forces in shaping sexual experience are discussed and illustrated with concrete historical and anthropological examples. Even in contemporary times sexuality continues to be socially structured, especially by large-scale social and economic forces in general and the state in particular.

(VII.C.4.) Gadlin, Howard
            1976 "Private Lives and Public Order: A
                  Critical View of the History of Intimate
                  Relations in the U.S." Massachusetts Review
                  17 (Summer): 304-330.

Both the repression of sexuality in 19th century America and the liberation of sexuality in the 20th century are related to the more general changes in the meaning and function of the family and interpersonal relations necessitated by the development of industrial capitalism and the growth of urban centers. These transformations are examined in four epochs in U.S. history marked by strikingly different attitudes toward sexuality: the colonial (mid-1600s), the Jacksonian (1825-1840), the second decade of the 20th century, and the contemporary period (post 1950). The separation

of life into public and private spheres, into work vs. home, the twin
emergence of individualism and intimacy, the loosening of social control
and support, and the rise of romantic love are all discussed.

This is an interpretative essay which identifies, for each epoch, the
complex interrelationships (and tensions) among sexuality, identity,
interpersonal relations, the larger society and its institutions.

More than a history of sexuality, GADLIN's article attempts to make sociological sense out of the entire span of U.S. history as it affected
people's everyday family lives and relationships.

(VII.C.5.) Shorter, Edward
              1971 "Illegitimacy, Sexual Revolution, and
                    Social Change in Modern Europe." Journal
                    of Interdisciplinary History 11 (Autumn):
                    237-272.

This article provides a quantitative documentation of the existence of
a late 18th century "revolution" in premarital sexual behavior and a
speculative interpretation about why that revolution may have occurred.

Premarital sexuality among young people, studied from the evidence of
illegitimacy, is considered to be but one indicator of a more-general
revolution of eroticism which occurred in the lower classes roughly
between 1790 and 1880 in England and Western Europe. This "illegitimacy
explosion" is attributed primarily to changes in lower-class attitudes
toward sexuality (from manipulative to expressive sexuality) and in the
situational pressures/opportunities to marry if pregnant (from stable to
unstable social situation). He speculates that there were four chronological
stages in illegitimacy: peasant bundling (manipulative/stable), master-
servant exploitation (manipulative/unstable), hit-and-run (expressive/
unstable), and true-love (expressive/stable). The illegitimacy explosion
represents the hit-and-run stage.

SHORTER then suggests several reasons why expressive sexuality (the wish
to be free) and social instability (discouraging marriage) may have both
increased at this time. That the lower classes and not the middle classes
were in the vanguard of the sexual revolution is attributed to differences
in social stability (weakening of the lower class family's social control).

(VII.C.6.) Berlanstein, Lenard
              1980 "Illegitimacy, Concubinage, and Proletarianization
                    in a French Rural Town, 1760-1914." Journal
                    of Family History 5 (Winter): 360-374.

Illegitimacy and concubinage are analyzed within one small French town,
Bezons, from 1760 to 1914. The focus is on the impact of rapid industrialization (transition from a village to a factory town in the second half of
the 19th century) upon sexual behavior. The creation of a specifically
factory proletariat did not produce a profound break in the "marriage
orientedness" of coitus, but this group's poverty and mobility did reduce
the likelihood that matrimony would follow. Concubinage (cohabitation),

too, was not subversive of stable domestic life but rather a means to achieve it, and it was far more often a prelude to marriage than a substitute for it. BERLANSTEIN concludes that the final upturn of the illegitimacy curve and the rise in concubinage did not reflect a weakening of social controls, although the meaning of marriage had been transformed by the infusion of urban working class culture into the commune.

(VII.C.7.) Barrett, Richard E.
                1980 "Short-Term Trends in Bastardy in
                Taiwan." Journal of Family History
                5 (Fall): 293-312.

Bastardy was, by international standards, a relatively common occurrence in Taiwan during the Japanese colonial period (1895-1945). It varied by prefecture but not by degree of urbanization, ethnicity, or availability/scarcity of unmarried women.

Drawing upon an hitherto unused data source, BARRETT weighs possible alternatives as to which groups of women (prostitutes, servants, widows, divorcees, never-married women) contributed most to the illegitimacy rate, in part by comparing the age-specific fertility rates generated under alternative assumptions with the actual marital and non-marital age-specific fertility rates. The evidence suggests sizeable numbers of divorcees and widows bearing illegitimate children but is insufficient to make definite statements about prostitution.

The rise in illegitimacy during the colonial period does not appear to have been directly associated with any "modernization" of social conditions during that time.

On sexuality and illegitimacy, see also V.C.5., IX.D.2., V.D.4., VII.C.5., VII.C.3., and X.B.8.

VII.D. BIRTH AND FERTILITY: NON-DEMOGRAPHIC APPROACHES

(VII.D.1.) Suitor, J. Jill
                1981 "Husbands' Participation in Childbirth:
                A Nineteenth-Century Phenomenon." Journal
                of Family History 6 (Autumn): 278-293.

Work on the social history of birth has often neglected the husband's
involvement. During the 19th century, many husbands attended birth to
provide emotional support to their wives.

American husbands began participating in their wives' childbirth experiences
sometime aroung 1830, according to SUITOR's analysis of pre-1911 books on
midwifery/obstetrics and marriage/health guides. The presence of male
physicians, beginning around 1750, was probably a necessary but not a
sufficient condition for the emergence of husbands' participation. Such
participation appears to have been related--as it was in England as well--
to three important changes in the family occurring during the late 18th
and early 19th centuries: (1) the emergence of companionate marriage
(greater marital intimacy); (2) a greater popular emphasis on children,
childhood, and parent-child relations; and (3) a decrease in family size.
Husbands' participation in childbirth continued until hospital births
became popular (about 1910-1920), at which time both husbands and female
social-support attendants were excluded from birth scenes.

(VII.D.2.) La Sorte, Michael A.
                1976 "Nineteenth-Century Family Planning
                Practices." History of Childhood
                Quarterly 4 (Autumn): 163-184.

LA SORTE describes in some detail a large number of techniques and drugs
used in 19th century United States (when family size began to decline) to
try to prevent pregnancy and to abort an unwanted fetus. Subtopics
include criminal (intentional) abortion, male initiative, vaginal
extraction of sperm, barrier methods, and continence and the sterile
period. The desire to control marital fertility was strongest among the
"older Americans" (native born, Protestants, middle and upper classes,
in longer-settled areas such as New England). The rise in the abortion
rate in the 19th century reflects an evolving interest in smaller
families under conditions of imperfect contraception techniques. In
the absence of reliable and safe family planning techniques, individual
motivation becomes a prime factor in fertility reduction.

For other non-demographic works on birth and fertility, see also V.B.1.,
V.B.3., and VIII.A.5.

VII.E. BIRTH AND FERTILITY: DEMOGRAPHIC APPROACHES

(VII.E.1.) Knodel, John and Susan DeVos
1980 "Preferences for the Sex of Offspring
and Demographic Behavior in Eighteenth-
and Nineteenth Century Germany: An
Examination of Evidence From Village
Genealogies." Journal of Family History
5 (Summer): 145-166.

This is one of a large number of articles on the demographic transition
in Germany by KNODEL and colleagues. Some other publications are listed
below. Via village genealogies (Ortsippenbücher), up to 14 villages
representing diverse regions of Germany are followed as they pass through
this transition. Together, these various publications document that--
contrary to prior interpretations based on macro-level data--micro-level
changes in reproductive patterns began in the 19th century prior to the
onset of socio-economic improvements and that, in villages where fertility
limitation emerged early, it occurred prior to the decline in infant
and child mortality rates. Preferences for sex of children had at most
a weak influence on demographic behavior, as discussed by KNODEL and DeVOS.

The fertility transition was not purely an adjustment process to socio-
economic development, which implies it probably would not--in contemporary
third-world nations--"automatically" follow from economic development.

Other relevant publications by John Knodel include:

"The Influence of Child Mortality on Fertility in European
Populations in the Past: Results from Individual Data."
Chapter 2 in The Effects of Infant and Child Mortality on
Fertility, edited by Samuel H. Preston. New York: Academic
Press, 1978.

"Natural Fertility in Preindustrial Germany." Population
Studies 32 (3): 481-510, November 1978.

(with Etienne van de Walle) "Lessons from the Past: Policy
Implications of Historical Fertility Studies." Population
and Development Review 5 (2): 217-245, June 1979.

"An Exercise on Household Composition for Use in Courses
in Historical Demography." Local Population Studies, No. 23:
10-23, Autumn 1979.

"From Natural Fertility to Family Limitation: The Onset of
Fertility Transition in a Sample of German Villages."
Demography 16 (4): 493-521, November 1979.

"Demographic Transitions in German Villages." Paper presented
at the Summary Conference on European Fertility, Princeton,
N.J., July 1979. (to be published in a volume based on the
conference proceedings, edited by A.J. Coale).

(with E. Van de Walle) "Europe's Fertility Transition: New
Evidence and Lessons for Today's Developing World." Population
Bulletin 34 (6), February 1980.

"The Influence of Child Mortality on Fertility in a Natural
Fertility Setting: An Analysis of Individual Level Data for
Selected German Villages," in Natural Fertility: Concepts,
Evidences, Implications, and Theory, edited by Henri Leridon
and Jane Menken, Liége, Ordina Editions, 1980.

"Remarriage and Marital Fertility in 18th and 19th Century
Germany: An Exploratory Analysis Based on German Village
Genealogies," in Marriage and Remarriage in Past Populations,
edited by J. Dapâquier, et al., New York, Academic Press, 1981.

"Birth Spacing and Family Limitation: A Critique of the
Dupâquier-Lachiver Technique for Detecting Birth Control
from Family Reconstitution Data." Annales Économies Sociétés
Civilisations, May/June 1981.

(with Chris Wilson) "The Secular Increase in Fecundity in
German Village Populations: An Analysis of Reproductive
Histories of Couples Married 1750-1899." Population Studies
35 (1): 53-84, March 1981.

"Child Mortality and Reproductive Behavior in German Village
Populations in the Past: A Micro-Level Analysis of the
Replacement Effect." PSC Research Report No. 81-1, Population
Studies Center, University of Michigan, 1981.

For additional information on this data source on German villages, see:

Imhof, Arthur E.
        1977 "Historical Demography and Social History:
              Possibilities in Germany." Journal of
              Family History 2: 305-332.

(VII.E.2.) Tolnay, Stewart E., and Avery M. Guest
        1982 "Childlessness in a Transitional Population:
              The United States at the Turn of the Century."
              Journal of Family History 7 (Summer): 200-219.

Most analyses of childlessness among white U.S. women before 1920
have perceived it as being primarily due to involuntary factors such
as poor health and nutrition. In contrast, TOLNAY and GUEST analyze
childlessness around 1900 across various geographic areas and find that
the substantial variations in childlessness were due largely to
voluntary choice on the part of many women, particularly in the North
Atlantic region. In other areas, such as the agricultural South,
almost all childlessness was probably involuntary. On the whole,
variations in childlessness seem to reflect the stage of these areas in
the general transition toward low fertility occurring in the United
States. However, some evidence suggests that urban industrialism may have
had an independent positive influence on the degree of childlessness.

117

(VII.E.3.) McFalls, Joseph A., Jr., and George S. Masnick
              1981 "Birth Control and the Fertility of the U.S.
                    Black Population, 1880-1980." Journal of
                    Family History 6 (Spring): 339-357.

The fertility rate of the U.S. black population declined sharply
between 1880 and 1940. Most previous studies--despite inadequate
evidence--have concluded that this was not due to contraception, according
to McFALLS and MASNICK. Recent findings, especially from the Philadelphia
Fertility Study, indicate that birth control did play a significant role
in this fertility decline. Blacks often had access to effective birth
control methods, made effective use of them, and used them early enough
in their reproductive careers to make an impact on their fertility.
However, other factors--especially a rise in subfecundity and a decrease
in time spent in stable unions--also played a role.

(VII.E.4.) Vinovskis, Maris A.
              1981 "An 'Epidemic' of Adolescent Pregnancy?
                    Some Historical Considerations." Journal
                    of Family History 6 (Summer): 205-230.

Historical research is often justified in terms of helping us understand
and solve contemporary social problems. Surprisingly enough, the present
U.S. preoccupation with adolescent pregnancy has led to little historical
analysis of teenage childbearing in the past. VINOVSKIS reviews and
critiques the efforts of policy-makers in Washington, considers how
this issue might profit from an historical perspective, and suggests
a number of possible questions for future research.

Contrary to the beliefs of policy makers, the current rate of teenage
childbearing does not represent a dramatic increase. In fact, the
actual rate of adolescent childbearing has sharply decreased (by 44.8
per cent) during the past twenty years--which is remarkable, given the
increase in their sexual activity. But almost all of this decline
occurred among older (18-19 year old) teenagers; rates among 10-to-14
year old girls have increased considerably, as have out-of-wedlock
pregnancies in general.

On fertility in the U.S.-in-general, see also IX.C.1.

(VII.E.5.) Haines, Michael R.
              1980 "Fertility and Marriage in a Nineteenth-
                    Century Industrial City: Philadelphia,
                    1850-1880." The Journal of Economic History
                    40 (March): 151-158.

This paper examines age-specific and differential fertility, both marital
and total, and nuptiality for 1850-1880 census samples of white Philadelphia
(USA) families headed by native white Americans, Germans, and Irish.
Using Philadelphia Social History Project data, own-children techniques
are employed to construct age-standardized child-woman ratios and age-
specific total and marital fertility rates.

HAINES concludes that the low fertility among native whites was due to both low marital fertility and later marriage, that rapid declines in marital fertility occurred among second generation migrants, and that variations existed in marital fertility across occupational groupings within ethnic groups.

(VII.E.6.) Laidig, Gary, Wayne A. Schutjer, and C. Shannon Stokes
1981 "Agricultural Variation and Human Fertility in Antebellum Pennsylvania." Journal of Family History 6 (Summer): 195-204.

Previous research on the decline in U.S. fertility in the 19th century has found that fertility declined as the settlement process reduced the availability of inexpensive, good farm land. LAIDIG, SCHUTJER, and STOKES' study suggests that the importance of agricultural opportunity extended beyond the frontier period. It examines fertility variation in 59 Pennsylvania counties in 1850 and 1860. Although the state was already largely settled, the relative availability of farmsites and land of varying quality continued to influence fertilty. The importance of agricultural factors did decline between 1850 and 1860, however, giving way to demographic structural variables as the major determinants of fertility.

This study is notable for its inclusion of measure of land quality and labor requirements. Higher quality land was associated with lower fertility. The linking mechanism between land quality and fertility may be income. Alternative mechanisms--date of settlement and different labor requirements of various cropping patterns--were investigated and found inadequate.

(VII.E.7.) Leet, Don R.
1976 "The Determinants of the Fertility Transition in Antebellum Ohio." The Journal of Economic History 36 (June): 359-378.

It now appears evident that the decline in U.S. birth rates preceded any significant urbanization and that changes in rural fertility played a major role even during this most-rapid period of industrialization. To clarify the circumstances which produced such substantial fertility declines, the major determinants of the 1810-1860 Ohio fertility transition--when fertility (indirectily standardized child-woman ratios) declined by well over 40 per cent despite little urbanization-- are identified and the relative importance of these factors is established via the use of multiple regression analysis of cross-sectional data on Ohio counties.

A new measure of population pressure, reflecting the relative costs of obtaining an acre of agricultural land, is developed by LEET. The full testing of the land-availability hypothesis requires a more micro-level analysis than had been previously done; Ohio offered just such a test, results of which supported the hypothesis. Between one-half and three-quarters of the variance in county fertility ratios was explained by a combination of five major independent variables, of which population pressure (value of non-urban land) was clearly the most important cause of declining fertility, followed by cultural heritage of new settlers (proportion of New Englanders). Education (illiteracy), the sex ratio, and urbanization had much less effect.

(VII.E.8.) Steckel, Richard H.
                1979 "Antebellum Southern White Fertility: A
                      Demographic and Economic Analysis." The
                      Journal of Economic History 40 (June): 331-350.

This is the first systematic study of the fertility patterns of whites in the U.S. South during the antebellum period, the time when the overall U.S. fertility decline got underway. STECKEL investigates the decline and regional differentiation in southern white fertility, using published census materials and population schedules, primarily for the year 1860. Demographic analysis is conducted with a synthetic total fertility rate that has four components: age at first birth, age at last surviving birth, surviving-child spacing, and the proportion of women who eventually have surviving children. The socioeconomic analysis (1860) employs regressions and focuses on causes of the underlying changes in the components. Family limitation appears to have been unimportant in this population. The distribution of wealth was probably an important factor shaping the time trend and regional differential in fertility.

(VII.E.9.) Sanderson, Warren C.
                1979 "Quantitative Aspects of Marriage,
                      Fertility and Family Limitation in
                      Nineteenth-Century America: Another
                      Application of the Coale Specifications."
                      Demography 16 (August): 339-357.

This methodological paper from the Stanford Project on the History of Fertility Control deals with three aspects of the decline in the fertility of white women in the U.S. from 1800 to 1920, in each case deriving estimates by utilizing the functional form specifications, parameter values, etc. of Ansley Coale and co-workers. Such analytical devices as the Coale marital fertility function and the Coale-McNeil nuptiality function are powerful tools for the study of situations in which demographic data are sparse.

Based on these estimates, it is shown that: (1) reductions in marital fertility rates accounted for more of the white fertility decline (74 per cent) than did changes in marriage rates (26 per cent); (2) depending on the assumptions used (upper vs. lower bounds), the proportion of never-married white women who reduced their fertility increased between the cohorts of 1838 and 1873 from 71 to 84 per cent (upper bounds) or from 38 to 61 per cent (lower bounds); (3) given several additional assumptions, induced abortions could have been the proximate cause of between 18 and 34 per cent of all births averted by never-married white women in the cohort of 1838 and between 20 and 27 per cent in the cohort of 1873.

The above illustrate a few of the many types of demographic magnitudes which may be computed with such techniques.

(VII.E.10) Krishnamoorthy, S.
            1979 "Family Formation and the Life Cycle."
            Demography 16 (February): 121-130.

This methodological article develops mathematical expressions--when only the age-specific birth and death rates are available--for estimating probabilities of certain events in the life cycle of a girl child (rather than a couple) from birth to death. Calculated are: probability at birth that she will have a specified number of children; expected length of time before the first birth, between the first and last child, and between the last child and her own death; probability of at least one child outliving the mother; and expected number outliving the mother. The latter two are illustrated using mid-1960 data for three selected countries having different birth and death rates (USA, Venezuela, and Madagascar). KRISHNAMOORTHY finds, for instance, that the probability of at least one child outliving the mother is influenced more by mortality than by fertility.

This approach is suggested as being useful for producing estimates necessary to test life cycle hypotheses of socioeconomic behavior when only limited aggregate data are available.

For other works on demographic methodology, see also Section X.I.

F

VII.F. BOTH FERTILITY AND MORTALITY: NON-DEMOGRAPHIC APPROACHES

(VII.F.1.) Davies, Mel
1982 "Corsets and Conception: Fashion
and Demographic Trends in the Nineteenth
Century." Comparative Studies in Society
and History 24 (October): 611-641.

This essay suggests that an accident of fashion--the tightlaced corset--
unintentionally served as a mode of birth control among the middle
classes in the West from the middle of the nineteenth century. Without
implying that this was the only factor which contributed to the decline
in fertility, DAVIES presents sociobiological evidence suggesting
that the tightlaced corset had an adverse effect on fecundity, led to
a decline in coital frequency, and resulted in an increase in the
number of spontaneous abortions and stillborns. Hence, tight lacing
may have been the element which set the decline in birth rates in
motion. It is also argued that, as the size of the middle-class
family declined, the small family became fashionable and desirable.
This pattern implies benefits in the form of a higher standard of living
to the family unit. Both economic benefits (as well as possible social
and psychological benefits to many parents) and the new small-family
norm made intentional contraception acceptable to the public. According
to Davies, the evidence supports a new and important variable which
complements the more conventional explanations found in demographic
literature, with the essential difference involving the path to those
conclusions.

(VII.G.1.) Lithell, Ulla-Britt
                1981 "Breast-Feeding Habits and Their
                      Relation to Infant Mortality and
                      Marital Fertility." <u>Journal of</u>
                      <u>Family History</u> 6 (Summer): 182-194.

LITHELL's study analyzes, at the family level, the influence of
biological factors, particularly breastfeeding, upon the levels of
age-specific infant mortality and of marital fertility (interval
before next birth after the survival or death of the preceding child)
in a Swedish-speaking parish in western Finland, as compared to two rural
Swedish parishes, in the first half of the 19th century. Breastfeeding
was practiced in only one of the three parishes.

The "breastfeeding parish" had lower infant mortality rates, no seasonal
variation in infant mortality, and a long birth interval if the first
child survived. Reasons for early weaning and low rates of breastfeeding
in the other two parishes are also explored.

(VII.G.2.) Fogel, Robert W. and Stanley L. Engerman
                1979 "Recent Findings in the Study of
                      Slave Demography and Family Structure."
                      <u>Sociology and Social Research</u> 63
                      (April): 566-589.

Recent works on the demographic patterns of slave and white populations
in the United States and on the slave population of the British West
Indies are examined here. Studies presenting new data on fertility,
mortality, and family structure are analyzed to determine those factors
contributing to the differing demographic performances of each slave
group, and to point to certain similarities in patterns between U.S.
slaves and southern whites. By offering a summary of the principal
new findings, and highlighting several still-unresolved issues in this
field of study, FOGEL and ENGERMAN provide scholars with a variety of
data sources and findings, organized according to the following subtopics:
fertility patterns; mortality, and family and household structure.

(VII.G.3.) Smith, Daniel Scott
                1972 "The Demographic History of Colonial
                      New England." <u>The Journal of Economic</u>
                      <u>History</u> 32 (March): 165-183.

                      Also: "Comments on Papers by Smith,
                      Vinovskis," written by J.J. Spengler
                      (214-215) and Richard Sutch (216-218).

The central fact of the demographic history of early North America is
rapid growth, writes SMITH. Since Franklin and Malthus, interpretations
of early American demography have centered on the high fertility associated
with near universal marriage for women at a low average age. This
high growth and its explanation have been long recognized and virtually
unquestioned until recently. In this essay, Smith integrates knowledge
of population trends on the colony-wide level with findings forthcoming
from recent intensive demographic analyses of New England communities,
in order to present generalizations about three central issues: (1) the
demographic sources of the higher colonial growth rate compared to a
reliably documented European society; (2) decadal variation in the pattern
of population growth, particularly the central role of lower fertility
in the apparent pause in rapid growth around 1700; and (3) the determinants
of the level of marital fertility, especially evidence for the conscious
limitation of family size before the "demographic transition" of the
first half of the 19th century.

For demographic works dealing with both fertility and mortality, see
also IV.C.5.

VII.H. DEATH AND MORTALITY: DEMOGRAPHIC APPROACHES

(VII.H.1.) Fogel, Robert W., Stanley L. Engerman, James Trussell,
            Roderick Floud, Clayne L. Pope, and Larry T. Wimmer
                    1978 "The Economics of Mortality in
                          North America, 1650-1910: A
                          Description of a Research Project."
                          Historical Methods 11 (Spring): 75-108.

This is a description of a collaborative research project involving research
groups at the National Bureau of Economic Research, the Office of Population
Research (Princeton University), Brigham Young University, Harvard University,
the University of London, and the University of Rochester. The new data
base described here will make it possible to construct previously unavailable
time series on vital rates for whites in the United States and Canada over
the entire period from 1650 to 1910 and for blacks in the United States and
the British West Indies over a substantial proportion of this period,
according to FOGEL et al. It will also permit construction of previously
unavailable time series of a number of social and economic variables.
These, in turn, will then make it possible to evaluate the determinants
of the trend and variation in mortality rates during this period, as well
as to assess the effect of changes in mortality rates upon such aspects
of social and economic behavior as fertility rates, family structure, the
distribution of wealth, and the increase in labor productivity. Practical
and theoretical considerations will dictate the linkage method used
from issue to issue. The sample of roughly 29,000 genealogies will make
it possible to construct both generational and cross-sectional life
tables and associated mortality rates. Finally, once completed, these
data will be made available to interested scholars. Comment: this set
of data on families would appear to be of potential use to family historians,
as well as to economists and economic demographers. On this research, see
also X.K.1.

(VII.H.2.) Sly, David F., and Peter S. K. Chi
                    1972 "Economic Development, Modernization, and
                          Demographic Behavior: Longitudinal Analysis
                          of Mortality Change." The American Journal
                          of Economic Sociology 31 (October): 376-386.

From a review of the literature, SLY and CHI find that no previous study
has empirically investigated the relative importance of economic development
and the more general process of modernization upon demographic behavior.
This paper attempts to do just that, for one type of demographic behavior
(mortality). It examines the relative contributions of two indicators of
economic well-being and four indicators of structural modernization to
the United States mortality trend between 1916 and 1962. In addition,
separate analyses were conducted for gender- and race-specific sub-
populations over the same period.

The analyses suggest that changes in the level of structural modernization have a greater effect on mortality trends than do changes in the level of economic well-being (or economic development). Moreover, the data suggest that the sub-populations studied are affected differentially by economic well-being and structural modernization. Finally, the authors suggest that this analysis approach could be beneficially applied to longitudinal data from other societies and to other types of demographic behavior such as fertility.

(VII.H.3.) Vinovskis, Maris A.
                        1972   "Mortality Rates and Trends in
                               Massachusetts Before 1860." The
                               Journal of Economic History 32 (March):
                               184-213. Also: "Comments on Papers by
                               Smith, Vinovskis," written by J.J. Spengler
                               (214-215) and Richard Sutch (216-218).

VINOVSKIS's paper offers tentative hypotheses on mortality trends in the U.S. state of Massachusetts before 1860. Particular attention is given to differences among earlier studies in sources and methodology; differences which might affect the validity of comparing mortality rates from these various studies. It is not the cause of the significance of changes in mortality rates which is at issue here, but rather the attempt to establish exactly what did happen to mortality rates before 1860. In so doing this essay introduces some new mortality data for Massachusetts, re-examines the methodology and the reliability of some of the earlier studies, and provides preliminary guidelines that will facilitate the future investigation of mortality rates in the United States before 1860.

VII.I. MIGRATION: DEMOGRAPHIC APPROACHES

(VII.I.1.) Bodnar, John, Michael Weber, and Roger Simon
1979 "Migration, Kinship, and Urban
Adjustment: Blacks and Poles in
Pittsburgh, 1900-1930." The Journal
of American History 66 (December):
548-565.

This article examines the differential pattern of urban adaptation of
Black migrants and Polish immigrants in America, by focusing on the actual
process of moving to the city and securing work. Urban adaptation is
analyzed by comparing the migration experiences, socialization practices,
and occupational patterns of these two groups in the U.S. city of
Pittsburgh between 1900 and 1930. BODNAR, WEBER, and SIMON offer
explanations for differences between immigrant and Black patterns of
adjustment, and also suggest the pernicious effects of urban racism.

Their analysis is based upon 94 oral histroy interviews conducted
among Polish immigrants and Black migrants who had arrived in Pittsburgh
before 1917. In addition, a 20 per cent random sample of Christian
Polish and Black families was taken from the 1900 United States census.
Their findings clearly show that not all newcomers to the city functioned
in the same way. However, these differences were not simply the result
of pre-migration cultures or of the disintegrating effects of the urban
milieu. For example, though kinship attachments operated in different
ways, both groups evidenced strong kinship attachments before and
during the migration process. Also, neither pre-migration culture nor
urban racism functioned independently; adjustment was ultimately a
product of the interaction of one with the other. Finally, neither
Blacks nor Poles moved rapidly upward in occupational mobility, but
Poles avoided intense racial hostility and became firmly planted on
the lower rungs of the occupational hierarchy by following kin into
the workplace.

(VII.I.2.) Moch, Leslie Page
1981 "Adolescence and Migration: Nîmes,
France, 1906." Social Science History
5 (Winter): 25-51.

This article examines the place of adolescent and migrant in urban
society during the 19th and early 20th century. Using 1906 information
for the French city of Nîmes, MOCH investigates the quantifiable
attributes of adolescence--residence and employment patterns--in relation
to migration. The specific questions posited are: (1) Were adolescent
and migrant mutually exclusive categories for young people? (2) What can
groups of migrants tell us about the relationships among adolescence,
migration, and changes in urban society at the turn of the century?

Important findings include that migration was a significant determinant of adolescent status and that, among migrants, the primary determinant of young people's residence and work patterns was whether they moved to the city with their family. Geographic origins and parentage together divided the experience of urban youth at the turn of the century, creating three possibilities for young people in Nîmes. The first kind of experience, found among natives and those who migrated with their middle-class parents, is the one associated with adolescent status--that of cohabitation with family and economic dependence. Cohabitation with family combined with labor force participation is another pattern, found among working-class native youth and among young people who migrated with working-class parents. The third category of experience belonged almost entirely to migrant youth and is the antithesis of the first type. It was the experience of young people who did not live with their own families and who consequently were employed. Because they lived alone in rented quarters or on the peripheries of other families as employees or servants, the isolation of this experience (in familial and economic terms) was probably a liability for these young people. In summary, most migrant youth did not participate in the context which gave rise to "adolescence" for native and middle-class youth.

(VII.I.3.) Swierenga, Robert P.
                1980 "Dutch Immigrant Demography, 1820-1880."
                      Journal of Family History 5 (Winter):
                      390-405.

Using ship passenger lists of arrivals to the U.S. (ports of Baltimore, Boston, New Orleans, New York, and Philadelphia), SWIERENGA analyzes the demographic characteristics of Dutch immigrants between 1820 and 1880. The pattern, different from that of many other nationality groups, reflects the fact that the Dutch "missed the train of the first industrial revolution." Overseas migration remained a pre-industrial one (heavily rural and in family units).

Migration was selective of pre-industrial rather than industrial-type movers and was a response to the mid-century religious and economic crisis in the Netherlands rather than to the structural changes associated with modernization.

(VII.I.4.) Kamphoefner, Walter D.
                1982 "Predisposing Factors in German-
                      American Urbanization." Unpublished
                      paper read at annual meeting of the
                      Organization of American Historians.

Notable among studies of German-Americans because it links 19th century German emigrant lists with American census data is that by KAMPHOEFNER. Immigrants from different parts of Germany experienced different rates of urbanization in the U.S. Upward mobility often followed the pattern of a transition period of urban residence, followed by a move to farms or small towns. On German immigrants in the U.S., see also I.D.4.

VII.J. DISSERTATIONS

(VII.J.1.) Avery, Roger Christopher
1974 The Age Pattern of Fertility and the Demographic Transition. Unpublished Ph.D. dissertation, University of California, Berkeley.

(VII.J.2.) Harper, John Paull
1975 'Be Fruitful and Multiply': The Reaction to Family Limitation in Nineteenth-Century America. Unpublished Ph.D. dissertation, Columbia University.

(VII.J.3.) Hodgson, Dennis George
1976 Demographic Transition Theory and the Family Planning Perspective: The Evolution of Theory Within American Demography. Unpublished Ph.D. dissertation, Cornell University.

(VII.J.4.) Kern, Louis John
1977 Love, Labor, and Self-Control: Sex-Roles and Sexuality in Three Nineteenth-Century American Utopian Communities. Unpublished Ph.D. dissertation, Rutgers University, The State University of New Jersey (New Brunswick).

(VII.J.5.) Lemieux, Christine Marie
1976 Living to Die: Nineteenth-Century Culture of Death and Dying in Delaware County, Pennsylvania. Unpublished Ph.D. dissertation, University of Pennsylvania.

(VII.J.6.) Muncy, Raymond Lee
1971 Sex and Marriage in Nineteenth Century Utopian Communities in America. Unpublished Ph.D. dissertation, University of Mississippi.

(VII.J.7.) Musallam, Basim Fuad
1973 Sex and Society in Islam: The Sanction and Medieval Techniques of Birth Control. Unpublished Ph.D. dissertation, Harvard University.

(VII.J.8.) Smith, J. E., and P. R. Kuntz
1976 "Polygyny and Fertility in 19th-Century America." Population Studies (London) 30 (Number 3): 465-480.

(VII.J.9.) Swedlund, Alan Charles
1970 The Genetic Structure of an Historical Population: A Study of Marriage and Fertility in Old Deerfield, Massachusetts. Unpublished Ph.D. dissertation, University of Colorado, Boulder.

VII.K. PUBLICATIONS

(VII.K.1.)   Burch, T. K.
             1979 "Household and Family Demography--Bibliographic
                   Essay." Population Index 45 (Number 2): 173-195.

(VII.K.2.)   Darroch, A. G.
             1981 "Migrants in the 19th-Century--Fugitives or
                   Families in Motion." Journal of Family History
                   6 (Number 3): 257-277.

(VII.K.3.)   Eng, R. Y., and T. C. Smith
             1976 "Peasant Families and Population-Control in
                   18th-Century Japan." Journal of Interdisciplinary
                   History 6 (Number 3): 417-445.

(VII.K.4.)   Fildes, V.
             1980 "Neonatal Feeding Practices and Infant-Mortality
                   During the 18th-Century." Journal of Biosocial
                   Science 12 (Number 3): 313-324.

(VII.K.5.)   Haines, M. R.
             1977 "Fertility, Nuptiality, and Occupation--Study
                   of Coal Mining Populations and Regions in England
                   and Wales in Mid-19th Century." Journal of
                   Interdisciplinary History 8 (Number 2): 245-280.

(VII.K.6.)   Hansen, E. D. R.
             1979 "Overlaying in 19th-Century England--Infant-
                   Mortality or Infanticide." Human Ecology 7
                   (Number 4): 333-352.

(VII.K.7.)   Lantz, H, and L. Hendrix
             1978 "Black Fertility and Black Family in 19th-
                   Century--Re-examination of Past." Journal of
                   Family History 3 (Number 3): 251-261.

(VII.K.8.)   Lockwood, R.
             1978 "Birth, Illness and Death in 18th-Century New
                   England." Journal of Social History 12 (Number 1):
                   111-128.

(VII.K.9.)   Marcy, P. T.
             1981 "Factors Affecting the Fecundity and Fertility
                   of Historical Populations--A Review." Journal
                   of Family History 6 (Number 3): 309-326.

(VII.K.10.) McCaskie, T. C.
             1981 "State and Society, Marriage and Adultery--Some
                   Considerations Towards a Social-History of Pre-
                   Colonial Asante." Journal of African History 22
                   (Number 4): 477-494.

(VII.K.11.) Mineau, G. P., L. L. Bean, and M. Skolnick
1979 "Mormon Demographic History II. Family-Life
Cycle and Natural Fertility." Population Studies
London 33 (Number 3): 429-446.

(VII.K.12.) Moch, L. P.
1981 "Marrige, Migration, and Urban Demographic-
Structure--A Case From France in the Belle
Epoque." Journal of Family History 6 (Number 1):
70-88.

(VII.I.13.) Shorter, E.
1973 "Female Emancipation, Birth Control, and Fertility
in European History." American Historical Review
78 (Number 3): 605-640.

(VII.K.14.) Smith, R. M.
1981 "Fertility, Economy, and Household Formation in
England Over Three Centuries." Population and Development
Review 7 (Number 4): 595-622.

(VII.K.15.) Strong, B.
1973 "Toward a History of Experiential Family--Sex
and Incest in Nineteenth-Century Family."
Journal of Marriage and the Family 35 (Number 3):
457-466.

(VII.K.16.) Wargon, S. T.
1978 "Households and Family in Canada--General Review
of Recent Demographic Trends." International
Journal of Sociology of the Family 8 (Number 1):
53-68.

(VII.K.17.) Barker-Benfield, G. J.
1972 "The Spermatic Economy: A Nineteenth-Century View
of Sexuality." Feminist Studies 1 (Number 1):
45-74.

(VII.K.18.) Degler, Carl N.
1974 "What Ought to Be and What Was: Woman's Sexuality
in the Nineteenth Century." American Historical
Review 79 (December): 1467-1490.

(VII.K.19.) Easterlin, Richard A.
1976 "Factors in the Decline of Farm Family Fertility
in the United States: Some Preliminary Research
Results." Journal of American History 63
(December): 600-614.

(VII.K.20.) Rothman, Ellen K.
1982 "Sex and Self-Control: Middle-Class Courtship in
America, 1770-1870." Journal of Social History
15 (Spring): 409-425.

(VII.K.21.)   Smith, Daniel Scott
              1973 "The Dating of the American Sexual Revolution:
                    Evidence and Interpretation." In Michael Gordon,
                    editor, 1978, The American Family in Social-Historical
                    Perspective, Second Edition, 426-438. (Prepared
                    especially for the first edition of this volume.)

(VII.K.22.)   Vinovskis, Maris A.
              1977 "Angel's Heads and Weeping Willows: Death in
                    Early America." Proceedings of the American
                    Antiquarian Society 86 (Part 2): 273-302.

(VII.K.23.)   Wells, Robert V.
              1975 "Family History and Demographic Transition."
                    Journal of Social History 9 (Fall): 1-20.

VIII. KINSHIP, LINEAGE, AND INHERITANCE

VIII.A. *KINSHIP AND LINEAGE*

A

(VIII.A.1.) Mogey, John
1976 "Residence, Family, Kinship: Some Recent Research." Journal of Family History 1 (Number 1): 95-105.

Review of: Jean Cuisenier, 1975, Economie et Parenté: Leur Affinités de Structure Dans le Domaine Ture et Dans le Domaine Arabe. Paris, France: Mouton.

Because family historians have devoted little attention to the interaction between domestic group and kin outside the household, MOGEY discusses a number of books and articles relating to kin arragements and interaction. In particular, an in-depth discussion of Cuisenier's study of two bilateral kinship systems (Arab and Turkish) offers further information on these issues. Cuisenier chose two complex societies, one in which marriage choices were governed by considerations of prestige or status (Turkish society) and one in which choices were governed by considerations of market production (Arab society). Behavior and beliefs about marriage were then contrasted in order to gain a theoretical understanding of the forces at work.

The conclusion emphasizes the need for recognizing the importance of kinship as an influential source of goals and desires that lead to decisions about marriage mates, the birth of children, and the adoption of a particular or satisfying life style. To come to grips with the theoretical issues raised in this essay, historians will have to reconstruct not only households but also kinship systems as well.

(VIII.A.2.) Dupâquier, Jacques
1981 "Naming-Practices, Godparenthood, and Kinship in the Vexin, 1540-1900." Journal of Family History 6 (Summer): 135-155.

The study of naming practices should permit us eventually to detect the existence of more or less tacit rules and hidden family structures, writes DUPÂQUIER, and to learn whether, even in those regions where the conjugal family unit prevailed, ideas related to lineage and to extended kinship remained active. This essay examines the allocation of given (baptismal) names between 1540 and 1900 in the Vexin region of France, in order to determine the degree to which given names attributed to children were those of the godparent, or of the parent, or of another family member. Parts of the analysis required family reconstitution and were limited to instances for which there were three complete family records--of the paternal grandparents, of the maternal grandparents, and of the parents themselves. The results show that, first, the corpus of given names became progressively restricted until the last quarter of the 17th century, and then was enlarged again by the fashion of double and triple names, until the explosion of the romantic period. Second, the new fashions in naming and in godparent choice were spread at the same time socially (down the social class hierarchy) and geographically (from urban to rural). Finally, the rules which governed the choice of godparents and the attribution of given names are of less universal importance than has been thought: there existed social and regional variants.

(VIII.A.3.) Plakans, Andrejs
                1982 "Ties of Kinship and Kinship Roles
                      in an Historical Eastern European
                      Peasant Community: A Synchronic
                      Analysis." Journal of Family History
                      7 (Spring): 52-75.

The transfer of anthropological techniques of kinship analysis to historical research is not easily accomplished, writes PLAKANS, yet historians studying the pre-industrial European past can do no better than to draw upon the century of experience of social anthropology. Focusing especially upon kinship in Eastern Europe, this article first explores the questions which can and should be asked, sources of information, and existing literature. Detailed subsections deal with such topics as linked household and genealogical data sets, and specific problems in using the parish registers in the Russian Baltic province of Kurland, including using them to trace kinship across household boundaries, to identify dyadic ties of family members in addition to the household head, and to identify the primary and secondary kin of a given Ego. This article offers one strategy for the (quantitative) analysis of social structure, with specific illustrations from the author's ongoing research on kinship in the Latvian estate of Spahren. Theoretical and conceptual issues relating to kinship roles and structural analysis are also touched upon.

(VIII.A.4.) Fischer, Claude S.
                1982 "The Dispersion of Kinship Ties
                      in Modern Society: Contemporary
                      Data and Historical Speculation."
                      Journal of Family History 7 (Winter):
                      353-375.

FISCHER develops a picture of contemporary American kinship networks and uses that picture to examine the following issue: did industrialization, urbanization, and "modernization" isolate the nuclear family and reduce the functional role of kinship? Or, do extended kin ties persist in some altered form (spatially extended, mobile, voluntaristic, etc.)? This debate is addressed in two parts. Part one of this essay presents descriptive data on the kinship patterns of almost 1,000 adults living

in northern California in 1977. Part two is speculative and briefly
reviews three alternative ways of explaining the development of contemporary
kinship patterns, namely industrialization, cultural change, and--
suggested as the most important factor--the growth of transportation
and communication technologies.

(VIII.A.5.) Harrell, Stevan
        ca. 1978 "The Rich Get Children: Segmentation,
                Stratification and Population in Three
                Zhejiang Lineages, 1550-1850." Unpublished
                paper.

This paper demonstrates (admittedly on a small scale) the connection
between two important social processes in late Ming and Qing Chinese
society: the growth and segmentation of patrilineages and the growth
of populations. These two processes were closely connected because
the upper classes produced more children. Thus wealthy branches of
lineages became numerically dominant as well until they grew so large
that they became differentiated internally and they themselves segmented
into wealthy and poor branches, and the cycle repeated itself. Simply
stated, the rich, as they get richer, get children, and by doing so some
of them get poorer. HARRELL illustrates the connection between segmentation,
stratification, and population in the He, Lin, and Wu lineages of
Xiao-shan xian, Zhejiang, between the years 1550 and 1850. The findings
have implications both for the study of the Chinese lineage and for
the study of population. The process of growth, segmentation, and
stratification in Chinese lineages has now been shown to be traceable
over the centuries by the use of genealogies. This means the validation
of Freedman's (1958) original model of segmentation in the Chinese
lineage: that it is asymetrical and based on wealth.

On kinship and lineage, see also I.C.1., II.F.2., II.B.1., II.B.2.,
and Section X.C.

VIII.B.   INHERITANCE

(VIII.B.1.)   Vinovskis, Maris
                   1971   "American Historical Demography: A
                   Review Essay." Historical Methods
                   Newsletter 4 (September): 141-148.

                   Review of: Philip J. Greven, Jr., 1970,
                   Four Generations: Population, Land, and
                   Family in Colonial Andover, Massachusetts.
                   Ithaca, New York: Cornell University Press.

The study of the structure of society via analysis of families within
their communities, particularly the re-examination of family life in
colonial New England, emerged in the late 1960s. The results of these
efforts by historians include the following three major (1970) works:
Demos', A Little Commonwealth, Lockridge's A New England Town--The First
Hundred Years, and Greven's Four Generations. Because of its detailed
demographic analysis, VINOVSKIS reviews only Greven's work, focusing
specifically on the topic of mortality rates. This volume, a study of
Andover, Massachusetts in the 17th and 18th centuries, is concerned
with population, land, and family patterns and how these factors
affected the lives of four successive generations. Greven's findings
indicate a dramatic increase in the death rate and suggest that Andover
was becoming much less healthy in the 18th century. While Vinovskis
recognizes the strength of these data, he does suggest exercising caution
in interpretation of the evidence and offers alternative explanations
for the findings.

(VIII.B.2.)   Salamon, Sonya
                   1980   "Ethnic Differences in Farm Family
                   Land Transfers." Rural Sociology
                   45 (2): 290-308.

This study demonstrates the persistence--over a century after migration
to America--of ethnic values for family and behavior in two communities
(Irish and German) in east central Illinois. Field studies of these
farming communities (1975-1978) reveal contrasts in family size,
interpersonal relations, marriage patterns, size of holdings, and out-
migration all relating to inheritance values. The differences are
shown to be linked to Germans favoring partible inheritance in land
transfer. They display fragmentation of holdings, suspicion between
relatives, and an increase in density of the population over a period
of a century. The Irish utilize de facto impartible inheritance
through a process of sibling cooperation in settling estates. They are
characterized by larger holdings and greater celibacy, out-migration,
and sibling cooperation. SALAMON also makes predictions about future
continuity of farm families in the present situation of scarce land,
when either partible or impartible land transfer is used. The Irish
community is likely to remain competitive at a time when larger holdings
are required (due to the balance between land use and numbers staying
and leaving).   The German community is in a near-crisis situation in

the people-to-land ratio; holdings are becoming too small for farm viability if the same numbers of Germans continue to value farming within the community boundaries.

(VIII.B.3.) Hoffman, Philip T.
                1981 "Pious Bequests in Wills: A
                      Statistical Analysis." Social
                      Science Working Paper #393. Pasadena,
                      California: Division of Humanities
                      and Social Sciences, California
                      Institute of Technology.

This paper is the first to employ maximum likelihood methods to analyze and account for the increase in pious bequests (i.e., for posthumous masses and charity) in wills, in this case for early modern France.

Family historians with sufficient mathematical training may find this a helpful example of the use of maximum likelihood methods (especially tobit, but also probit) for estimating relationships with limited dependent variables.

A number of other sources on such techniques are cited, including:

                Maddala, G. S.
                     1977 Econometrics. New York, Düsseldorf, and
                           other cities: McGraw-Hill. See pages
                           162-182, especially 168-170.

                Tobin, James
                     1958 Estimation of Relationships for Limited
                           Dependent Variables, Econometrics 26: 24-36.

                Yatchew, Adonis, and Zvi Griliches
                     1979 Specification Error in Probit and Logit
                           Models, Harvard Institute of Economic
                           Research Discussion Paper 717.

(VIII.B.4.) Douglass, William A.
                1981 "Sheep Ranchers and Sugar Growers: Property
                      Transmission in the Basque Immigrant Family
                      of the American West and Australia." Paper
                      prepared for the Wenner-Gren Foundation
                      Symposium on "Households: Changing Form and
                      Function," October 8-15, 1981.

Noting that it is somewhat myopic to examine immigrant families without reference to the preimmigration system of familism from which they came--although such an approach is difficult and hence seldom done-- DOUGLASS addresses this issue in his analysis of a sample of Basque sheep ranchers in the American West and Basque sugar farmers in North Queensland, Australia. This comparative treatment of intergenerational property transmission is critical both to the study of New World family systems and to a fuller understanding of the constraints and potentialities within European family systems as they adapt to changing conditions.

This study focuses on the founding immigrant and his first-gerneration offspring; the very recency of events precludes speaking of an "institution-alized" immigrant family system having its own explicit value system. The findings indicate that over half of the families did not follow the Old World stem family pattern of property inheritance, often exhibiting a pattern of patrilineal extension, e.g., two or more married sons sharing ownership with their parents. Had the Old World Basques not been limited by a non-expandable land base, Douglass suggests that they might have done the same. As with certain other findings, the relative influence of Old World and New World factors cannot be clearly delineated; even informants themselves provide conflicting rationales regarding their behavior. Hence the study of immigrants in the Old World context provides clues, but not definitive answers, for understanding family behavior.

For a study of Basque families in contemporary Spain, focusing on how inheritance norms influenced the decision to leave farming, see: William A. Douglass, "Rural Exodus in Two Spanish Basque Villages: A Cultural Explanation." American Anthropologist 73 (October 1971): 1100-1114.

(VIII.B.5.) Ditz, Toby L.
            1982 Family, Law and Economy: Inheritance
                  Practices in Five Connecticut Towns,
                  1750-1820. Unpublished Ph.D. dissertation
                  in Sociology, Columbia University.

This study compares inheritance patterns in four upland, subsistence-plus communities and one river-valley, commercial agriculture town. A quantitative analysis of inheritance practices is made from probate and land records, while a supplementary qualitative analysis of letters and sermons provides evidence on sentiments and norms surrounding transfer of property. Also, legislation and dispute cases concerning the law of succession and property law are examined. The comparative and over-time research design allows the identification of links between degree of town integration (into developing regional and national markets) and types of inheritance practices. DITZ argues that the timing and nature of variation in familial strategies that attempt to both maintain a viable agricultural enterprise and provide for children, displays dynamics similar to those found in family farm regions of Western Europe. This research also provides the basis for a discussion of the issue of American "exceptionalism" (the degree to which American institutions and values differ from those of European society).

On inheritance, see also X.E.1. and VI.C.1.

VIII.C. <u>*DISSERTATIONS*</u>

(VIII.C.1.) Bissell, Linda Auwers
        1973 <u>Family, Friends, and Neighbors: Social</u>
             <u>Interaction in Seventeenth-Century Windsor,</u>
             <u>Connecticut.</u> Unpublished Ph.D. dissertation,
             Brandeis University.

D

VIII.D. <u>PUBLICATIONS</u>

(VIII.D.1.)   Bonfield, L.
              1979 "Marriage Settlements and the Rise of
                    Great Estates--Demographic Aspect." <u>Economic</u>
                    <u>History Review</u> 32 (Number 4): 483-493.

(VIII.D.2.)   Chaytor, M.
              1980 "Household and Kinship--Ryton in the Late
                    16th and Early 17th Centuries." <u>History</u>
                    <u>Workshop: A Journal of Socialist Historians</u>
                    1980 (Number 10): 25-60.

(VIII.D.3.)   Lafitte, F.
              1973 "History of Family Help." <u>New Society</u> 25
                    (Number 564): 206-208.

(VIII.D.4.)   Smith, R. M.
              1979 "Kin and Neighbors in a 13th-Century Suffolk
                    Community." <u>Journal of Family History</u> 4
                    (Number 3): 219-256.

(VIII.D.5.)   Cody, Cheryll Ann
              1982 "Naming, Kinship, and Estate Dispersal: Notes
                    on Slave Family Life on a South Carolina Plantation,
                    1786-1833." <u>William and Mary Quarterly</u> 39
                    (January): 192-211.

IX. OTHER INSTITUTIONS AND THE FAMILY

THE ECONOMY AND EDUCATION

IX.A. *THE FAMILY ECONOMY AND FAMILY STRATEGIES*

(IX.A.1.) Goldin, Claudia
1979 "Household and Market Production of
Families in a Late Nineteenth Century
American City." Explorations in Economic
History 16: 111-131.

GOLDIN examines the determinants of child labor in the late 19th century
through the use of microlevel data from the 1880 U.S. manuscript census
for Philadelphia. Certain variables are tested (father's unemployment
and income, the presence of nuclear and non-nuclear members in the household, ethnicity, and others) in a probit analysis of the labor force
participation of children over ten years old within the context of family
economy. The findings support the economic theory of household and market
production, including the substitutability of daughters for their mothers.
Economic, demographic, and cultural factors influenced decisions about
sending children outside the home to work, and simple demographics
generally determined which of the children in the family was to work.
Two important implications for this study involve economists and historians.
For economists studying the allocation of time in the family, the
determinants of children's labor involve many of the same issues found
in analyses of working wives. For historians interested in 19th century
American social history, ethnicity was important only in determining
whether first-generation daughters worked in the market. This study is
notable as an illustration of how economic methods and historical data
can be integrated.

Goldin and associates have a number of other papers on the economic
history of the family, including:

Goldin, Claudia, and Kenneth Sokoloff, 1981, "Women, Children,
and Industrialization in the Early Republic: Evidence from
the Manufacturing Censuses." National Bureau of Economic
Research (1050 Massachusetts Avenue, Cambridge, Massachusetts
02138) Working Paper number 795.

Goldin, Claudia, and Donald O. Parsons, 1981, "Economic
Well-being and Child Labor: The Interaction of Family
and Industry." National Bureau of Economic Research,
Working Paper number 707.

(IX.A.2.) Harding, Susan
1979 "Family Reform Movements: Recent Feminism and its
Opposition." Michigan Occasional Paper number 16.
(Dept. of Anthropology, University of Michigan,
Ann Arbor, Michigan 48106.)

HARDING's working paper develops--for post-World War II America--an analytic framework and argument about the connections between the family movements for and against feminist reforms. It is argued that groups of women in contemporary America have conflicting interests defined by competing strategies for forming and maintaining a family, and that these conflicting interests yield opposing positions regarding feminist reforms. The discussion extends to the general concept of family strategy and the particular concepts of "moral" versus "rational" family strategies. Both feminism and its opposition are family reform movements: they represent women's interests as they are rooted in their family lives or, more broadly, in issues of gender identity, sexuality and reproduction. The conflict between groups of women over family reforms during the last decade is not a "cover" for other struggles, but rather a political expression of enduring social interest groups responding to long-term social trends.

(IX.A.3.)   Early, Frances H.
            1982   "The French-Canadian Family Economy and
                   Standard of Living in Lowell, Massachusetts,
                   1870." Journal of Family History 7 (Summer):
                   180-199.

In the spirit of the revisionist approach to immigrant history and in contrast to traditional interpretations of the immigrant experience in America, EARLY's paper investigates the working lives of French Canadians in Lowell, Massachusetts, in the 1870s. The focus is on the way French Canadians, as recent immigrants, accommodated their institution of the family farm economy to meet the exigencies of the limited occupational opportunites of a one-industry textile town. The success of this adaptive mechanism is then assessed by showing the relationship between culture (family-economy tradition) and day-to-day survival (standard-of-living). Finally, Early briefly addresses the question which lies at the heart of the disagreement between revisionist and orthodox interpretations: To what extent were French Canadians makers and shapers of their lives, and to what extent were they victims of circumstances beyond their control?

On family economy and family strategies, see also VI.C.1.

(IX.B.1.) Kanter, Rosabeth Moss
1978 "Families, Family Processes, and Economic
Life: Toward Systematic Analysis of Social
Historical Research." In John Demos and
Sarane Spence Boocock, editors, Turning
Points: Historical and Sociological Essays
on the Family, S316-S339. Chicago, Illinois:
University of Chicago Press. (Supplement to
Volume 84 of American Journal of Sociology.)

KANTER views the task of systemization--identifying variables and issues
that lend themselves to comparative analysis across times and places--
as an area where the sociologist can make a contribution to family history.
Such variables can be used to examine the differing ways in which
families interact with their social and economic context, as well as to
examine historical variations in processes within families. The topics
under discussion in this essay include: the family as an "independent
variable" in economic life; variations in the relationship between
families and organizations; work system variables and their impact on
families (including time and timing, rewards and resources, occupational
cultures and world view, and emotional climate); and finally, variables
for comparative analysis of relationship processes (including meaning,
power, and intimacy). Kanter concludes by noting that the sociologist's
attention to concepts and relationships apart from their immediate
context can serve as a corrective to the historian's tendency to see
only uniqueness and change.

(IX.B.2.) Smelser, Neil J., and Sydney Halpern
1978 "The Historical Triangulation of Family, Economy,
and Education." In John Demos and Sarane Spence
Boocock, editors, Turning Points: Historical and
Sociological Essays on the Family, S288-S315.
Chicago Illinois: University of Chicago Press.
(Supplement to Volume 84 of American Journal of
Sociology.)

This essay introduces a number of concepts and perspectives that are useful
for the study of the dynamics of change in the family. In the first
section, the focus is on the structural differentiation of family,
economy, and education, especially as it enhances the understanding of
the social structuring of authority and affective relations. In the
second section, the discussion broadens to include cultural values,
ideologies, and purposive group action in addition to social-structural
relations. SMELSER and HALPERN use these concepts to develop a general
model of change through which new structural arrangements relevant to
family life are generated. It not only accounts for some of the social-
historical developments under discussion, but also helps to explain
the "invention" and evolution of age categories and age norms. The
third and final section focuses on the study of the life cycle. The
authors posit that the concept of structural differentiation, which has

been widely applied in institutional analysis but seldom to the organization
of the life course, is useful in explaining a number of broad historical
trends in age grading.

(IX.B.3.) Kolko, Gabriel
                1978 "Working Wives: Their Effects on the Structure
                      of the Working Class." Science and Society 42
                      (Fall): 257-277.

The history of the American working class and how it has been shaped
by the structural dilemmas of capitalism, has thus far devoted too little
attention to defining the role of working women, writes KOLKO. The
phenomenon of the working woman has been erroneously viewed as a question
of the "white collar" occupations rather than a problem of defining
the exact social character of these workers and their fundamental relationship to working men, whom they marry, and of the forces which push them
into the labor market. Kolko proceeds to outline certain of the main
facts about changes since 1900 and then briefly explores the analytical
conclusions which can be reasonably drawn from these facts. Subtopics
include the growth of the female workforce, expansion and transformation
of the labor supply, growth of the available labor mass, the structure
of women's occupations, the expansion of the proletariat, and the
income of the working class. His focus is on married women workers,
including some consideration of their impact upon family life.

(IX.B.4.) Fruin, W. Mark
                1980 "The Family as a Firm and the Firm as a
                      Family in Japan: The Case of Kikkoman Shōyu
                      Company Limited." The Journal of Family
                      History 5 (Winter): 432-449.

It is often argued that the key relationship in Japanese social structure
in both preindustrial and industrial periods is that of kinship. Business
firms are commonly said to operate "like a family." Yet this family-firm
analogy is often misleading, says FRUIN, because its character is usually
symbolic or ideological--not descriptive. In this article he examines
the relationship between family and firm in the case of the Kikkoman Shōyu
Company Limited, which is known in Japan as a "family firm" and has for
nearly 300 years used the combined efforts of family and firm for
entreprenurial success. The findings indicate the close and constant
interaction of family and firm, but family and firm were and are different
and distinguishable. The family-firm analogy is held to be historically
inappropriate when applied to Kikkoman as well as other larger, more
mature, more diversified, and internationally known firms in Japan today.
The genealogical, the ideological, the culutral, and the socio-economic
uses of the family analogy in Japan must be descriptively and conceptually
separated in order to avoid ambiguity and imprecision.

(IX.B.5.) Vanek, Joann
           1980 "Work, Leisure, and Family Roles: Farm
                 Households in the United States, 1920-1955."
                 Journal of Family History 5 (Winter): 422-431.

Based on time-budget data for U.S. farm households, this study identifies
several changes between 1920 and 1955; industrialization segregated the
work activities of husbands and wives, encouraged segregated leisure
activities for husbands but not for wives, and lessened the interweaving
of work and family activities throughout the day. Hence the nature of
family interaction changed. The specific activities and daily/weekly
routines during the 1920s are sketched. VANEK calls for more study of
the forces that held women in the home for such a long time after the loss
of their gainful role in the household economy.

On the family in the larger economy, see also V.E.2., I.B.1., IV.D.7.,
X.G.6., and VI.A.5.

IX.C. EDUCATION

(IX.C.1.) Graff, Harvey J.
                1979 "Literacy, Education, and Fertility, Past
                and Present: A Critical Review." Population
                and Development Review 5 (March): 105-140.

Many contemporary and historical studies on the role of literacy and
education in changing fertility patterns are reviewed and critiqued,
including special attention to inadequacies in how the role of education
is conceptualized. Subtopics include major theoretical explanations
(economic demographic transition and modernization theories) as well as
problems common to education-fertility analysis. GRAFF concludes that
future research would benefit from a more basic, critical, and realistic
conceptualization of the role of education; education should more often
be seen as exerting its influence over fertility less directly and less
linearly, functioning and meditating through and with other structural
and attitude-shaping factors.

On education, see also IX.B.2.

IX.D. WELFARE AND PUBLIC POLICY: REVIEWS OF MAJOR BOOKS

(IX.D.1.) Sennett, Richard
1980 "Exploding the Nuclear Family." New York
Times Book Review (Februray 24): 3,39.

Review of: Jacques Donzelot (translated by
Robert Hurley), 1979, The Policing of Families.
New York: Pantheon.

The history of the family became a primary concern of historians and
sociologists in the United States, in part because of the feminist
movement, in part because of the interest in the connection between the
family and poverty spurred by the Moynihan report, and in part because
of the work a number of European scholars who influenced a new generation
of scholars in the United States did, writes SENNET. One such scholar
is French sociologist Jacques Donzelot, whose book has now been translated
into English. His Policing of Families describes how the laws of the
state and the precepts of the professions have shaped middle-class and
working-class families in very different ways. The central question
is the relation between sociability and family life. Because two centuries
of educators, psychologists, and doctors defined sociability in terms
of family images, more and more pressure has been put on the family as
a place in which the idealized virtues of socability should be realized.
From this perspective, the very instability of the family is what
makes it such an attractive target for the forces of regulation, inviting
continual "policing"--the creation of ever-new forms of control.

Sennett compares this book with Lasch's Haven in a Heartless World, which
pictured the history of the modern bourgeois family as one of the state
"invading" the functions of the family via welfare bureaucracies,
psychiatric controls, etc. For Donzelot, the invasion image is wrong;
since the mid-18th century, the state has actively participated in
creating the forms of family life that we know today. He lacks Lasch's
nostalgia for the virtues of the 19th century bourgeois family and also
has a sharper interest in questions of social class.

On Donzelot (1979), see also IX.D.2. On Lasch (1977), see IX.D.4-7 and
V.C.2.

(IX.D.2.) Lasch, Christopher
1980 "Life in the Theraputic State." The New
York Review of Books 27 (June 12): 24-32.

Review of:

Carl N. Degler, 1980, At Odds: Women and the
Family in America from the Revolution to the
Present. New York: Oxford University Press.

Michel Foucault (Robert Hurley, translator),
1978, The History of Sexuality. Volume 1: An
Introduction. New York: Pantheon.

Jacques Donzelot (Robert Hurley, translator),
1979, The Policing of Families. New York: Pantheon.

LASCH reviews three recent books on the history of the family and sexuality,
with a detailed discussion of their contributions to our understanding
of how outside agencies gained more control over domestic life. Degler's
book on the American family points out that women actively used Victorian
sexual norms and the "cult of domesticity" ideology to win greater
autonomy and control. Unfortunately, according to Lasch, the achievement
of individualism and autonomy for middle-class women represented part
of a larger process that ended in the ascendancy of professional experts,
who expanded their jurisdiction over domestic life not only at the
expense of patriarchal authority but also at the expense of the authority
formerly exercised by women over childbirth, child rearing, and domestic
economy. Foucault takes issue for France, as Degler does for America,
with the notion that 19th century sex was surrounded by a conspiracy
of silence. The achievement of sexual freedom is seen as an aspect of
the medicalization of life, the extension of medical jusrisdiction over
sex. Donzelot extends Foucault's line of analysis to the French family per
se; women's role as cultural missionaries, closely bound up with their
domestic confinement but simultaneously serving to justify their demands
for wider social influence, was to some extent the deliberate creation
of physicians seeking to make wives and mothers agents of medical
influence. He also discusses the "domestication of the poor," where
reformers sought to encourage orderly habits of domesticity by using
wives as arbitrators of domestic morality. See also V.B.8., V.B.9.,
V.C.5., and IX.D.1.

(IX.D.3.) Lasch, Christopher
            1977 "The Siege of the Family." New York Review
            of Books 24 (November 24): 15-18.

            Review of: Kenneth Keniston and the Carnegie
            Council on Children, 1977 (paperback edition
            1978), All Our Children: The American Family
            Under Pressure. New York: Harcourt, Brace,
            Jovanovich.

This is not so much a summary as a critique of Keniston's report on
the family, which LASCH uses as a starting point for discussing his
own views about the "invasion" of the modern family by outside experts
and agencies. The family's dependence on professional services over
which it has little control is one form of a more general phenomenon,
the erosion of self-reliance and ordinary competence by the growth
of giant corporations and of the bureaucratic state which serves them,
according to Lasch. Keniston is right in his observation that experts
have taken over much of the authority and work of child rearing yet
left parents with most of the blame for whatever goes wrong; but he merely seeks to regularize and regulate the relationship between family and

experts, to use federal policy to equalize the relationship between experts and parents. Keniston's hope that the state can provide needed services to the family without undermining parental authority and competence even further is unrealistic; not the family but only the professions are strengthened by well-meaning increases in professional services.

(IX.D.4.) Berman, Marshall
             1978 "Family Affairs." New York Times Book
                   Review (January 15): 6-7, 20.

                   Review of: Christopher Lasch, 1977, Haven
                   in a Heartless World: The Family Besieged.
                   New York: Basic Books.

(IX.D.5.) Joffe, Carole
             1978 "What Haven? For Whom?" Social Policy 9
                   (May/June): 58-60.

                   Review of: Christopher Lasch, 1977, Haven
                   in a Heartless World: The Family Besieged.
                   New York: Basic Books.

(IX.D.6.) Davis, David Brion
             1978 "The Invasion of the Family." New York
                   Review of Books 25 (February 23): 37-39.

                   Review of: Christopher Lasch, 1977, Haven
                   in a Heartless World: The Family Besieged.
                   New York: Basic Books.

(IX.D.7.) Rosenberg, Bella H.
             1979 "Private Lives, Public Lies." Harvard
                   Educational Review 49 (May): 231-239.

                   Review of: Christopher Lasch, 1977, Haven
                   in a Heartless World: The Family Besieged.
                   New York: Basic Books.

Christopher Lasch's controversial book, Haven in a Heartless World: The Family Besieged, has received much attention and even more criticism. BERMAN notes that he has produced a study, not of the family, but of the study of the family. Lasch plays Marxism and psychoanalysis off each other, in the end offering a pseudo-Marxist conspiracy theory, blaming the crisis of the family upon The Professionals (teachers, pediatricians, social workers, psychoanalysts, sociologists, etc.). Other reviewers such as JOFFE accuse him of denying the historical complexity of family life, neglecting the obvious point that family life is experienced differently by different family members. Lasch's mourning for the lost authority of the family (really lost male authority in the patriarchal family) neglects the fact that what may have been satisfying to fathers may have been oppressive to children and mothers. Also, he underestimates the real benefits achieved by social services.

DAVIS's review gives more attention to the first section of the book, where the ideas of such social theorists as Talcott Parsons, Willard Waller, and Erik Erikson are discussed. ROSENBERG notes that this book is more an indictment of the theory and practice of social science than it is family history. Lasch sees an unmistakable relation between social science and the modern capitalism which has (together with government and professionals) essentially destroyed private life; professionals socialized reproduction and thereby consummated the process that began with the socialization of production. Much as political economy justified capitalism, social science provided the rationale to justify making families dependent on professionals.

On Lasch (1977), see also V.C.2. For other book reviews regarding welfare and public policy, see VI.A.1.

IX.E. WELFARE AND PUBLIC POLICY: *OTHER WORKS*

(IX.E.1.) Cavallo, Dom
             1976 "Social Reform and the Movement to
                   Organize Children's Play During the
                   Progressive Era." The Journal of
                   Psychohistory: History of Childhood
                   Quarterly 3 (Spring): 509-522.

One of the most distinctive features of the Progressive Era (1890-1920)
was the concern of American reformers with the impact of urban-industrial
life upon the moral, intellectual and physical welfare of children.
CAVALLO discusses a previously ignored dimension of "child-saving"
during this era, namely the movement to organize the play and games
of children, particularly immigrant children living in urban slums.
The play movement emphasized peer group moral sanctions, group interaction
premised upon traditional American democratic values, and loyalty and
cooperation. The team experience was viewed by reformers as a panacea
for three of the most acute problems of urban-industrial America: the
demise of pre-industrial institutions for the socialization of the child,
the conundrum of immigrant acculturation, and the economic and social
anarchy spawned by unrestrained individualism. As envisioned by play
advocates, the team experience would render inocuous the youth's
"insides"--his wholly personal realm of affects, ideals and moral
decision-making--by transforming them into rational procedures necessary
for successful participation in the means-end structure of the team
game. Hence, the positive response of his age-peer groups--without
which these games had neither meaning nor value--would be exchanged
in later life for positive responses from his class or professional
group.

(IX.E.2.) Featherstone, Joseph
             1979 "Family Matters." Harvard Educational
                   Review 49 (February): 20-52.

That the family has become a major focus for American educators, policy
makers, and researchers is partially the result of the particular
constellation of events that are now referred to as "the sixties,"
which FEATHERSTONE recounts in detail. His essay also includes a
discussion of such influential works as Christopher Lasch's The Culture
of Narcissism (New York: Norton, 1979), Mary Jo Bane's Here to Stay
(New York: Basic Books, 1977), and Kenneth Keniston's All Our Children
(New York: Harcourt, Brace, Jovanovich, 1977).

He warns of the danger inherent in seeking private solutions to problems
that are collective in nature and presents his perspective on why the
family is now the focus of so many political and policy debates. The
new interest in families has its merits, says Featherstone, but it will
have done us all a disservice if it turns us away from public issues
to private matters: a vision of things that has no room for the inner
life is bankrupt, but a psychology without social analysis or politics
is both powerless and very lonely.

(IX.E.3.) Laslett, Peter
              1979 "The Family and the Collectivity." <u>Sociology</u>
                    <u>and Social Research</u> 63 (3): 432-442.

LASLETT writes that the collectivity is all of society which is outside
the little knot of father and mother, man and wife, parent and child,
cousin, uncle, and other relatives we think of as "the family." An
important feature of the collectivity, which includes Church, State,
economic and volunteer organizations, is that it performs welfare
functions, i.e., functions which families themselves cannot always
accomplish alone. To study the history of the family adequately, the
relationship between the family and collectivity must be realized;
all social relations--not only emotional and familial ones--must be
taken into account. This article, admittedly an exploratory and preliminary
statement, discusses the interdependency of the family and the collectivity
and applies this concept to western European and Anglo-Saxon familial
systems where the family is small, where it contains few relations, and
where old people--widowed mothers and ailing kinfolk--are and have been
required to live by themselves as far as possible. To the extent that
the family system has been nuclear, it has probably always required
the support of some form of collectivity or welfare state, hypothesizes
Laslett.

(IX.E.4.) Zaretsky, Eli
              1982 "The Place of the Family in the Origins
                    of the Welfare State." In Barrie Thorne
                    with Marilyn Yalom, editors, <u>Rethinking</u>
                    <u>the Family: Some Feminist Questions</u>, 188-224.
                    New York: Longman.

ZARETSKY re-examines the origins of the welfare state in America,
acknowledging the importance of trade-union protectionism and middle-
class reform as well as early 20th century urban liberalism and,
especially, feminism. It is the class and sexual structure of American
society, rather than the intentions of any single group, which has
shaped the meaning of diverse reform efforts in unforseen (and still
untheorized) ways. He argues that the family, in the conventional sense
of a private self-supporting nuclear unit, was to a large extent
created or at least reconstituted by the modern state, first in the liberal
or laissez-faire and then in the welfare phases of its history. The
welfare state has had destructive effects on women; reasons for the
failure of the feminist movement to forsee the negative side of the
reforms it endorsed are explored. Far from the state "invading" or
"replacing" the family, a certain kind of alienated public life and a
certain kind of alienated private life have expanded together. The
form in which the welfare state expanded was public, the content private.

THE MILITARY

IX.F. <u>WAR AND THE FAMILY</u>

(IX.F.1.) Taylor, Peter, and Hermann Rebel
            1981 "Hessian Peasant Women, Their Families, and
                  the Draft: A Social-Historical Interpretation
                  of Four Tales from the Grimm Collection."
                  <u>Journal of Family History</u> 6 (Winter): 347-378.

This study deals with the impact of the military draft system on rural
peasant life. Late 18th century Hesse-Cassel--a state financed by the
leasing of drafted mercenaries--is the case in point. The focus is on
the peasant mentalité, on the perceived effects of the draft upon such
aspects of rural life as the relations between the sexes and among family
members, the devolution of rights and properties, and social success
and failure. The sources for this investigation are four stories from
the Grimm collection. Treated as historical sources, whose largely
feminine origins make them especially relevant to the history of Hessian
peasant women, these German fairy tales reveal a relatively sophisticated
social intelligence capable of identifying the connections among the
state system, the draft, the private family, and the larger society.
TAYLOR and REBEL's subtopics include: mentalité, fairy tales, and historical
change; the storytellers; the tales; and the draft, dispossessions,
and women's action.

IX.G. <u>*DISSERTATIONS*</u>

(IX.G.1.)   Uttrachi, Patricia Branca
            1973 <u>Health and Household: Material Culture of</u>
                  <u>Middle-Class Women in Nineteenth-Century</u>
                  <u>Britain</u>. Unpublished Ph.D. dissertation,
                  Rutgers University, New Brunswick, New Jersey.

(IX.G.2.)   Sa, Sophie
            1975 <u>Family and Community in Urban Taiwan: Social</u>
                  <u>Status and Demographic Strategy Among Taipei</u>
                  <u>Households, 1885-1935</u>. Unpublished Ph.D.
                  dissertation, Harvard University.

(IX.G.3.)   Shaffer, John Wesley
            1979 <u>Family and Farm: Agrarian Change and Household</u>
                  <u>Organization in the French Nivernais</u>. Unpublished
                  Ph.D. dissertation, UCLA, Los Angeles, California.

IX.H. PUBLICATIONS

(IX.H.1.) Johnson, A. H.
          1978 "Impact of Market Agriculture on Family and
               Household Structure in 19th-Century Chile."
               Hispanic American Historical Review 58 (Number 4):
               625-648.

(IX.H.2.) Moran, G. F.
          1979 "Religious Renewal, Puritan Tribalism, and the
               Family in 17th-Century Milford, Connecticut."
               William and Mary Quarterly 36 (Number 2): 236-254.

(IX.H.3.) Scott, R. B., and M. R. Winston
          1976 "Health and Welfare of Black Family in United
               States--Historical and Institutional Analysis."
               American Journal of Diseases of Children 130
               (Number 7): 704-707.

(IX.H.4.) Goldin, Claudia
          1981 "Family Strategies and the Family Economy in
               the Late Nineteenth Century: The Role of
               Secondary Workers." In Theodore Hershberg,
               editor, Philadelphia: Work, Space, Family, and
               Group Experience in the 19th Century, 277-310.
               London, England, and New York: Oxford University
               Press.

(IX.H.5.) Haines, Michael R.
          1981 "Poverty, Economic Stress, and the Family in
               a Late Nineteenth-Century American City:
               Whites in Philadelphia, 1880." In Theodore
               Hershberg, editor, Philadelphia: Work, Space,
               Family, and Group Experience in the 19th Century,
               240-276. London, England, and New York: Oxford
               University Press.

X. METHODOLOGY: RESEARCH AND TEACHING

RESEARCH: COMPUTER MICRO-SIMULATION

X.A. COMPUTER MICROSIMULATION: REVIEWS OF MAJOR BOOKS

(X.A.1.) Haines, Michael R.
          1980 "Computer Simulation and Modelling in
                Historical Demography." Journal of
                Family History 5 (Winter): 450-454.

                Review of: Kenneth W. Wachter with Eugene
                A. Hammel and Peter Laslett, 1977, Statistical
                Studies of Historical Social Structure. New
                York: Academic Press.

Under review here is the joint effort in historical household simulation
by Wachter, Hammel, and Laslett. HAINES explains that the book's first
five chapters contain the "core" of the research effort, and that the
last six chapters are actually a series of essays exploring simulation
experiments and the application of statistical techniques to historical
evidence. Chapter four is of special interest because it is the introduction
of a method for presenting three dimensions of data in a two dimensional
plane--otherwise known as a triangular plot. This is a technical book
aimed at readers interested in the mechanics of simulation and statistical
modelling. The reviewer notes that one of the major questions raised in
this study is still unanswered, namely why there were so few complex
households in early modern England. For another review of Wachter et al.
(1977/78), see also X.B.5.

X.B.   COMPUTER MICROSIMULATION: OTHER WORKS

(X.B.1.)   Hammel, E. A.
           1979 "Experimental History." Journal of
                 Anthropological Research 35 (Fall):
                 274-291.

(X.B.2.)   Hammel, E. A., and Kenneth W. Wachter
           1977 "Primonuptiality and Ultimonuptiality:
                 Their Effects on Stem-Family-Household
                 Fequencies." In R. Lee, editor, Population
                 Patterns in the Past, 113-134. New York:
                 Academic Press.

(X.B.3.)   Hammel, E. A., D. W. Hutchinson, K. W. Wachter, R. T. Lundy,
           and R. Z. Deuel
           1976 SOCSIM: Demographic-Sociological
                 Microsimulation Program Operating
                 Manual. Research Series 27. Berkeley:
                 University of California, Institute for
                 International Studies.

(X.B.4.)   Hammel, E. A., and R. Z. Deuel
           1977 Five Classy Programs: Computer Procedures
                 for the Classification of Households.
                 Research Series 33. Berkeley: University
                 of California, Institute for International
                 Studies.

(X.B.5.)   Fitch, Nancy
           1980 "The Household and the Computer: A Review."
                 Historical Methods 13 (Spring) 127-137.

                 Review of: Kenneth W. Wachter, with Eugene
                 A. Hammel and Peter Laslett, 1978, Statistical
                 Studies of Historical Social Structure. New
                 York: Academic Press.

(X.B.6.)   Hammel, E. A.
           1980-a "Household Structure in Fourteenth Century
                 Macedonia." Journal of Family History 5 (Fall):
                 242-273.

(X.B.7.)   Hammel, E. A.
           1980-b "Sensitivity Analysis of Household Structure
                 in Medieval Serbian Censuses." Historical
                 Methods 13 (Spring): 105-118.

(X.B.8.)   Hammel, Eugene A., Chad K. McDaniel, and Kenneth W. Wachter
           1980 "Vice in the Villefranchian: A Microsimulation
                 Analysis of the Demographic Effects of
                 Incest Prohibitions." In B. Dyke and W. Morrill,
                 editors, Genealogical Demography, 209-234. New
                 York: Academic Press.

(X.B.9.) Hammel, E. A.
         1976   "The Matrilateral Implications of Structural
                Cross-Cousin Marriage." In E. Zubrow, editor,
                Demographic Anthropology: Quantitative Approaches,
                145-168. Albuquerque, New Mexico: University of
                New Mexico Press.

Microsimulation, it is claimed, is frequently more reliable than "analytic
modelling" (the latter involving mathematical calculations of central
tendencies of statistical aggregates, done either with pencil and paper
or by computer macrosimulation). A microsimulation begins with a computerized
model of a population having the demographic characteristics, kinship
structures, modes of inheritance, and other traits thought to have been
typical for a given village or region at a particular historical time-point.
Using the Monte Carlo technique, the computer repeatedly "spins the
roulette wheel" for each of the individuals in the population. Individuals
are followed from birth to death, as are their children and their
children's children, etc., their chances of marrying or divorcing,
giving birth, changing households, inheriting property, or dying at
a particular age being determined by average risk-rates (derived from
empirical data or from a theory being tested). After a number of "years"
have passed, the end-state of the model is compared with empirical data
about this later historical time-period; the goodness-of-fit between
model and observed data is one way to evaluate the plausibility of the
theory/explanation/principle being tested. It can also be used to
evaluate whether actual empirical differences found, e.g., between two
villages, could have been due to sampling errors or to chance variation
alone.

In the U.S., much microsimulation has been done at Berkeley by Eugene
Hammel, Kenneth Wachter, Chad McDaniel, and others.

The best non-technical introduction to this work is HAMMEL (1979), which
provides a bibliography and a readable introduction to how microsimulation
has been applied in several areas: the effect of marriage impediments,
such as incest prohibitions of varying severity, upon population size;
the extinction of patrilines; testing the utility of genealogical
indicators as substitutes for data on demographic rates; projecting the
kindred which the aged will have in the year 2000 under varying fertility
levels; and the frequency of stem families which would obtain under
three rules of household formation and 15 different sets of (plausibly
possible) demographic conditions (on the latter, see also HAMMEL and
WACHTER, 1977).

Researchers who want to use the SOCSIM Demographic-Sociological Microsimulation Program should correspond first with Hammel (Anthropology,
University of California, Berkeley, California 94720). The current
version is only for the CDC 7600 computer, although rewriting to make
it less machine-dependent is underway. For approximately $150, payable
to the Regents of the University of California, one receives the operating
manual (HAMMEL, HUTCHINSON, WACHTER, LUNDY, and DEUEL, 1976), plus
updates, documentation tapes, and five additional programs(HAMMEL and
DEUEL, 1977).

The major book-length collection on microsimulation is Wachter, Hammel, and

Laslett (1978). For a criticism of the shortcomings of this book, see FITCH (1980). For very recent microsimulation studies on household structures, see HAMMEL (1980 a and b); on demographic effects of incest, see HAMMEL, McDANIEL, and WACHTER (1980). An older article on cross-cousin marriage is HAMMEL (1976).

See X.A.1. for another review of Wachter et al. (1977/78).

X.C. _QUANTITATIVE HANDLING OF ANTHROPOLOGICAL AND CROSS-CULTURAL DATA_

(X.C.1.) Hammel, E. A., and Djordje Šoć
1973 "The Lineage Cycle in Southern and Eastern Yugoslavia." American Anthropologist 75 (June): 802-814.

(X.C.2.) Hammel, E. A.
1972 "The Zadruga as Process." In Peter Laslett with Richard Wall, editors, Household and Family in Past Time. Oxford, England, and New York: Cambridge University Press.

(X.C.3.) Hammel, E. A.
1975 "Reflections on the Zadruga." Ethnologia Slavica 7 (Bratislava): 141-151.

(X.C.4.) Hammel, E. A., and Charles Yarbrough
"Social Mobility and the Durability of Family Ties." Journal of Anthropological Research 29 (Autumn): 145-163.

(X.C.5.) Hammel, E. A., and Peter Laslett
1974 "Comparing Household Structure Over Time and Between Cultures." Comparative Studies in Society and History 16 (January): 73-109.

Computer-assisted analysis of empirical data (i.e., "real" rather than simulated data) has been a second branch in the family history work of Hammel and certain colleagues. Although relevant to various substantive topics, most of these articles are of special interest for their quantitative handling of anthropological and historical data and hence are listed together here. His empirical studies in the last decade have concerned the development of Serbian kinship systems and household structures (HAMMEL and ŠOĆ, 1973; HAMMEL 1972 and 1975), the effect of migration and social mobility upon kinship and family systems in modern times (HAMMEL and YARBROUGH, 1973), and medieval studies in search of a tradition baseline-of-comparison (see X.B.6. and X.B.7.). Also see HAMMEL and LASLETT (1974) for a consideration of how to compare household structure across time and cultures.

X.D. RECORD LINKAGE AND FAMILY RECONSTITUTION

(X.D.1.) Hastings, Donald W., and Jerry N. Harrison
1979 "A Note on the Use of SPSS Control Cards
to Create Selected Algorithms for Manipulation
of Data Obtained from Family Reconstruction
Forms." Historical Methods 12 (Summer):
129-136.

After nominal record linkage has been completed, there still remains
the sizeable task of preparing data derived from family reconstitution
forms for statistical analysis. The exact control cards necessary to
accomplish this job using the Statistical Package for the Social Sciences
(SPSS) are specified by HASTINGS and HARRISON, including those necessary
to compute (for husband-wife units) age, marital rank of each spouse,
fertility variables of parity and childspacing and age of mother at
birth, husband's age at first marriage, time interval between marriages,
age differences between spouses, husband's total years spent in marriage,
etc. How to create fixed-length card sets for each family unit (husband
plus his wife or wives and any children) is also briefly described. The
appendix reproduces the variable list, recode, and other control cards
used for a study of Mormon records on a Utah (USA) community between
1849 and 1948.

(X.D.2.) Bouchard, Gerard, and Christian Pouyez
1980 "Name Variations and Computerized Record
Linkage." Historical Methods 13 (Spring):
119-126.

As a part of a family reconstitution project for the whole Saguenay
region in Quebec, Canada, a set of record-linkage computer programs
has been developed. A major problem in record linkage is that the same
person's name may be spelled differently in different records. These
four programs, applied sequentially, resulted in the automatic linkage
of 98.5 per cent of the pairs which could be linked, in one test on
2,000 records. For maximum reliability, the most fundamental rule
is never to link records for individuals but rather for pairs of
individuals (e.g., for married couples).

X.E. *INVENTORY ANALYSIS*

(X.E.1.) Carr, Lois Green, and Lorena S. Walsh
               1980   "Inventories and the Analysis of Wealth
                      and Consumption Patterns in St. Mary's
                      County, Maryland, 1658-1777." Historical
                      Methods 13 (Spring): 81-104.

CARR and WALSH provide an introduction to one source of historical
data, probate inventories (lists of the property people own at death)
of the English colonies in America, particularly those in the Chesapeake
Bay region. As an example of inventory analysis, the authors' study
of lifestyles in St. Mary's County, Maryland (1658-1777) is described
in detail. The appendix discusses techniques for standardization of
inventory data (controlling for price inflation and the adjustments
necessary before one can make valid inferences about the living from
records of the dead).

X.F. *MULTIVARIATE STATISTICAL ANALYSIS: PROBIT, LOGIT, TOBIT, ETC.*

(X.F.1.) Shammas, Carole
1981 "Dealing with Dichotomous Dependent
Variables." Historical Methods 14
(Winter): 47-51.

Certain types of quantitative analysis are only appropriate for specific
levels of measurement (interval, ordinal, or nominal variables). Some
nominal-level variables are dichotomous, for example, gender (male/
female), a woman's labor-force participation (yes/no), etc. When the
dependent variable is dichotomous--or can be made into a dichotomous
dummy variable--probit analysis (employing maximum likelihood estimates)
is superior in accuracy to ordinary least squares regression in many
situations where the relationship between variables is not linear. The
SHAMMAS article describes probit analysis, in as non-technical language
as possible, as compared to ordinary least squares regression. Probit
analysis cannot be used if there is only one independent variable or if
the dependent variable cannot be collapsed into two categories, and its
advantages are lost if the sample size is too small. (If the dependent
variable is nominal level but has three or more categories, logit or
discriminant analysis may be used. For "limited" dependent variables--
i.e., basically interval but bounded in some manner--a maximum likelihood
estimation model such as tobit is applicable.) Additional references
are cited for probit, logit, tobit, and discriminant analysis.

For an example of tobit analysis with limited dependent variables, see
VIII.B.3. An example of probit analysis is IX.A.1.

(X.F.2.) Kousser, J. Morgan, Gary W. Cox, and David W. Galenson
1982 "Log-Linear Analysis of Contingency Tables:
An Introduction for Historians With an
Application to Thernstrom on the 'Floating
Proletariat.'" Social Science Working Paper
417, California Institute of Technology,
Division of Humanities and Social Sciences.
(Pasadena, California 91125.)

For historians or other social scientists whose data are available in
discrete (nominal or ordinal level) form, recently developed "log-linear"
multivariate statistical techniques are in many respects superior to
such multivariate methods as multiple classification analysis, weighted
least-squares, and logit. Reanalyzing Thernstrom's Boston data on geographic
mobility, KOUSSER, COX, and GALENSON explain the ideas behind and the
procedures of log-linear analysis explicitly, step-by-step. Someone
already familiar with statistics such as multiple regression, they
claim, should be able to perform log-linear analysis after reading this
paper. Additional references on this technique are cited in endnote 5
of their paper.

G

X.G. *DATA BANKS AND DATA SETS*

(X.G.1.) Bean, Lee L., Dean L. May, and Mark Skolnick
1978 "The Mormon Historical Demography
Project." Historical Methods 11
(Winter): 45-53.

This paper outlines one component of a major research effort involving
physicians, epidemiologists, statisticians, biostatisticians, geneticists,
demographers, sociologists, and historians. While teams of these researchers
pursue certain independent objectives, they are all linked together
through the development and use of a single core data base: a set of
family records for Mormon families who experienced a birth, death, and/or
marriage on the Mormon pioneer trail or in the U.S. state of Utah. This
data base includes over 8 million "family group sheets"; its history and
contents are briefly described.

The major focus of the article is the work of one research team, the
Mormon Historical Demography Project. BEAN, MAY, and SKOLNICK describe
their goals and also discuss the quality and evaluation of the data,
completeness of the genealogical records, representativeness of these
records, and preliminary findings. Other researchers are encouraged to
utilize this computerized data base, located at the University of Utah
in Salt Lake City, Utah, to study populations in both the United States
and Europe.

(X.G.2.) Skolnick, Mark, Lee L. Bean, Sue M. Dintelman, and Geraldine
Mineau
1979 "A Compterized Family History Data Base
System." Sociology and Social Research
63 (Number 3): 506-523.

Described here is the development of a unique, computer-based data
management system designed to increase the ability of social historians
and historical demographers to collate and analyze large quantities
of historical data (data manipulation and automatic record linkage).
The Mormon historical demography research project, for which the system
was developed, is briefly described. Three features of the system
are outlined in detail--the file structure, input systems, and data
access facilities. The paper includes an illustration of the types
of analysis which are possible through this type of computerized
system.

(X.G.3.) Austin, Erik W.
1979 "The Historical Data Resources of the
Inter-University Consortium for Political
and Social Research." Historical Social
Research/Historische Sozialforschung Number
12 (October): 43-45.

German readers are already familiar with the German journal Historical Social Research, which is published in the English language. Its offerings include brief descriptions of historical data sources in various contries, including the U.S. For example, see AUSTIN's report on computer-readable holdings of the Inter-University Consortium for Political and Social Research (University of Michigan, Ann Arbor, Michigan 48106, U.S.A.). This data bank gives researchers access to such data sets as the U.S. census (1790 to 1970) and the French census (1801 to 1926), part of Fogel and Engermann's Time on the Cross data on slavery in the U.S., and Goldin's population samples for 1870 and 1880 for seven southern U.S. cities. Write Austin at the above address for a free copy of the ICPSR's Guide to Resources and Services.

(X.G.4.) Soliday, Gerald L.
            1977 "Marburg in Upper Hesse: A Research
                  Project." Journal of Family History
                  2: 164-168.

SOLIDAY's project is a social history of Marburg, Germany, from the mid-16th century to the beginning of the 19th, and investigates urban social groups and institutions in their larger regional context. This brief progress report focuses on the use of Marburg sources, and indicates the direction of the research and some preliminary findings as well.

An abundance of sources were available for early modern Marburg, including municipal and territorial tax records, surveys of property holdings, and censuses. Together, these data will help to determine the size of the population and to examine property relations, the occupational and social structure, and the social geography of the city for five time points (1580, 1620, 1676-77, 1731, and 1771).

The tax registers provide assessments of each taxpayer's wealth and his tax payments, in addition to identifying the propertyless and the privileged elite, and will provide an important basis for analysis of economic stratification. Further, a series of Kontributionsrechnungen from 1721 to 1771 breaks the wealth assessments into distinct categories that make it possible to identify the exact nature of an individual's wealth as well as the class structure of the community. Perhaps the most remarkable of the sources described is the Marburger Sippenbuch assembled by Dr. Kurt Stahr, a twenty-three volume reconstitution of all Marburg families.

On data resources on Germany, see also the Imhof citation under VII.E.1.

(X.G.5.) National Immigration Archives
            forthcoming A series of volumes of passenger lists of
                          immigrants entering U.S. ports. See
                          description below.

From the "Immigration Data Base" of the National Immigration Archives, a number of publications are in preparation, including lists of British immigrants who arrived in New York between 1846 and 1850 (forthcoming

ca. 1984) and passenger lists of "famine" Irish arrivals in New York
for the same dates (Baltimore, Maryland: Genealogical Publishing Co.).
Ultimately, the data base will index immigrants arriving in the port
of New York from 1846 until 1896. Direct inquiries to: I.A. Glazier,
Director, National Immigration Archives, Temple University at the Balch
Institute, 18 South 7th Street, Philadelphia, Pennsylvania 19106.

(X.G.6.) Kleinberg, Susan J.
                1975 "The Systematic Study of Urban Women."
                      Historical Methods Newsletter 9 (December):
                      14-25.

This essay examines the relationship of urbanization and industrialization
to women's economic, cultural, social, and political activities, primarily
in the United States. The first part explores the determinants of female
labor force participation and the nature of women's work, while the second
part concentrates on the methodology and techniques for use in the study
of women in the city. Some findings noted in part one include: (1) the
occupational structure within the area as the most important factor in
determining whether or not a woman worked outside the home; (2) a dramatic
variance in the percentage of the female labor force as a function of
the industrial, social, ethnic, and racial composition of the area;
and (3) cities with mixed industrial bases allowed women more opportunities
to work, either in industry or domestic service. In the second part of
this paper, KLEINBERG suggests utilizing collective sources and quantitative
techniques to aid in the systematic study of urban women. The detailed
list of suggested sources and their specific uses includes census
returns, marriage and death records, city records, etc., which provide a
wide variety of analysis possibilities for the study of such topics as
female occupational and social mobility. Court records (especially
of neighborhood courts) offer another means of examining women's behavior,
and the technique of oral history allows for the understanding of people's
attitudes towards women and women's lives, particularly in the 20th
century. This article presents a quite systematic inventory of questions
to be answered, pointing out key literature and noting topics where
more research is especially needed. A number of relevant publications
are cited in the endnotes.

X.H. ARCHIVAL AND OTHER SOURCES

(X.H.1.) Hughes, Diane Owen
     1974 "Toward Historical Ethnography: Notarial
          Records and Family History in the Middle
          Ages." Historical Methods Newsletter 7
          (March): 61-71.

Historical method is intimately linked to sources. After briefly discussing
various sources on the family in the Middle Ages, and their implications for
methodology, HUGHES turns to formal legal and survey documents such as
notarial records. The advantages and limitations of notarial records
are mentioned. Notarial records lend themselves to a type of anthropological
analysis based on concepts of action set, kin set, and network.

See endnote 12 for the location and holdings of various notarial archives
in Mediterranean Europe, including some holdings also available on
microfilm in certain U.S. libraries.

On archival and other sources, see also VII.C.2., I.E.3., and X.G.6. On
sources for U.S. women's history, see I.F.17.

X.I. _PROBLEMS IN DEMOGRAPHIC ANALYSIS_

(X.I.1.) Spagnoli, Paul G.
    1977 "Population History from Parish Mongraphs:
    The Problem of Local Demographic Variations."
    Journal of Interdisciplinary History 7
    (Winter): 427-452.

There have been many research monographs based on family reconstitution
techniques applied to European and North American parish registers of
baptisms, marriages, and burials. If one wants to be able to generalize--
i.e., to move from parish registers to the history of population--one
must ascertain how representative a parish is of the larger region (in
particular, whether there were sizeable intra-regional variations in
demographic rates). Evidence from France suggests that substantial local
demographic variations did exist in pre-industrial Europe. SPAGNOLI offers
suggestions for future research aimed at developing sampling methods to
overcome the difficulties created by local variations.

(X.I.2.) Smith, Daniel Scott
    1978 "A Community-Based Sample of the Older
    Population from the 1880 and 1900 United
    States Manuscript Census." Historical
    Methods 11 (Spring): 67-74.

SMITH's paper on sampling strategy reports on the decisions and associated
reasoning underlying the samples for a project on the demographic and
social history of old age in late 19th century America. The focus is on
the experience of the black population, in the South, with whites
serving only as a comparison group. Independent samples were drawn
from the 1880 and 1900 U.S. manuscript censuses. A high priority was
assigned to minimizing the difficulties of data gathering. A coding
scheme was devised to obtain the fullest possible information on each
old person and his familial and socioeconomic environment. (Copies of
this codebook are available from the Family and Community History Center,
Newberry Library, 60 West Walton Street, Chicago, Illinois 60610.)
This paper also discusses in detail, for this particular study, the use
and selection of primary sampling units, stratification of primary
sampling units, sampling within the PSU, and sampling and nonsampling
errors. The author notes the importance of sampling design and procedure
as an integral part of research design, emphasizes the importance of
sample stratification, and recommends the utility of the ICPSR tape
for those scholars investigating populations in counties of the United
States.

(X.I.3.) Smith, Daniel Scott
          1979 "The Estimates of Early American Historical
                Demographers: Two Steps Forward, One Step
                Back, What Steps in the Future?" Historical
                Methods 12 (Winter): 24-38.

Inadequate training in demography has led to many errors in the published
demographic history literature written by historians and social scientists,
including some well-knows scholars. SMITH examines many such errors in
the literature on early America, including the problems historians have
had in estimating life tables and the problems of social scientists who
fail to examine the original data or who use questionable methods and
adjustments. Although particularly useful for those who study early
American history, this article's lessons about what mistakes to avoid
and how not to do historical demography may help other scholars as well.

(X.I.4.) Espenshade, Thomas J., and Rachel Eisenberg Braun
          1982 "Life Course Analysis and Multistate
                Demography: An Application to Marriage,
                Divorce, and Remarriage." Journal of
                Marriage and the Family 44 (November):
                1025-1036.

Transitions made by individuals are fundamental to our understanding
of changes in the form and function of families and households. Life
course analysis is a useful framework in which to study these transitions
because individuals spent time in different discrete statuses over their
lifetimes. But individuals' experiences of these statuses do not follow
a linear pattern. Not all individuals experience the same statuses, and
the order in which they occur may differ.

The techniques of multistate demography provide a methodology for analyzing
such transitions in a life course context, according to ESPENSHADE and
EISENBERG. An application of multistate demography to marriage, divorce
and remarriage behavior is described and results of current research on
marital histories are presented.

On problems in demographic analysis, see also VII.E.9. and VII.E.10.

X.J. _ORAL HISTORY_

(X.J.1.) Shopes, Linda
            1981 "The Baltimore Neighborhood Heritage
                  Project: Oral History and Community
                  Involvement." Radical History Review
                  25 (October): 27-44.

This neighborhood history project, which began in 1977, had several aims:
to "democratize" the historical record, from the perspective of the local
citizens themselves; to nurture the self-respect of senior citizens; to
communicate to younger generations a sense of their own family, neighborhood,
and city identities; and finally, to help people in the community to
connect their personal histories with the broader social processes,
and subsequently be moved to a more activist, critical stance with respect
to their own social and economic circumstances.

SHOPES' essay presents the oral history aspect of this project. She
discusses the notion of the "insider's view" of a community, the involvement
of community residents as historians of their own community, and the
potential for community history projects to expand people's understandings
of their own individual histories into a broader social perspective.
Both the limitations and successes of this project are mentioned. Shopes
concludes by suggesting that links between community history projects
and community organizations be developed. The development of such links
may then give a political edge to the historian's work and some perspective
to the community organization's concerns, providing an institutional
framework for bringing historians and residents into a more sustained and
broad-based interaction than is possible from oral history interviews
alone and providing the practical mechanisms by which feelings of
identity and pride evoked by projects can be channeled in the ongoing
lives of communities.

(X.J.2.) Blatt, Marty
            1981 "United States: Massachusetts History
                  Workshop." Radical History Review 25
                  (October): 184-185.

BLATT describes the Massachusetts History Workshop, patterned after
the British History Workshop Movement, which seeks to bring together
historians and the people who actually had--in their younger days--
participated in making the history which historians study. Primarily
focused on community-level labor history, meetings so far have involved
groups of Massachusetts textile workers and former shoe workers.

This brief article is part of a special journal issue on "public history,"
most of which concentrates on communicating historical knowledge to the
general public. But the History Workshop Movements in England and the U.S.
also invite the public to participate in the writing of their own history
and provide historians with an opportunity to receive first-hand feedback
on the accuracy of their research findings. The activities of the British
Movement, described in a related piece by Green, indicate that this approach
can also be applied to topics ranging from the history of education to
ideologies surrounding the home.

X.K. *HANDLING HISTORICAL TIME-CHANGE*

(X.K.1.) Fogel, Robert W., Roderick Floud, Clayne L. Pope, and
          Larry T. Wimmer
                    1982 "Uses of Intergenerational Data Sets in
                          Economic History: The Problem of Time Scales."
                          Unpublished manuscript.

As part of the National Bureau of Economic Research Program in Development
of the American Economy, FOGEL and co-workers are planning to construct
several representative data sets of intergenerationally linked families,
for study of long-term changes in the economy at the microeconomic level.
These data sets require the linking of family histories, probate records,
tax records, manuscript schedules of the census, and medical records.
A series of pilot studies have produced encouraging results, but also
methodological problems such as the handling of the time-variable.

The authors feel that historical events need to be measured on more than
one time scale (e.g., event-specific, life-cycle, intergenerational
scales) in order to maximize explanatory power. Many examples illustrating
the fruitfulness of this multiple-time-scale approach are cited. On this
study, see also VII.H.1.

(X.K.2.) Patterson, Orlando
                    1982 "Persistence, Continuity, and Change in the
                          Jamaican Working-Class Family." Journal of
                          Family History 7 (Summer): 135-161.

One of the most difficult problems facing the student of culture,
writes PATTERSON, is that of deciding whether two corresponding patterns,
separated by time and/or space, are continuous or whether they resemble
each other purely by coincidence. Historians and sociologists concerned
with social change in a general way, however, tend to overlook the
extreme importance of this problem, operating instead within an implicitly
dogmatic criterion of continuity. This essay attempts to clarify this
problem and to underscore its importance to all students of social and
cultural change. He defines and distinguishes between three closely
related concepts (continuity, congruence, and "social persistence")
and establishes criteria for using them. These concepts are then applied
to a case study of social change in the familial patterns of lower-class
Jamaicans. Various types of lower-class mating and familial patterns
are described and related to their socio-ecological contexts, so that
the temporal relationship between these different types of social
organization can be shown.

On handling historical time change, see also IV.B.3.

X.L. OTHER ARTICLES ON RESEARCH METHODOLOGY

(X.L.1.) Kousser, J. Morgan
1982 "Criticisms of Quantitative Social Scientific
History: A Response." Paper given at the First
International Conference on Quantitative
History, Washington,D.C. The author is located
at the Division of Humanities and Social Sciences,
California Institute of Technology, Pasadena,
California 91125.

Under the assumption that quantitative social science history (QUASSH, for
short) has not yet won its battle for legitimacy and that it still needs
to be defended, this paper provides a rebuttal of 13 anti-QUASSH criticisms--
that it is a passing fad, that it hasn't answered the big questions, that
the available historical data is too imprecise to warrant sophisticated
methods of analysis, that it is too expensive and time-consuming, etc.

Other methodology articles: on coding categories, see IV.D.2. and IV.D.3.

X.M. COURSE SYLLABI FOR COLLEGE CLASSES

(X.M.1.) Lyman, Kathleen, and Richard B. Lyman
1981 "History of the Family." Unpublished course syllabus for History 119-2, Spring 1981, Simmons College, Boston, Massachusetts 02115.

(X.M.2.) Johnson, K., M. Slater, F. White, and B. Yngvesson
1982 "Family in Cross Cultural Perspective." Unpublished course syllabus, Spring 1982, School of Social Science Hampshire College, Amherst, Massachusetts 01002.

(X.M.3.) Cerullo, M., K. Johnson, and F. White
1981 "Comparative History of the Family." Unpublished course syllabus for SS 214, Spring 1981, School of Social Science Hampshire College, Amherst, Massachusetts 01002.

(X.M.4.) Lee, Gary R.
1982 "Comparative Family Systems." Unpublished course syllabus for Sociology 451, Spring 1982, Washington State University, Pullman, Washington 99164.

(X.M.5.) Goldfrank, Walter L., editor
1980 Teaching Historical Sociology: A Report Plus Selected Syllabi. Available from: American Sociological Association, ASA Teaching Resources Center, 1722 N. Street, N.W., Washington, D.C. 20036.

(X.M.6.) Thorne, Barrie
1982 "Feminist Theory." Unpublished course syllabus for Sociology 242B, Spring 1982, University of California at Santa Cruz. (Thorne is now at the Sociology Department, Michigan State University, E. Lansing, Michigan 48824.)

A number of scholars have shared with us their unpublished descriptions of college courses, which may provide teachers with ideas about course organization and reading assignments.

For undergraduate courses on the family, see: LYMAN and LYMAN (western history with U.S. focus); JOHNSON et al. and also CERULLO, JOHNSON, and WHITE (two similar interdisciplinary social science courses, including traditional, transitional, and contemporary coverage of Europe, Africa, China, and U.S.); and LEE (cross-cultural sociology course with an historical component).

For a graduate seminar on historical demography, see John Knodel (in GOLDFRANK volume). There is an extensive bibliography on data sources,

analysis techniques (aggregative, household listing, nominal record
linkage, and family reconstitution) and on selected substantive areas
(pre-industrial mortality, migration and mobility and turnover, the
inheritance-family formation link, protoindustrialization and proletarian-
ization, natural fertility and family limitation, fertility-mortality
links). A more recent version is available upon request from Knodel.

For an undergraduate course on feminist theory, see THORNE 1982. Lyman
(see above) also will share a syllabus of his new History of Childhood
course (aimed at master's degree candidates majoring in children's
literature).

X.N. TEXTBOOKS FOR COLLEGE CLASSES

(X.N.1.) Watts, Jim, and Allen F. Davis
1982 Generations: Your Family in Modern American
History. New York: Alfred A. Knopf, Inc.

One way to introduce undergraduate college students--particularly non-history
majors--to family history is to have them do oral-history interviews with
older members of their own families, older neighbors, etc. A widely-used
U.S. history textbook for use with such an approach is WATTS and DAVIS.
It guides students toward questions of how family life was linked to larger
historical forces and events (the great migrations, the Depression, the
World Wars, etc.). The book's 400 pages include many readings covering
the past century up through the 1970s.

A number of other works are also appropriate for classroom use.

> For European family history, see I.D.3. (Mitterauer and Sieder)
> and also V.B.6. on European women's and family history.

> For "readers," see Section I.J. (general family history),
> I.F.1. (European women's history), I.F.2. (U.S. women's
> history), VII.B.1. (U.S. historical demography), and I.F.14
> (U.S. feminist theory).

> Brief introductory articles for adding an historical dimension
> to otherwise non-historical social science courses are cited
> in Section I.K. Also particularly appropriate for such courses
> might be VII.E.4. (social problems courses) and VII.C.4.
> (sociology, psychology, and family relations classes).

> The articles in Section X.O. all have extensive annotated
> bibliographies of articles and books useful for college courses
> in family history.

> Information about a series of recent publications for high school
> students can be obtained by consulting the journal issue cited
> in VII.C.2.

X.O. IDEAS AND TECHNIQUES FOR TEACHING FAMILY HISTORY

(X.O.1.) Beall, Pamela E., Warren Leon, Peter S. O'Connell, and
         Ellen K. Rothman
                1981 "Students and Family History: The View From
                      Sturbridge Village." Journal of Family History
                      6 (Spring): 5-14.

Based upon their extensive teaching experience, BEALL et al. present a
descriptive model of the teaching strategies used in the Old Sturbridge
Village outdoor museum in Massachusetts, for courses on family history.
Step by step, they describe how an extended unit on family history is
taught. The strategy is to select initial student activities which
generate data and hypotheses about family life, first in the present and
then in the past; the students look first at their own lives analytically
and then search for general patterns. The first historical materials
given to students are quantitative--"family role cards" which supply
1820 demographic data on 35 Sturbridge families. These data are evaluated,
starting with one particular individual and working outward to consider
the impact of certain historical forces on his or her life. The use of
artifacts, personal documents, paintings, engaging in activities such
as spinning wool and chopping wood, and the museum environment are also
discussed. The article concludes with five general guidelines for using
this teaching strategy successfully.

A resource packet on Households and Families is also available from Old
Sturbridge Village. (See X.O.2. for address.)

(X.O.2.) Rothman, Ellen K.
                1981 "The Written Record." Journal of Family
                      History 6 (Spring): 47-56.

Collaboration with college teachers and our own field study teaching
at Old Sturbridge Village, writes ROTHMAN, have demonstrated the value
of giving primary sources an important place in the history curriculum.
Toward this objective, a number of teaching approaches were developed
that use primary sources to engage students in thinking about the past.
This essay suggests ways in which documents can be integrated into classroom
teaching. The appendix offers an introductory list of primary sources for
the study of U.S. family history on the college level.

Sample activities described deal with the classroom use of diaries,
autobiographies and correspondences, sometimes in combination with maps,
genealogies, census and tax records. Approaches include the event-
centered and the problem-centered case study, and the structured
research experience (which can also be combined with the case study
approach, focusing on the student's own family). For information about
Old Sturbridge Village Resource Packets of primary sources on childhood,
youth, and courtship and marriage in rural 19th century New England,
contact: Museum Education, Old Sturbridge Village, Sturbridge, Massachusetts
01566.

(X.O.3.) O'Connell, Peter S.
                 1981 "Putting the Historic House Into the Course
                 of History." Journal of Family History 6
                 (Spring): 28-40.

This essay describes the value of a field study of an historic house
to students of family history, and offers suggestions about resources
and activities that help to realize its educational potential. A
successful field experience for students depends on a strong conceptual
framework, knowledge of the relevant resources, and proper sequencing
of problems to investigate. O'CONNELL describes the teaching and learning
strategies to accomplish these objectives, and presents a case study of
the Towne family of Charlton, Massachusetts, as an example of these
strategies in actual practice. The historical house can bring the issues
of family history into focus, and can be an essential component in a
course on family history. Students participate with greater understanding
as they learn how the house can reveal the values and lifestyles of
families in the past.

Specific teaching techniques are described, ranging from scripted historical
drama about the family that lived in the house to techniques of "room
reading" and "mapping." An appendix cites and describes related
literature for teachers and their students.

For teaching U.S. women's history, see also I.F.17.

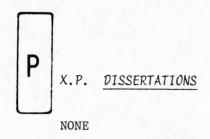

X.P. <u>DISSERTATIONS</u>

NONE

The best general source on research methods is the journal Historical Methods. For the reader's convenience, some relevant articles which were not annotated are listed below. Previously known as the Historical Methods Newsletter, it adopted the current name beginning with Volume II.

Historical Methods, Volume 16 (Number 1): Winter 1983:

(X.Q.1.) Goheen, Peter G.
"Methodology in Historical Geography: The 1970s in Review," 8-15.

Historical Methods, Volume 16 (Number 2): Spring 1983:

(X.Q.2.) Alter, George
"Estimating Mortality from Annuities, Insurance, and Other Life Contingent Contracts," 45-58.

(X.Q.3.) Goldin, Claudia
"Historian's Consensus on the Economic Role of Women in American History: A Review Essay," 74-81.

Historical Methods, Volume 15 (Number 3): Summer 1982:

(X.Q.4.) Tolnay, Stewart E., Stephen N. Graham, and Avery M. Guest
"Own-child Estimates of U.S. White Fertility, 1886-99," 127-138.

Historical Methods, Volume 15 (Number 2): Spring 1982:

(X.Q.5.) Borchert, James
"Historical Photo-analysis: A Research Method," 35-44.

(X.Q.6.) McCaa, Robert
"Modeling Social Interaction: Marital Miscegenation in Colonial Spanish America," 45-66.

(X.Q.7.) Dietrich, Donald J.
"Psychohistory: Clio on the Couch--or Off?" 83-90.

Historical Methods, Volume 15 (Number 1): Winter 1982:

(X.Q.8.) Laslett, Barbara
"Rethinking Household Structure: A New System of Classification," 3-10.

(X.Q.9.) Dobbert, G. A.
"An On Line System for Processing Loosely Structured Records," 16-22.

(X.Q.10.) Lynch, Katherine A.
"Local and Regional Studies in Historical
Demography," 23-29.

(X.Q.11.) Special Issue: The Historical Study of Diet and Nutrition
Volume 14 (Number 1): Winter 1981.

Historical Methods, Volume 14 (Number 4): Fall 1981:

(X.Q.12.) Gutmann, Myron P., and Randy Wyrick
"Adapting Methods to Needs: Studying Fertility
and Nuptiality in Seventeenth- and Eighteenth-
Century Belgium," 163-172.

(X.Q.12a) Degler, Carl N.
"Can a Historian or Social Scientist Learn
Anything from Sociobiology?" 173-180.

Historical Methods, Volume 14 (Number 3): Summer 1981:

(X.Q.13.) Crackel, Theodore J.
"Longitudinal Migration in America, 1780-1840:
A Study of Revolutionary War Pension Records," 133-138.

(X.Q.14.) Kocolowski, Gary P.
"Alternatives to Record-linkage in the Study of
Urban Migration: The Uses of Naturalization
Records," 139-142.

(X.Q.15.) Wilson, Adrian
"Inferring Attitudes from Behavior," 143-144.

Historical Methods, Volume 14 (Number 2): Spring 1981:

(X.Q.16.) King, T. J.
"The Use of Computers for Storing Records in
Historical Research," 59-164.

(X.Q.17.) Conk, Margo A.
"Accuracy, Efficiency and Bias: The Interpretation
of Women's Work in the U.S. Census of Occupations,
1890-1940," 65-72.

(X.Q.18.) Condran, Gretchen A., and Jeff Seaman
"Linkage of the 1880-81 Philadelphia Death
Register to the 1880 Manuscript Census: A
Comparison of Hand- and Machine-Record Linkage
Techniques," 73-84.

(X.Q.19.) Jensen, Richard
"Crunching Numbers by Hand," 97 ff.

(X.Q.20.) Special Issue: Approaches and Methods in Early American
           History Volume 13 (Number 1): Winter 1980.

Historical Methods, Volume 13 (Number 4): Fall 1980:

(X.Q.21.) Moore, Peter W.
                     "Measuring Residential Environmental Quality,"
                     193-203.

(X.Q.22.) Fitch, Nancy E.
                     "Statistical and Mathematical Methods for
                     Historians: An Annotated Bibliography of Selected
                     Books and Articles," 222-231.

Historical Methods, Volume 13 (Number 3): Summer 1980:

(X.Q.23.) Davis, James A., and Tom W. Smith
                     "Looking Backward: A National Sample Survey of
                     Ancestors and Predecessors, 1980-1850," 145-162.

(X.Q.24.) Crimmins, Eileen M.
                     "The Completeness of 1900 Mortality Data Collected
                     by Registration and Enumeration for Rural and
                     Urban Parts of States: Estimates Using the Chandra
                     Sekar-Deming Technique," 163-170.

(X.Q.25.) Dubnoff, Steven
                     "A Method for Estimating the Economic Welfare
                     of American Families of Any Composition: 1860-1909,"
                     171-180.

Historical Methods, Volume 12 (Number 1): Winter 1979:

(X.Q.26.) Condran, Gretchen A., and Eileen Crimmins
                     "A Description and Evaluation of Mortality Data
                     In the Federal Census: 1850-1900," 1-23.

(X.Q.27.) Wetherell, Charles, and Darrett B. Rutman
                     "QANTAS: A Plotting Program For the Social Sciences,"
                     46-51.

Historical Methods, Volume 11 (Number 1): Winter 1978:

(X.Q.28.) Imhof, Arthur E.
                     "The Analysis of Eighteenth-Century Causes of
                     Death: Some Methodological Considerations," 3-35.

Historical Methods Newsletter, Volume 10 (Number 4): Fall 1977:

(X.Q.29.) Doucet, Michael J.
                     "Discriminant Analysis and the Delineation of
                     Household Structure: Toward a Solution to the
                     Boarder/Relative Problem on the 1871 Canadian
                     Census," 149-156.

Historical Methods Newsletter, Volume 10 (Number 3): Summer 1977:

(X.Q.30.) Imhof, Arthur E.
"Historical Demography in Germany: A Research
Note," 122-126.

Historical Methods Newsletter, Volume 10 (Number 2): Spring 1977:

(X.Q.31.) The Historical Figures Assessment Collaborative
"Assessing Historical Figures: The Use of
Observer-Based Personality Descriptions."

(X.Q.32.) Baker, Reginald
"Teaching Quantitative History: A Review Essay."

Historical Methods Newsletter, Volume 10 (Number 1): December 1977:

(X.Q.33.) Guth, Gloria
"Surname Spellings and Computerized Record
Linkage," 10-21.

Historical Methods Newsletter, Volume 9 (Numbers 2 & 3): March/June 1976:

(X.Q.34.) Hershberg, Theodore
"The Philadelphia Social History Project: An
Introduction," 43-58.

(X.Q.35.) Hershberg, Theodore, Alan N. Burstein, and Susan M. Drobis
"The Historical Study of Urban Space," 99-136.

(X.Q.36.) Hershberg, Theodore, Alan Burstein, and Robert Dockhorn
"Record Linkage," 137-163.

Historical Methods Newsletter, Volume 8 (Number 1): December 1974:

(X.Q.37.) Main, Gloria L.
"The Correction of Biases in Colonial American
Probate Records," 10-28.

Historical Methods Newsletter, Volume 7 (Number 1): December 1973:

(X.Q.38.) Laslett, Barbara
"Family Structure and Social History: A
Methodological Review Essay," 2-8.

(X.Q.39.) Schoenwald, Richard L.
"Using Psychology in History: A Review Essay,"
9-24.

(X.Q.40.) Markoff, John, and Gilbert Shapiro
"The Linkage of Data Describing Overlapping
Geographical Units," 34-46.

Historical Methods Newsletter, Volume 6 (Number 4): September 1973:

(X.Q.41.) Bateman, Fred, and James D. Foust
"A Matched Sample Of Households Selected From
The 1860 United States Census," 141-148.

Historical Methods Newletter, Volume 6 (Number 3): June 1973:

(X.Q.42.) Cerny, James W.
"Computers as Cartographic Tools," 97-98.

Historical Methods Newsletter, Volume 6 (Number 1): December 1972:

(X.Q.43.) Friedberger, Mark
"Cohorting With the State Census: The Concept
of the Cohort, and its Use in Manuscript Census
Research," 1-3.

(X.Q.44.) Holland, Reid A.
"Urban History and Computer Mapping," 4-9.

(X.Q.45.) Kelley, R., M. H. Skolnick, and N. Yasuda
"A Combinatorial Problem in Linking Historical
Records," 10-16.

****

(X.Q.46.) Crafts, N. F. R., and N. J. Ireland
1976 "Family Limitation and English Demographic
Revolution--Simulation Approach." Journal of
Economic History 36 (Number 3): 598-623.

(X.Q.47.) Cohen, L.
1975 "How to Teach Family History by Using an Historic
House." Social Education 39 (Number 7): 466-469.

(X.Q.48.) Culbert, D. H.
1975 "Family History Projects--Scholarly Value of
Informal Sample." American Archivist 38 (Number 4):
533-541.

(X.Q.49.) Des Jardins, B., P. Beauchamp, and J. Legare
1977 "Automatic Family Reconstitution--French-Canadian
17th-Century Experience." Journal of Family History
2 (Number 1): 56-76.

(X.Q.50.) Jeay, M.
1979 "Sexuality and Family in 15th-Century France--
Are Literary Sources a Mask or a Mirror?"
Journal of Family History 4 (Number 4): 328-345.

(X.Q.51.) Kyvig, D. E.
            1975 "Family History--New Opportunities for Archivists."
                  American Archivist 38 (Number 4): 509-519.

XI. SPACE AND ARCHITECTURE

XI.A. *DOMESTIC SPACE*

(XI.A.1.) Clark, Clifford E., Jr.
　　　　　　1976 "Domestic Architecture as an Index to
　　　　　　Social History: The Romantic Revival
　　　　　　and the Cult of Domesticity in America,
　　　　　　1840-1870." Journal of Interdisciplinary
　　　　　　History 7 (Summer): 33-56.

This essay examines popular literature about home design and compares
that literature to the houses that were actually built in the U.S.
from 1840 to 1870. CLARK argues that the housing crusade shared
similar values and priorities (particularly the vision of middle-
class society) with the abolitionist crusade and temperance movement,
and that the housing crusade's social impact and indirect behavioral
influence was as great as that of these reform movements. It is said
that by contrasting the values and assumptions expressed in the reform
literature with the plans of houses still in existence, some idea
may be gained about the discrepancies between the reformer's ideals
and actual practice. Clark finds that the success of the house
reformers can be seen ultimately in the way in which the family
home came to be the major symbol of middle-class values at mid-
century; it stood for the individual's tastes and virtues, for
dedication to one's family and belief in the ideals of efficiency,
order, sobriety, and domesticity.

(XI.A.2.) Lawrence, Roderick J.
　　　　　　1982 "Domestic Space and Society: A Cross-
　　　　　　Cultural Study." Comparative Studies
　　　　　　in Society and History 24 (January):
　　　　　　104-130.

This is a study of the influence of certain cultural, social, and
architectural factors upon the meaning and use of domestic space in
England and Australia during the last two centuries. Using an historical
and cross-cultural framework, LAWRENCE promotes an understanding of
the history of the kinds of ideas which are invested in spatial form
and use of houses. He establishes the principle that the meaning and
use of domestic space are not intrinsic to a set of physical characteristics.

The manner in which houses are the material expression of a matrix of
sociocultural influences--influences that vary between two societies
stemming from the same Anglo-Saxon culture--are discussed. First, an
historical review of house forms in England and Australia are offered.
Second, an ethnographic approach to the design and use of domestic
facilities for eating food is presented. The findings indicate minor,
yet interesting differences between the structure of family activities in
Australia and England.

On domestic space and architecture, see also X.O.3.

XI.B. __URBAN SPATIAL PATTERNS__

(XI.B.1.) Modell, John
        1979 "Suburbanization and Change in the
        American Family." Journal of Inter-
        disciplinary History 9 (Spring): 621-646.

MODELL explores the effect of urban spatial differentiation--in particular,
suburbanization--upon families. This study is notable for its finding
that, in the initial stages of suburbanization, changes in urban form
did little to promote change in family patterns. The pace of suburbanization
may have to exceed some threshhold-level, as it apparently did after
World War II, before such effects on the family will be evident.

The focus is on the process of suburbinazation over time (the concentration
of single-family dwellings, home ownership, etc.) and its relationship
to families (including selective location according to family life
stage). Special emphasis is given to the era of electric street car
suburbanization (1890-1920) in four U.S. cities (Boston, Baltimore,
Chicago, and St. Louis), using ward-level (pre-1940) and census-tract-
level (1940-1950) data. Although family suburbs and new family patterns
were both discernible by 1920, spatial location of families at this time
was more a function of ethnicity and socioeconomic status than of family
life stage.

(XI.B.2.) Wekerle, Gerda R.
        1980 "Women in the Urban Environment." Signs
        5 (Spring, Supplement): 188-214.

WEKERLE outlines major themes and directions in the newly emerging
area of study of women in urban settings. Much literature is discussed,
a mixture of many contemporary and some historical works from the disciplines
of urban and architectural history, urban geography, urban sociology,
economics, political science, planning, architecture, and appropriate
technology. Many of these are "pioneering" works, i.e., the first of
their kind in the field.

Topics include the private-public dichotomy (housework and the single-
family home, the industrialization and collectivization of housework,
women in public space), the fit between the urban environment and
women's changing role (women and suburbia, women in the city), and
primarily contemporary studies of women and environmental equity (in
transportation, housing, etc.).

The appendix provides a useful list of the key review essays, bibliographies,
books, newsletters, professional organizations, and special-issues of
journals in this field. On urban women, see also X.G.6.

XI.C. _DISSERTATIONS_

NONE

C

D

XI.D. <u>PUBLICATIONS</u>

NONE

NAME INDEX

Alter, George   III.E.1.,
         X.Q.2.
Anderson, Barbara A.   V.B.6., VII.B.1.,
         VII.B.3.
Anderson, Michael   I.M.1., II.B.6.,
         II.C.3.
Armitage, S. H.   V.G.1.
Austin, Erik W.   X.G.3.
Avery, Roger Christopher   VII.J.1.

Baker, Reginald   X.Q.32
Barker-Benfield, G. T.   VII.K.17
Barrett, Richard E.   VII.C.7.
Bateman, Fred   X.Q.41.
Beall, Pamela E.   X.O.1.
Bean, Lee L.   VII.K.11., X.G.1.,
         X.G.2.
Beauchamp, P.   X.Q.4.
Becker, Gary S.   III.A.1.-III.A.4.
Bell, Susan Groag   I.F.1.
Benjamin, Jessica   I.F.16
Ben-Porath, Yoram   III.A.4.
Berkin, Carol R.   V.B.9.
Berkner, Lutz K.   I.A.6., VI.D.1.
Berlanstein, Lenard   VII.C.6.
Berman, Marshall   IX.D.4.
Birnbaum, Bonnie   I.E.2.
Bissell, Linda Auwers   VIII.C.1.
Blatt, Marty   X.J.2.
Bloch, R. H.   V.G.2.
Blumberg, Rae Lesser   II.B.1., II.B.2.
Bodnar, John   VII.I.1.
Bolin, Winfred Dorothy Wandersee
         V.D.6., V.F.1.
Bonfield, L.   VIII.D.1.
Boocock, Sarane Spence   I.J.4.,
         IV.F.1.
Borchert, James   X.Q.5.
Bouchard, Gerard   X.D.2.
Boulding, E.   V.G.3.
Bower, Ames Sheldon   I.F.17
Braun, Rachel Eisenberg   X.14
Breines, Wini   VI.A.1.
Brennan, E. R.   III.F.2.
Bridenthal, Renate   I.F.1., I.F.9.,
         I.F.10.
Brobeck, Stephen   VI.B.1.
Brøgger, Jan   VI.C.4.
Brown, Bruce W.   V.D.5.
Brown, Clair   V.E.5.
Brown, Irene Q.   III.D.3.
Brown, Keith   VI.C.5.
Brownlee, W. Elliot   V.D.7.
Burch, T. K.   VII.K.1.

Burr, Wesley R.   II.B.1.
Burstein, Alan   V.Q.35, X.Q.36
Burton, Orville Vernon   VI.A.11.
Bushman, Claudia Lauper   VI.D.2.

Carr, Lois Green   X.E.1.
Cavallo, Dominick   I.G.5., IX.E.1.
Cerullo, M.   X.M.3.
Chambers, Clarke A.   I.F.17
Chaytor, M.   VIII.D.2.
Cherlin, Andrew   IV.B.1.
Chi, Peter S. K.   VII.H.2.
Chrisman, Miriam   VI.C.2.
Chudacoff, Howard P.   IV.C.1.
Clark, Clifford E., Jr.   XI.A.1.
Clark, Elaine   IV.E.4.
Clement, P. F.   IV.H.1.
Coale, Ansley J.   VII.B.3.
Cobb, Richard   V.B.5.
Cody, Cheryll Ann   VIII.D.5.
Cohen, L.   X.Q.2.
Cohen, Miriam   I.A.2., V.D.4.
Condran, Gretchen A.   X.Q.18, X.Q.26
Conk, Margo A.   X.Q.17
Cooper, Sandi E.   V.C.2.
Cott, Nancy F.   I.F.2., III.C.1.,
         III.F.3., V.B.2., V.B.3.
Cowan, Ruth Schwartz   V.E.1.
Cox, Gary W.   X.F.2.
Crackel, Theodore J.   X.Q.13
Crafts, N. F. R.   X.Q.46
Crimmins, Eileen M.   X.Q.24, X.Q.26
Cuisenier, Jean   VIII.A.1.
Culbert, D. H.   X.Q.48
Czap, Peter, Jr.   II.C.4.

Darroch, A. G.   VII.K.2.
Davies, Mel   VII.F.1.
Davis, Allen F.   X.N.1.
Davis, David Brion   IX.D.6.
Davis, J.   VI.C.4.
Davis, James A.   X.Q.23
Davis, Natalie Zemon   VI.B.2.
Degler, Carl N.   I.A.4., V.B.8.,
         V.B.9., VII.K.18, IX.D.2.,
         X.Q.12a.
deMause, Lloyd   I.G.2., IV.D.5.,
         IV.D.6.
Demos, John   I.J.4., I.M.2., IV.B.1.,
         IV.B.2., IV.B.4., IV.D.4.,
         IV.H.9., VI.B.4.
DesJardines, B.   X.Q.4.
Deuel, R. Z.   X.B.3., X.B.4.
DeVos, Susan   VII.E.1.

Diefendorf, Barbara B. III.D.1.
Dietrich, Donald J. X.Q.7.
Dintelman, Sue M. X.G.2.
Ditz, Toby L. VIII.B.5.
Dobbert, G. A. X.Q.9.
Dockhom, Robert X.Q.36
Donzelot, Jacques IX.D.1., IX.D.2.
Doucet, Michael J. X.Q.29.
Douglas, Ann V.B.2., V.B.3.
Douglass, William A. VI.C.3., VI.C.4.,
                VIII.B.4.
Drobis, Susan M. X.Q.35
Dublin, Thomas V.B.9.
Dubnoff, Stevan X.Q.25
Dunn, Patrick VI.A.9.
Dupâquier, Jacques VIII.A.2.

Early, Frances H. IX.A.3.
Easterlin, Richard A. VII.K.19.
Easton, Barbara V.C.1.
Ebel, Henry IV.D.6.
Ehrenreich, Barbara V.B.2., V.B.3.
Eisenstein, Zillah I.F.12
Elder, Glen H., Jr. I.B.2., I.B.3.,
        IV.A.3., IV.A.4., IV.A.6.,
        IV.B.1., IV.B.3., IV.C.2.,
        IV.C.3., IV.C.4., IV.D.12.,
        IV.H.2.
Eng, R. Y. VII.K.3.
Engerman, Stanley L. II.B.7.,
        VII.G.2., VII.H.1.
English, Deidre V.B.2., V.B.3.
Espenshade, Thomas J. X.I.4.
Evans, Richard J. I.D.2., I.D.3.
Ewbank, Douglas C. VII.B.2.
Ewen, Stuart V.B.2.

Farber, Bernard I.H.4., II.B.2.
Featherstone, Joseph IX.E.2.
Ferber, Marianne A. I.E.2.
Fildes, V. VII.K.4.
Fischer, Claude S. VIII.A.4.
Fitch, Nancy X.B.5., X.Q.22.
Fitzpatrick, John J. I.G.2.
Flandrin, Jean-Louis VI.A.1.
Floud, Roderick VII.H.1., X.K.1.
Fogel, Robert W. VII.G.2., VII.H.1.,
        X.K.1.
Folbre, Nancy V.C.3.
Foucault, Michel V.C.5., IX.D.2.
Foust, James D. X.Q.41.
Fox-Genovese, Elizabeth V.C.5.
Franzoi, Barbara V.D.8.
Freedman, Estelle B. VII.C.1.

Freiden, Alan III.A.3.
Friedberger, Mark IV.D.9.
Fruin, W. Mark IX.B.4.
Fuchs, Victor R. II.D.3.
Fügedi, Erik II.C.5.
Furstenberg, Frank F., Jr. II.E.3.,
                IV.H.12.

Gadlin, Howard VII.C.4.
Gagen, D. VI.E.1.
Galenson, David W. X.F.2.
Garcia, Maria-Pilar II.B.1., II.B.2.
Gavazzi, Milovan II.C.8.
Goheen, Peter G. X.Q.1.
Goldfrank, Walter L. X.M.5.
Goldin, Claudia IX.A.1., IX.H.4.,
                X.Q.3.
Gordon, D. IV.H.3.
Gordon, Linda V.B.1., V.B.3.
Gordon, Margaret II.B.1., II.B.2.
Gordon, Michael I.J.1.
Gottlieb, Beatrice III.E.2.
Graff, Harvey J. IX.C.1.
Graham, Stephen N. X.Q.4.
Greven, Philip J., Jr. IV.H.10,
                VIII.B.1.
Griliches, Zvi VIII.B.3.
Guest, Avery M. VII.E.2., X.Q.4.
Gunda Béla II.C.6.
Guth, Golria X.Q.33.
Gutman, Herbert G. II.B.7., II.E.2.,
                VI.A.12.
Gutmann, Myron P. X.Q.12

Haber, Barbara I.F.17.
Härm, Erna VII.B.3.
Haines, Michael R. VII.E.5., VII.K.5.,
                IX.H.5., X.A.1.
Hall, Peter Dobkin III.F.8.
Halpern, Sydney IX.B.2.
Hammel, Eugene A. X.A.1., X.B.1-9.,
                X.C.1-5.
Hanawalt, B. A. IV.H.5.
Hannan, Michael T. III.A.5.
Hansen, E. D. R. VII.K.6.
Harding, Susan IX.A.2.
Hareven, Tamara I.H.2., I.H.3., I.I.1.,
                I.K.1., II.B.3., II.D.2.,
                IV.A.1., IV.A.5., IV.A.7.,
                IV.B.1., IV.B.2., V.A.1.,
                VI.E.2.
Harper, John Paull VII.J.2.
Harrell, Stevan VIII.A.5.
Harris, Barbara J. I.A.5.

Harris, William II.E.4.
Harrison, Cynthia E. I.F.17.
Harrison, Jerry N. X.D.1.
Hartmann, Heidi V.E.2.
Hastings, Donald W. X.D.1.
Helmholz, Richard Henry III.E.3.
Hendricks, C. D. IV.H.6.
Hendricks, J. IV.H.6.
Hendrix, L. VII.K.7.
Hershberg, Theodore II.E.3., IV.H.12.,
        X.Q.34-36.
Hill, Christopher VI.A.4.
Hill, Reuben I.H.7.
Himmelfarb, Gertrude I.A.4.
Hinding, Andrea I.F.17.
Hiner, N. Ray IV.D.11.
Historical Figures Assessment
        Collaborative, The X.Q.31.
Historical Study of Diet and
        Nutrition, The X.Q.11.
Hodgson, Dennis George VII.J.3.
Hoffman, Philip T. VIII.B.3.
Hogan, Dennis P. VII.B.3.
Howard, Ronald Lee I.L.1.
Huber, Joan III.A.6.
Hughes, Diane Owen X.H.1.
Hunt, David IV.B.4.
Hutchinson, D. W. X.B.3.

Imhof, Arthur E. I.D.3., VII.E.1.,
        X.Q.28, X.Q.30.
Interrante, Joseph V.B.2.
Ireland, N. J. X.Q.46

Jackson, K.A. VI.E.3.
Jeay, M. X.Q.50
Jeffrey, K. I.M.3.
Jeffrey, Kirk, Jr. VI.D.3.
Jensen, Joan M. V.E.4.
Jensen, Richard X.Q.19.
Joffe, Carole IX.D.5.
Johnson, A. H. IX.H.1.
Johnson, David George VI.D.4.
Johnson, K. X.M.2., X.M.3.
Johnson, Mary Durham V.B.9.
Johnson, Thomas Hoevet VI.D.5.
Jones, A. David IV.D.3.

Kagan, Alexander II.C.9.
Kahk, Juhan II.C.7.
Kammen, Michael I.A.4.
Kamphoefner, Walter D. VII.I.4.
Kanter, Rosabeth Moss IX.B.1.
Kaplow, Jeffry VI.A.7.

Kelly, Joan I.F.14., I.K.3.
Keniston, Kenneth IV.A.8., IX.D.3.
Kennedy, Susan Estabrook V.B.9.
Kerber, Linda K. V.B.8.
Kern, Louis John VII.J.4.
Kertzer, D. I. II.H.1.
Kett, Joseph F. IV.H.11.
Keyes, J. I.M.4.
King, T. J. X.Q.16.
Kitson, Gay C. II.B.1., II.B.2.
Kittel, Margaret Ruth V.F.2.
Kleinberg, Susan J. X.G.6.
Knodel, John III.F.1., VII.E.1., X.M.5.
Kobrin, Frances II.D.1.
Kocolowski, Gary P. X.Q.14.
Kolko, Gabriel IX.B.3.
Koonz, Claudia I.F.1.
Kousser, J. Morgan X.F.2., X.L.1.
Kozak, Conrad M. IV.D.7.
Krech, S. II.H.2.
Krishnamoorthy, S. VII.E.10.
Kulikoff, Allan VI.E.10.
Kuntz, P. R. VII.J.8.
Kyvig, D. E. X.Q.51.

Lafitte, F. VIII.D.3.
Laidig, Gary VII.E.6.
Lammerme, P. J. II.H.3.
Lantz, Herman R. I.M.4., VI.B.3.,
        VI.E.4., VII.K.7.
Lasch, Christopher V.C.2., VI.A.10.,
        IX.D.2-7.
Laslett, Barbara I.B.1., I.B.4.,
        I.H.6., I.K.2., II.B.6.,
        X.Q.8., X.Q.38.
Laslett, Peter II.B.3-5., IX.E.3.,
        X.A.1., X.B.5., X.C.5.
LaSorte, Michael A. VII.D.2.
Lasser, Carol V.B.2.
Lawrence, Roderick J. XI.A.2.
Lee, Gary R. X.M.4.
Lee, W. R. I.D.1., I.D.2.
Leet, Don R. VII.E.7.
Legare, J. X.Q.4.
Lemieux. Christine Marie VII.J.5.
Leon, Warren X.O.1.
Lerner, Gerda I.F.3., I.F.4.,
        I.F.17., V.B.1.
Lesthaeghe, Ron J. VII.B.2.
Levine, David II.B.5.
Levy, Darlene Gay V.B.9.
Liker, Jeffrey K. IV.C.2.
Lindemann, Barbara S. V.B.7.
Lindemann, Mary IV.D.8.

Liston, Margaret I. I.E.3.
Litchfield, R. Burr II.B.5., IV.H.3.
Lithell, Ulla-Britt VII.G.1.
Lizaur, M. P. VI.E.5.
Lockwood, R. VII.K.8.
Lommitz, L. A. VI.E.5.
Lopez, Manual D. IV.D.1.
Lougee, Carolyn C. I.F.7.
Lovett, Clara M. V.B.9.
Lundy, R. T. X.B.3.
Lyman, Kathleen X.M.1.
Lyman, Richard IV.D.2., X.M.1.
Lynch, Katherine A. X.Q.10.

Macfarlane, Alan IV.B.4.
MacKinnon, Catharine A. I.F.15.
Maddala, G. S. VIII.B.3.
Main, Gloria L. X.Q.37.
Marcy, P. T. VII.K.9.
Markoff, John X.Q.40.
Masnick, George S. VII.E.3.
May, Dean L. I.H.5., X.G.1.
May, Elaine Tyler III.F.9.
Maynes, Mary Jo VII.A.1.
McCaa, Robert X.Q.6.
McCarthy, J. VI.E.6.
McCaskie, T. C. VII.K.10.
McDaniel, Chad K. X.B.8.
McDonald, John III.C.3.
McFalls, Joseph A., Jr. VII.E.3.
McLaughlin, Virginia Yans V.D.1.
Mechling, Jay Edmund IV.G.1.
Mendels, F. F. II.H.4.
Michael, Robert T. II.D.3.
Milden, James W. I.I.2., VI.D.6.
Milkman, Ruth V.D.9.
Mineau, Geraldine P. VII.K.11, X.G.2.
Minge-Kalman, Wanda IV.D.10.
Mitchell, Albert Gibbs, Jr. VI.D.7.
Mitterauer, Michael I.D.3., II.C.9.,
          II.C.10.
Moch, Leslie Page VII.I.2., VII.K.12.
Modell, John II.D.2., II.E.3.,
        IV.B.3., IV.H.12., XI.B.1.
Mogey, John VIII.A.1.
Moore, Peter S. X.Q.21.
Morgan, G. F. IX.H.2.
Muncy, Raymond Lee VII.J.6.
Musallam, Basim Fuad VII.J.7.

Nafziger, John Marvin VI.D.8.
National Immigration Archives X.G.5.
Netting, R. M. II.H.5.
Neugarten, B. L. IV.H.7.

Norton, Mary Beth I.F.6., V.B.7.

O'Connell, Peter S. X.O.1., X.O.3.
O'Hara, Mary VI.B.3.
O'Neill, William L. III.F.10.

Padgug, Robert A. VII.C.2.
Palli, Heldur II.C.7.
Parming, Tönu II.C.1.
Parsons, Donald O. IX.A.1.
Patterson, Orlando X.K.2.
Peale, E. V.G.4.
Pedlow, Gregory W. VI.C.1.
Phillips, R. V.G.5.
Pickens, K. A. III.F.4.
Pi-Sunyer, Mary Jane Richards II.G.1.
Plakans, Andrejs VI.E.7., VIII.A.3.
Platt, Gerald M. I.G.3., VI.A.10.
Pleck, Elizabeth H. I.F.2., VI.A.11.,
          VI.E.11.
Plumb, J. H. VI.A.3.
Pope, Clayne L. VII.H.1., X.K.1.
Poster, Mark VI.A.2.
Potts, Louis W. I.G.2.
Pouyez, Christian X.D.2.
Preston, Samuel H. III.C.3.

Quitt, Martin H. I.G.4.

Rabb, Theodore K. I.J.3.
Rapp, Rayna I.F.9., VI.C.3.
Rebel, Hermann IX.F.1.
Remy, Dorothy V.B.4.
Rich, Adrienne V.B.1.
Riegelhaupt, Joyce V.B.9.
Ring, R. R. VI.E.8.
Rippley, LaVern J. I.D.4.
Rishel, Joseph Francis VI.D.9.
Rodgers, R. H. IV.H.4.
Roman, Louis VII.A.2.
Rosenberg, Bella H. IX.D.7.
Rosenberg, Charles I.J.2.
Ross, Ellen I.F.9., VI.A.2., VII.C.3.
Rotberg, Robert I. I.J.3.
Roth, Darlene R. I.F.17.
Rothman, Ellen K. VII.K.20, X.O.1.,
          X.O.2.
Rubin, Gayle I.F.13.
Runck, Bette IV.C.4.
Rury, John VI.A.12.
Rutman, Darrett B. X.Q.27.
Ryan, Mary P. I.H.1.

Sa, Sophie IX.G.2.

Sacks, Karen V.B.4.
Safley, Tomas Max III.B.2.
Salamon, Sonya VIII.B.2.
Sanderson, Warren C. VII.E.9.
Sanjek, Roger II.F.3.
Sawhill, Isabel V. I.E.1.
Scammell, J. III.F.5.
Schmidtbauer, Peter II.C.2.
Schoenwald, Richard L. I.G.3., X.Q.39.
Schultz, Martin I.M.4., III.C.2.,
        VI.B.3.
Schutjer, Wayne A. VII.E.6.
Scott, Joan W. V.B.6., V.D.3.,
        V.D.4.
Scott, R. B. IX.H.3.
Scott, Sharon R. II.D.3.
Seaman, Jeff X.Q.18.
Searle, E. III.F.6.
Sennett, Richard IX.D.1.
Seward, R. R. II.H.6.
Shaffer, John Wesley V.G.6., IX.G.3.
Shammas, Carole VI.E.12., X.F.1.
Shanley, Mary Lyndon I.F.8.
Shapiro, Gilbert X.Q.40.
Sheingorn, P. III.F.7.
Shifflett, Crandall A. II.E.1.
Shopes, Linda X.J.1.
Shorter, Edward VI.A.5-9., VII.C.5.,
        VII.K.13.
Sicherman, BArbara I.F.5.
Sieder, Reinhard I.D.3.
Simon, Roger VII.I.1.
Sinofsky, Faye I.G.2.
Skinner, G. William I.I.3.
Skolnick, Arlene I.G.1.
Skolnick, Mark VII.K.11., X.G.1.,
        X.G.2.
Slater, Miriam VI.D.10., X.M.2.
Sly, David F. VII.H.2.
Smelser, Neil J. IX.B.2.
Smith, Bonnie G. V.B.5.
Smith, Daniel Blake I.A.3.
Smith, Daniel Scott III.F.11., VII.G.3.,
    VII.K.21., X.I.2., X.I.3.
Smith, James E. I.H.6., VII.J.8.
Smith, R. M. VII.K.14., VIII.D.4.
Smith-Rosenberg, Caroll V.B.3.
Smith, T. C. VII.K.3.
Smith, Tom W. X.Q.23
Šoč, Djordje X.C.1.
Sokoloff, Kenneth IX.A.1.
Sokoloff, Natalie J. V.C.4.
Soliday, Gerald L. I.D.3., I.I.1.,
        X.G.4.

Spagnoli, Paul G. X.I.1.
Spengler, J. J. VII.G.3., VII.H.3.
Spicker, Stuart IV.E.2.
Spitze, Glenna III.A.6.
Stage, Sarah V.B.3.
Stannard, David E. I.G.5.
Steckel, Richard H. III.B.1., VII.E.8.
Stewart, Abigail J. IV.D.3.
Stokes, C. Shannon VII.E.6.
Stone, Lawrence I.A.1., VI.A.3.,
        VI.A.4.
Strong, B. VII.K.15.
Struminger, L. S. VI.E.9.
Suitor, J. Jill VII.D.1.
Summer Institute on Women in American
    History, The I.F.17.
Sutch, Richard VII.G.3., VII.H.3.
Swedlund, Alan Charles S. VII.J.9.
Swerdlow, Amy V.E.3.
Swierenga, Robert P. VII.I.3.

Taylor, Michael D. III.B.3.
Taylor, Peter IX.F.1.
Terris, Virginia R. I.F.17.
Thorne, Barrie I.F.11., X.M.6.
Tilly, Charles VII.B.2.
Tilly, Louise A. I.A.2., V.B.6.,
    V.D.3., V.D.4., VI.A.5.
Tingley, Donald F. I.F.17.
Tingley, Elizabeth I.F.17.
Tobin, James VIII.B.3.
Tolnay, Stewart E. VII.E.2., X.Q.4.
Trussell, James VII.H.1.
Turshen, Meredith V.B.4.
Uhlenberg, Peter IV.E.1.
Uibu, Halliki II.C.7.
Uttrachi, Patricia Branca IX.G.1.

Valentin, J. H. I.M.5.
van de Walle, Etienne VII.E.1.
Vanek, Joann IX.B.5.
Vann, Richard T. I.I.1., II.B.4.
Van Tassel, David IV.E.2., IV.E.3.
Verdon, Michel II.A.1., II.A.2.
Vinovskis, Maris IV.A.2., IV.B.1.,
        VII.B.1., VII.E.4., VII.H.3.,
        VII.K.22., VIII.B.1.
Volkov, A. G. V.G.7.

Wachter, Kenneth W. X.A.1., X.B.2.,
        X.B.3., X.B.5., X.B.8., X.B.10.
Walkowitz, Daniel J. V.D.2.
Wall, Richard II.B.3., II.B.4.
Walsh, Lorena S. X.E.1.

Wargon, S. T.   VII.K.16.
Watkins, Susan Cotts   IV.B.2.
Watts, Jim   X.N.1.
Weber, Michael   VII.I.1.
Weber-Kellerman, Ingeborg   I.D.3.
Weinstein, Fred   I.G.3., VI.A.10.
Weisbrod, C.   III.F.7.
Weiss, N. P.   IV.H.8.
Wekerle, Gerda R.   XI.B.2.
Wells, Robert V.   II.F.1., IV.C.5.,
                   VI.A.8., VII.K.23.
Wetherell, Charles   X.Q.27.
Wheaton, Robert   I.I.1., II.F.2.
White, F.   X.M.2., X.M.3.
White, Harriet Branson Apple   V.B.9.
Whitney, G.   IV.H.4.
Wilson, Adrian   X.Q.15.
Wilson, Chris   VII.E.1.
Wimmer, Larry T.   VII.H.1., X.K.1.
Winch, Robert F.   II.B.1., II.B.2.
Winston, M. R.   IX.H.3.
Winter, David G.   IV.D.3.
Wolf, Arthur P.   I.I.3.
Woodard, Kathleen   IV.E.2.
Wright, Raymond Sanford III   VI.D.11.
Wrigley, E. Anthony   I.A.7.
Wyntjes, Sherrin Marshall   III.D.2.
Wyrick, Randy   X.Q.12.

Yanagasako, Sylvia Junko   I.C.1.
Yarbrough, Charles   X.C.4.
Yatchew, Adonis   VII.B.3.
Yngvesson, B.   X.M.2.

Zaretsky, Eli   VI.A.5., IX.E.4.
Zuckerman, Michael   II.D.4.